Marlborough's War Machine 1702–1711

Marlborough's War Machine 1702–1711

James Falkner

Pen & Sword
MILITARY

First published in Great Britain in 2014 by
PEN & SWORD MILITARY
an imprint of
Pen & Sword Books Ltd
47 Church Street
Barnsley
South Yorkshire
S70 2AS

Copyright © James Falkner, 2014

ISBN 978-1-84884-821-4

Typeset by Concept, Huddersfield, West Yorkshire, HD4 5JL.
Printed and bound in England by CPI Group (UK) Ltd, Croydon CR0 4YY.

Pen & Sword Books Ltd incorporates the imprints of Pen & Sword Archaeology, Atlas, Aviation, Battleground, Discovery, Family History, History, Maritime, Military, Naval, Politics, Railways, Select, Social History, Transport, True Crime, and Claymore Press, Frontline Books, Leo Cooper, Praetorian Press, Remember When, Seaforth Publishing and Wharncliffe.

For a complete list of Pen & Sword titles please contact
PEN & SWORD BOOKS LIMITED
47 Church Street, Barnsley, South Yorkshire, S70 2AS, England
E-mail: enquiries@pen-and-sword.co.uk
Website: www.pen-and-sword.co.uk

Contents

Death of Carlos II, 10; Philippe d'Anjou takes the throne, 11; Creation of the
Grand Alliance, 13; Death of William III, and War declared on France, 14;
Marlborough made Captain-General, 15; Slow progress in Flanders, 17; The 1704
campaign in Bavaria – Schellenberg and Blenheim, 18; A frustrating year in
1705, 21; France strengthens its position in Spain, 22; Victory for Marlborough at
Ramillies and for Eugene at Turin in 1706, 23; Alliance expands its demands, 24;
Renewed frustration in 1707, 25; Success at Oudenarde and Lille in 1708, 26;
The Great Frost and a failure to secure a good peace, 27; Bloody battle at
Malplaquet in 1709, 27; Failing influence of Marlborough, 28; Siege warfare in
1710 and 1711, 28; The victory at Bouchain, 29; Marlborough's dismissal and
renewed French confidence, 29; Peace with the Treaty of Utrecht in 1713, 29.

The Captain-General, 33; Troop numbers required by the Grand Alliance, 33;
The Dutch Army, 34; Foreign contingents, 34; Queen Anne's Army, 35; Financing
an army, 35; Terms of service, 36; Purchase of Commissions, 36; Brevet Rank, 37;
The Lingua Franca, 40; Recruiting methods, 41; Regimental strengths, 43; Dress,
arms and equipment, 44; Discipline and deserters, 48; Prisoners of war, 49;
The conduct of officers, 53; Foraging, pillaging and looting, 53; Good
administration, 54; Hardships on campaign, 55; Routine in camp, 56.

Marlborough, 58; Eugene, 69; Overkirk, 70; Cadogan, 72; Keppel, 74; Natzmer, 75;
Orkney, 75; Argyll, 76; Churchill, 78; Orange, 79; Lottum, 79; Stair, 80;
Anhalt-Dessau, 80; Lumley, 81; Rantzau, 81; Hesse-Kassel, 81; Sabine, 82; Van
Goor, 82; Baden, 83; Tilly, 84; Van Goslinga, 84; Parke, 85; Merode-Westerloo, 86;
Webb, 88; Tallard, 88; Villeroi, 89; Vendôme, 89; Villars, 90; The staff, 90;
Command and control, 91; Composition of the army, 93.

Classic role of cavalry, 98; Horse and dragoons, 101; Terms of service, 105;
Expense of cavalry, 105; Horsemanship, 106; Evolving tactics, 107; The
disciplined charge, 108; Swordsmanship, 111; Cavalry as a battle-winning
arm, 111; Declining influence, 113.

List of Illustrations

Maps

Plates

1. John Churchill, First Duke of Marlborough, by Godfrey Kneller.
2. The Duke of Marlborough at the Battle of Blenheim in 1704.
3. Prince Eugene of Savoy.
4. Henry of Nassau, Veldt-Marshal Overkirk.
5. John Churchill, First Duke of Marlborough.
6. Queen Anne of Great Britain.
7. Louis XIV of France, the 'Sun King'.
8. Louis-Guillaume, Margrave of Baden.
9. Major General William Cadogan.
10. Arnold Joost van Keppel, First Earl Albemarle.
11. Lieutenant General Charles Churchill.
12. George Hamilton, First Earl Orkney.
13. Claude-Louis-Hector de Villers, Marshal of France.
14. Major General Joseph Sabine.
15. Major General Lord John Cutts of Gowran.
16. George, the Elector of Hanover.

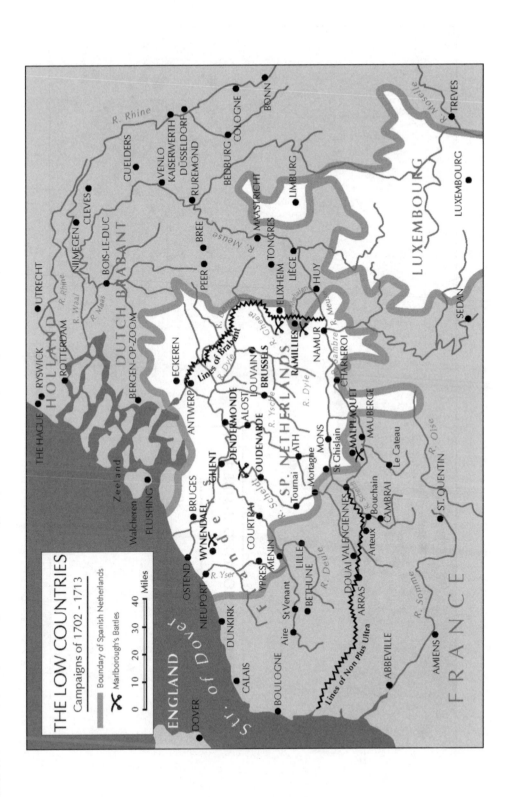

THE LOW COUNTRIES
Campaigns of 1702 - 1713

Boundary of Spanish Netherlands

✗ Marlborough's Battles

0   10   20   30   40
Miles

ENGLAND

Str... of Dover

DOVER

CALAIS

BOULOGNE

DUNKIRK

NIEUPORT

OSTEND

Walcheren

FLUSHING

Zeeland

THE HAGUE

RYSWICK

ROTTERDAM

UTRECHT

HOLLAND

R. Waal

R. Rhine

R. Maas

NIJMEGEN

CLEVES

BOIS-LE-DUC

BERGEN-OP-ZOOM

DUTCH BRABANT

GUELDERS

VENLO

RUREMOND

KAISERWERTH

DÜSSELDORF

R. Rhine

BEDBURG

COLOGNE

BONN

R. Moselle

TREVES

LUXEMBOURG

LUXEMBOURG

SEDAN

R. Meuse

PEER

BREE

LIMBURG

MAASTRICHT

TONGRES

LIÈGE

HUY

R. Meuse

R. Sambre

NAMUR

CHARLEROI

ELIXHEIM

RAMILLIES

Mehaigne R.

Geheele R.

Lines of Brabant

R. Dender

R. Dyle

R. Yssche

BRUSSELS

LOUVAIN

ECKEREN

ANTWERP

DENDERMONDE

ALOST

OUDENARDE

ATH

MONS

Mortagne

St.Ghislain

MALPLAQUET

MAUBERGE

Le Cateau

SP. NETHERLANDS

R. Dyle

Tournai

R. Scheldt

R. Schelde

BRUGES

GHENT

WYNENDAEL

COURTRAI

MENIN

LILLE

YPRES

BETHUNE

St Venant

Aire

R. Yser

R. Deule

F l a n d e r s

Bouchain

CAMBRAI

Arleux

VALENCIENNES

DOUAI

ARRAS

Lines of Non Plus Ultra

R. Scarpe

ABBEVILLE

AMIENS

R. Somme

ST. QUENTIN

R. Oise

FRANCE

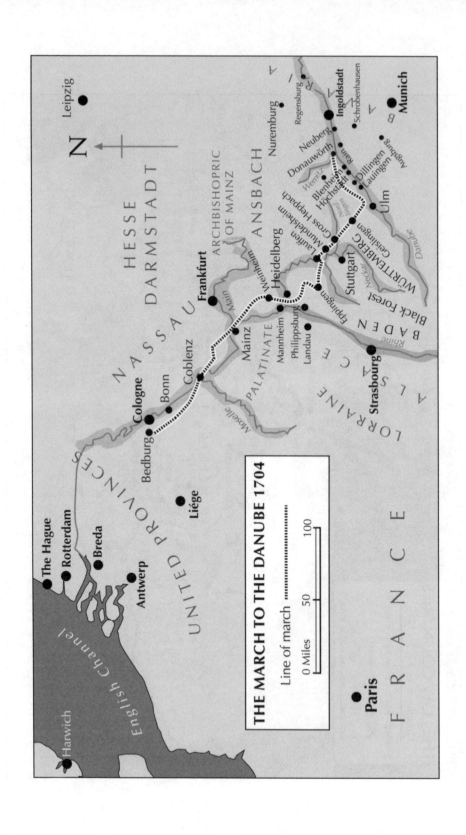

THE MARCH TO THE DANUBE 1704

Line of march ••••••••••

0 Miles   50   100

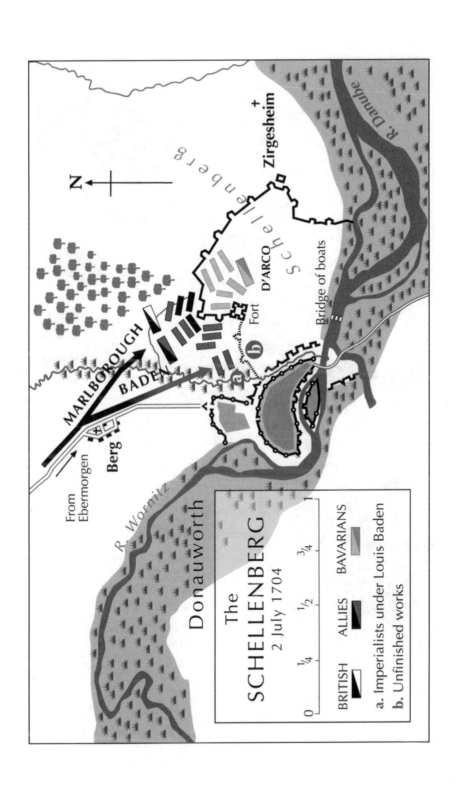

N

Zirgesheim +

S c h e l l e n b e r g

D'ARCO

Bridge of boats

R. Danube

Fort

b

a

MARLBOROUGH

BADEN

From
Ebermorgen

Berg

R. Wornitz

Donauworth

The
SCHELLENBERG
2 July 1704

| 0 | ¼ | ½ | ¾ | 1 |

BRITISH   ALLIES   BAVARIANS

a. Imperialists under Louis Baden
b. Unfinished works

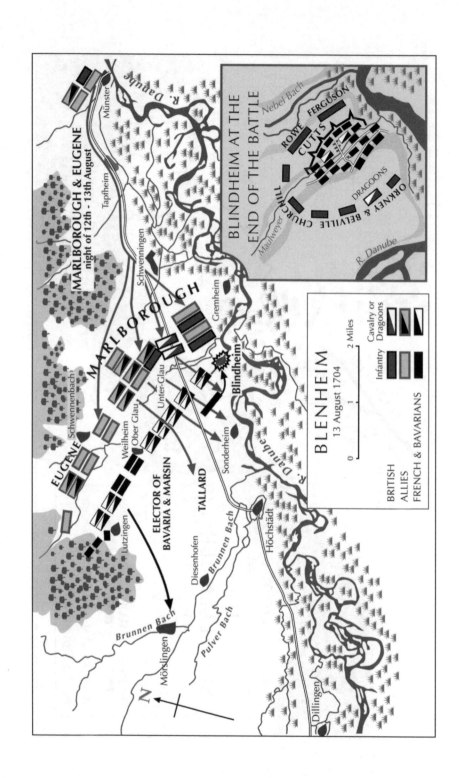

BLINDHEIM AT THE
END OF THE BATTLE

Nebel Bach

FERGUSON

ROWE

CUTTS

DRAGOONS

ORKNEY & BEVILLE CHURCHILL

Maulweyer Bach

R. Danube

MARLBOROUGH & EUGENE
night of 12th - 13th August

R. Danube

Münster

Tapfheim

Schwenningen

MARLBOROUGH

Gremheim

Unter-Glau

Blindheim

Schwennenbach

Weilheim

Ober Glau

Sonderheim

EUGENE

Lützingen

ELECTOR OF
BAVARIA & MARSIN

TALLARD

Diesenhofen

Brunnen Bach

Höchstädt

R. Danube

Brunnen Bach

Mörslingen

Pulver Bach

Dillingen

N

BLENHEIM
13 August 1704

0   1   2 Miles

BRITISH
ALLIES
FRENCH & BAVARIANS

Infantry

Cavalry or
Dragoons

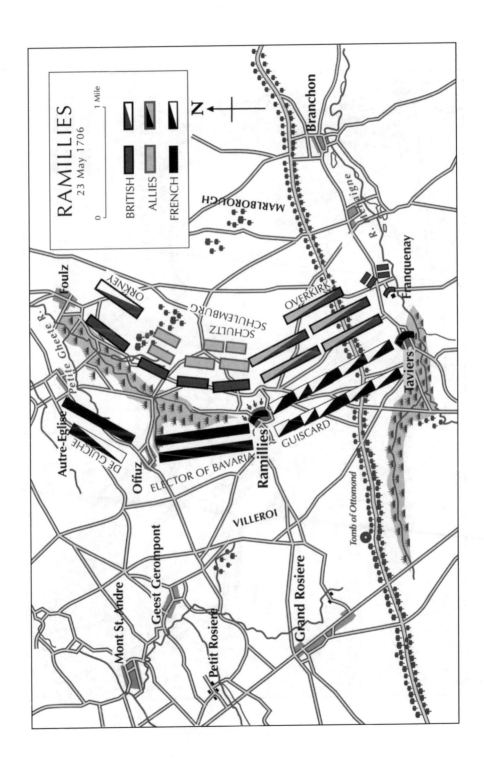

RAMILLIES
23 May 1706

0   1 Mile

BRITISH

ALLIES

FRENCH

N

Branchon

MARLBOROUGH

R. Mehaigne

Franquenay

Foulz

ORKNEY

SCHULTZ SCHULEMBURG

OVERKIRK

Taviers

Autre-Eglise

Petite Gheete R.

DE GUICHE

Offuz

ELECTOR OF BAVARIA

Ramillies

GUISCARD

Tomb of Ottomond

VILLEROI

Geest Gerompont

Mont St. Andre

Petit Rosiere

Grand Rosiere

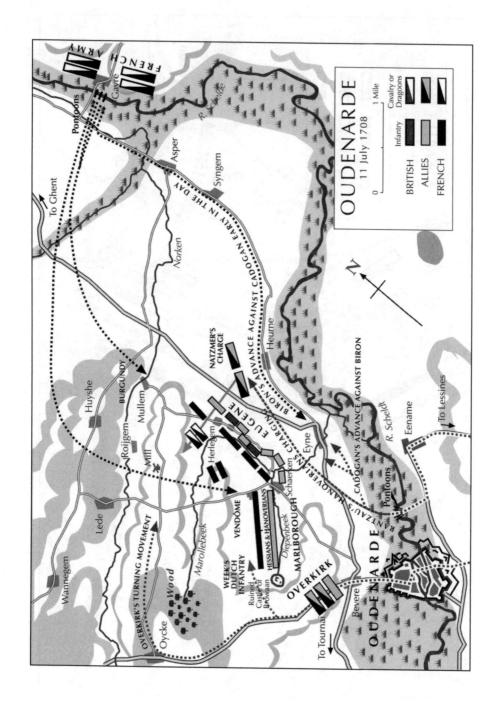

OUDENARDE
11 July 1708

BRITISH
ALLIES
FRENCH

Infantry
Cavalry or Dragoons

0   1 Mile

FRENCH ARMY

To Ghent

Pontoons

Gavre

R. Scheldt

Asper

Syngem

Norken

Heurne

To Lessines

Eename

R. Scheldt

Pontoons

CADOGAN'S ADVANCE AGAINST BIRON

BIRON'S ADVANCE AGAINST CADOGAN EARLY IN THE DAY

NATZMER'S CHARGE

EUGENE

CHARGING RANTZAU'S HANOVERIANS

Eyne

Burgundy

Huyshe

Mullem

Roijgem

Mill

Herlegem

Schaerken

VENDÔME

Diepenbeek

HESSIANS & HANOVERIANS

MARLBOROUGH

Lede

Marollebeek

WEEK'S DUTCH INFANTRY

Ruined Castle of Bevere

OVERKIRK

OVERKIRK'S TURNING MOVEMENT

Oycke Wood

Wannegem

OUDENARDE

Bevere

To Tournai

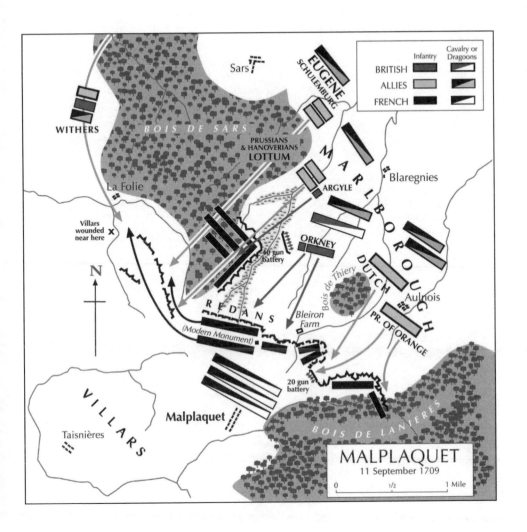

MALPLAQUET
11 September 1709

Introduction

To Flanders, Portugal and Spain
Queen Anne commands and we obey
Over the hills and far away
Courage boys, 'tis one to ten
That we return all gentlemen
To whore and rant as well as they
When over the hills and far away.[1]

Any army is a 'war machine', and whether it achieves success or failure, or is used for good or ill, that is its only purpose. First and foremost, however, an army is what its commander is – if the commander succeeds, then so too does the army with laurels and glory to match, but if he fails, then the army is in consequence led to ruin and disgrace. Accordingly, this book must primarily be about Queen Anne's Captain-General, John Churchill, First Duke of Marlborough, and his famous exploits as a military commander during the War of the Spanish Succession between the years 1702 and 1711. However, the story must plainly also be about the men whom the duke was entrusted to lead into battle by England (Great Britain, as it was known from the Act of Union in 1707 onwards) and the States-General of Holland. Those troops made up the only effective military force in northern Europe that could take the field to face the French, and so, just as the duke's fortunes were the fortunes of his men, so too were they the fortunes of those two countries and their allies at a time of acute European crisis. Of Marlborough's unsurpassed record of success it was said in perfect truth that 'He passed all the rivers and lines that he attempted, took all the towns he invested, won all the battles he fought, was never surprised by the enemy, was ever beloved by his own soldiers and dreaded by those of the enemy.'[2]

That his troops were led to astonishing and unprecedented victories in Germany and the Low Countries will soon be seen, but we should also look at just who and what that army was, how it was gathered together, equipped, trained, administered and supplied, and how the soldiers campaigned and how they lived, whored and ranted, as the old scurrilous rhyme had it, and how they died.

This is not intended to be a simple account listing in detail the composition and structure of the Duke of Marlborough's army at that time of war, for it was an ever-changing picture with complexity enough to gladden the heart of any Byzantine scholar, and at this remove of time the glass has darkened and the intricate detail is far from clear. What this book intends to do, rather, is to set out why that army was a war machine – a resoundingly winning machine at that – and how it moved, breathed, lived and, under the masterful hand of Marlborough, struck in deadly fashion at its opponents during almost ten years of hard campaigning. Those long years saw the war machine that the duke commanded, inspired with confidence and led from victory to victory, effectively laying the foundations for a military, and militant, reputation and legacy for Great Britain in particular that lasts to the present day. The duke showed his often-astonished countrymen what could be achieved, and while their opinions of him and suspicions of his vaulting ambitions might vary, the wider lesson of what they as a nation might become was not lost on them.

Marlborough's army, his war machine, achieved success on an almost unparalleled level; at the time, certainly, its exploits in humbling the armies of King Louis XIV of France were regarded as a true wonder. In part, this was because until only a few years before the outbreak of the war for Spain, England had been regarded as a relatively negligible military entity, seemingly irrelevant and riven by internal dissent and fractious civil wars. The exploits of Cromwell's well-disciplined New Model Army, which had achieved so much in the mid-seventeenth century, were disregarded, particularly as the dilettante and dissolute Restoration years of King Charles II saw marked military decline and cynical opportunism. That wily and impecunious monarch allied himself, both openly and covertly, to the French king in return for subsidies in ready cash, and English regiments were loaned into the French service to fight the Dutch and the Spanish, depending upon which opponent Louis XIV was engaged with at any particular time. It is true that these troops gained a good reputation for themselves as tough fighters, and handsome young John Churchill, who would one day become the Duke of Marlborough and a scourge of French army commanders, fought as a junior officer in these campaigns and was noted for his gallantry on more than one occasion, attracting the attention of Louis XIV. He was even offered a commission in the French army, but declined as a non-Roman Catholic could hardly hope to rise far in the service of the Sun King.[3] The reputation of the English troops, however, did not match that of the more battle-experienced Dutch, nor was their administration and logistical ability of the same high order. The States-General of Holland, of course, had learned hard lessons in the long years of their own war for independence from Spain, lessons reinforced when they were attacked by their erstwhile ally, France, and brought so close to complete ruin in the 1670s.

Louis XIV had long had a policy of aggressive forward defence, pushing out his borders, particularly in the north and north-east where major natural obstacles were lacking, at the expense of his weaker near neighbours. The flight from London of King James II in 1688, and the assumption of the thrones of England and Scotland by his Dutch son-in-law, the Stadtholder William of Orange, changed the scene in western Europe considerably. The Dutchman was an implacable opponent of the French, and from then on, the power and wealth of England would be joined with that of the United Provinces of Holland and turned against France, and what were widely and understandably seen to be the overbearing ambitions of the king. In the meantime, John Churchill gradually established his reputation as a good field commander, not only in France and with the English garrison in Tangier, but also at a key moment in the suppression of the Monmouth Rebellion in the West Country in 1685. He rose high in the service of King James II, but at the opportune moment allied himself to Dutch William readily enough, as did many of his brother officers.

The new monarch, uneasy on his throne, was reluctant to trust this gifted and ambitious man too much, but as time went by he came to appreciate Churchill's worth and to employ his services to good effect. By the time of the outbreak of the War of the Spanish Succession early in 1702, the Earl of Marlborough, as Churchill had become, was England's Captain-General, and soon would be appointed to be the commander of the Anglo-Dutch army when it was in the field. He was still an unknown quantity to a certain degree, regarded with some scepticism by more veteran commanders, men who had endured long and arduous campaigns against the French over the recent decades, and who might with good reason have felt that they had a better claim to the role. That Marlborough won such doubters over so completely, and enjoyed their almost unreserved support, speaks highly for both his tact and his natural abilities as a commander. It should be added that, at a time of acute crisis, he was perhaps the best and only widely acceptable choice, no matter how limited his experience at the head of an army might have been – that he was an eminently good choice would soon be demonstrated.

One of the duke's illustrious descendants gave an indication of how warfare was carried on in Marlborough's day, important background when considering how Marlborough, his allies, and his army, and of course his opponents, conducted their campaigns. The excesses and horrors of the Thirty Years War in the first half of the previous century had produced a reaction, and an attempt was made to make these affairs less barbarous with the implementation of some widely acknowledged rules of conduct, at least where they were applied in western Europe:

> After the fury of battle was spent both sides, and especially the victors, laboured to rescue the wounded, instead of leaving them to perish inch by inch in agony in No Man's Land. If in their poverty they stripped the dead of their clothing, they also exchanged prisoners with meticulous accounting. The opposing generals paid each other compliments and courtesy which did not hamper their operations, and in the winter season issued passports to prominent officers to traverse hostile territory on their shortest route home. Although the great causes in dispute were stated with a robust vigour and precision which we have now lost, no hatred, apart from military antagonism, was countenanced among the troops. All was governed by strict rules of war, into which bad temper was not often permitted to enter. The main acceptance of a polite civilization still reigned across the lines of the opposing armies, and mob violence and mechanical propaganda had not yet been admitted.[4]

There is an element of rose-tinting here, but there was undoubtedly a kind of rough and ready, if unspoken and grudging, camaraderie between the opposing armies. Soldiers on each side endured the same sort of discomfort and privation when on campaign and harboured, as a result, a lurking respect for their foes. At the siege of Ath in the summer of 1706, John Deane of the 1st English Foot Guards remembered that the Allied troops 'Entrenched themselves almost up to the palisades of the enemy's works, being so near that they could easily call to each other.'[5] Sentries minding their own business, men fetching water or firewood or 'easing nature' at a latrine or behind a bush were rarely fired on. Putting up a good fight was of course admired, and craven conduct, whether by friend or foe, appropriately despised. Such admirable sentiments and arrangements, while true, have to be viewed in the knowledge of the brutality that is naturally inherent in making war – the scarcely bridled licensed ferocity of combat with shot, sword, bayonet and musket butt on the battlefield. To this must be added the inevitable disruption of life for most ordinary people in any

region campaigned over: the bombardment of their towns and inhabitants, such as happened with merciless ferocity at Ostend in 1706; onerous
taxation; the levying of what were euphemistically known as 'contribu-
tions' and the confiscation of crops, stores of grain, herds and horses.
Impressment of ordinary men to labour on mending roads or in hazardous siege lines was common, and destitution and poverty were often the
consequence for the civilian population, who often had little or no interest
or stake in whatever great matter was being fought over.

After what may be regarded as something of a slow start for Marlborough, with two years of steady but uninspiring progress in the Low
Countries, the famously victorious Danube campaign of 1704 changed
everything forever. The defeat of a main French force in this decisive way
was an unheard of event, for the Marshals of France had a long record of
success; the Duc de St Simon at Versailles wrote that:

> We were not accustomed to misfortunes. There was scarcely an illus-
> trious family that had not one of its members killed, wounded, or
> taken prisoner . . . The grief of the King at this ignominy and this loss,
> at the moment when he imagined that the fate of the Emperor [of
> Austria] was in his hands, may be imagined . . . All was lost in
> Bavaria.[6]

The defeated Marshal Tallard was sitting in Marlborough's own coach,
while another French army, commanded by Marshal Ferdinand Marsin,
accompanied by their defeated Bavarian allies, was in flight and disarray.
Nothing would ever be the same, and, although the Imperial Austrian
commander, Prince Eugene of Savoy, played a major part in the achieving
of such a success, it was widely understood that Marlborough's had been
the guiding hand for the campaign, and his was the victory, Indeed, had
the campaign failed, the disgrace would have largely fallen on him with
potentially dire consequences, with his political opponents in London
only waiting for the chance to break him up 'like hounds upon a hare'. In
the event of such success, however, the laurels of the victory were rightly
heaped on the duke at home and abroad. In part, perhaps, this was the
first occasion for some hundreds of years that an English commander
could be said to have triumphed in such emphatic style over the French.[7]

The victory at Blenheim, wonder of the age that it was, was followed
less than two years later by the crowning triumph for Marlborough at
Ramillies in what was then the Spanish (or Southern) Netherlands.
Marshal Villeroi's fine French and Bavarian army was shattered in only a
short afternoon, and the duke quickly went on to seize almost the whole

of the strategically vital region for the Grand Alliance. The Austrian claimant to the Spanish throne, Archduke Charles, appeared to be on the very brink of success, able to take the throne in Madrid as King Carlos III, courtesy of Marlborough and his troops. To add to the general air of joyous disbelief at such relatively painless gains, it was acknowledged that Marlborough had achieved this success with no real superiority in numbers of men or guns. The duke had out-generalled and outfought the French commander and his allies; moreover, Prince Eugene had not been there to lend a hand, being engaged elsewhere in the conflict. This was Marlborough's victory, plain and simple, and as such it was also that of his war machine.

Unexpected success, warm, welcome and achieved at what appeared to be modest cost, has its drawbacks. After the apparent miracle for the Allied cause at Ramillies it seemed that everything was possible and any-thing could be, and indeed soon would be, demanded of the French king. This assumption of a certain victory already achieved, with the profits safely tucked away, was a significant miscalculation on the part of the Allies, who failed to appreciate the robust nature of Louis XIV and his long-suffering people. While demand was carelessly added to demand by the Grand Alliance, France fought doggedly on, and so in consequence the war had to continue. For all Marlborough's skill and the efforts of his soldiers, long and tiring years of war followed the glorious summer of 1706 when everything and anything had briefly seemed possible. The duke and his generals would confront and defeat the French on numer-ous occasions and yet, for all this litany of success – a lengthy passage of arms that is arguably unrivalled in European military history – the duke, even when combined with the skill and power of Prince Eugene and his Imperial troops, could not force a complete enough submission from France to satisfy the inflated demands of the Grand Alliance. Those demands, crucially, came to contain an absolute requirement that Arch-duke Charles should take possession of the throne in Madrid and that the French claimant, King Philip V (the Duc d'Anjou), should be ousted. Such a cocksure approach could not be borne in Versailles, for all the thread-bare state of France and French armies by the summer of 1709 and the mounting discontent amongst the hungry people. Louis XIV judged the mood of his army and his people well and would write to his provincial governors to explain his rejection of the latest Allied terms:

> Our enemies in their pretence to negotiate are palpably insincere, we
> have only to consider how to defend ourselves ... Let us show our

enemies that we are still not sunk so low, but that we can force upon them such a peace as shall be consistent with our honour and with the peace of Europe.[8]

Marlborough's army, operating under the guiding hand of one of the great captains in history, had achieved a victory over France and associated French interests in the huge Spanish Empire. Complete success and peace, measured and judicious, was at hand but those in the comfortable council chambers of the Grand Alliance proved unable to make this good. The reasons for the eventual incomplete outcome, and the unfulfilled hopes of the Allies, lay at the door of those same inept and self-serving politicians. The principal original demand when the Grand Alliance was formed in 1702 – that the Spanish Empire should be divided so that neither Austria nor France would gain too great an accrual of power from the demise of King Carlos II – was accomplished, but this was all forgotten. The inability of Marlborough and his army to force an abject submission from Louis XIV by victory on the field of battle was well remembered, though, and in the closing days of 1711, in spite of being fresh from a new triumph at the siege of Bouchain, the duke was dismissed from all his posts and appointments by an ailing and disappointed Queen Anne. 'That we must part from such a man, whose fame has spread throughout the world,' lamented veteran soldier John Wilson on hearing the news of the duke's dismissal.[9] As Marlborough left the scene, so the fortunes of the Grand Alliance noticeably dipped, and this did not go unnoticed, 'The affair of displacing the Duke of Marlborough', Louis XIV wrote on hearing the news from London, 'will do all for us that we desire.'[10] It was clearly apparent in Versailles just what was the mainspring in the effort to curb the power of France, no matter how little this was recognized by the queen and her ministers in London.

The Allied campaign in the Low Countries languished with British troops now under the ineffectual command of Marlborough's replacement by a political appointee, James Butler, Second Duke of Ormonde. By this point, even Prince Eugene seemed ill at ease and out of sorts now that his old friend and comrade was no longer on the active scene, and success was limited and harder to gain. Acting on covert instructions from London, Ormonde gradually withdrew British troops from the field, in effect leaving their Dutch, German and Imperial allies to fight on their own. Queen Anne's secretary of state, Henry St John, wrote on 1 July 1712 to the German princes and electors who, in return for payment from the

British Treasury, provided troops for the Grand Alliance and were now proving very reluctant to draw off from active campaigning:

> Her Majesty has ordered him [Ormonde] to notify the Ministers of the Princes, who have troops in Flanders, whether entirely in the pay of the Queen, or in conjunction with the States-General, that she will look upon such a refusal as a Declaration against Herself; and that she has resolved to issue no more pay, subsidy, or arrears, to those who make such a refusal.[11]

This was just bluster, an attempt to intimidate princes and electors who were not susceptible to such crude pressure. By then, of course, it was no longer Marlborough's army; his guiding hand was withdrawn, as Sir Winston Churchill eloquently wrote in the 1930s, and lesser men were leading his fine troops to defeat and disgrace. The French field commander, Marshal Villars, ever watchful and dangerous although lamed at Malplaquet, was able to regain much of the territory and many of the fortresses lost to Marlborough over the preceding few years, and the war stumbled to a tired end in northern Europe and on the Rhine in 1713 and 1714, and in Spain in 1715. The imperfect peace that came with the negotiated treaties of Utrecht in 1713, and Rastadt, Baden and Madrid in following years, satisfied no one, although inevitably some had through good management or good fortune gained more than others. In fact, no one was really in a mood to be fully satisfied after so much effort and expense had been lavished, and which at first glance had gained little.

The principal aim of the Grand Alliance had been achieved; to that end, the Allies' original intention to curb the power of France to an acceptable level was a distinct success, with a kind of balance of power established in Europe for decades to come. Without doubt, for all the fine words and lofty sentiments concerning amity and lasting peace expressed in comfortable council chambers, this success was to a large extent the product of the work of Marlborough and the soldiers who made up his army, his war machine. A new reputation for military endeavour and success had been established: the regiments might come home, some to be reduced or disbanded, others sent to campaign elsewhere, but the memory of what had been achieved could not be overlooked or erased. That reputation, founded by the duke and his men during the long years of war, lent a distinct and enduring lustre to the newly found martial image of Great Britain, establishing a confident legacy for projecting power that would last in various forms until the present day.[12]

Chapter 1

The War for Spain

By the close of the seventeenth century, it had become clear that, despite the administering of strange, fanciful and exotic potions, together with earnest prayers and incantations, the sickly Habsburg King Carlos II of Spain would never father children. He had no surviving brothers, sisters or close cousins to succeed him when he died, and so the vexed question across much of western Europe became, who would take the throne in Madrid once Carlos was gone and in his grave? The mid-sixteenth-century division of the great empire of Charles V into Spanish and Austrian portions had left two potential claimants, each arguably with as good a cause in their favour as the other. Without some sure-footed diplomacy and judicious calculation, the scope for mischief, misunderstanding, danger and even ruinous war was immense.

The question of who would succeed Carlos was one of prime importance for, although Spain was no longer the political and military power that it had once been, the empire ruled from Madrid encompassed much of the Iberian Peninsula (Portugal, while fiercely independent, being very much in the Spanish sphere of influence), the Balearic Islands and Sardinia in the Mediterranean, the wealthy Southern Netherlands, enclaves on the Barbary shore of the north coast of Africa, much of Sicily, Naples and northern Italy, wide stretches of the rich lands in the Americas, and even the Philippines, exotic and far off as they were. If the potential claimant from the House of Bourbon took the throne, then the power and influence of France would be enhanced to a degree that England and Holland could not countenance. The aggressive wars which King Louis XIV of France had waged against his near neighbours in the second half of the century made such a potential increase in French power, harnessed to the wealth of the Spanish Empire, a matter of great concern – concern that would prove to be worth going to war for.

If, on the other hand, the Habsburg claimant in Vienna should succeed to the throne in Madrid, then the power of Imperial Austria – although increasingly diverted by internal divisions and rebellion and the Ottoman threat from the east – would set out the possibility of the encirclement of France once again, a throwback to the old times of Charles V. Habsburg armies would perhaps gather to surround and threaten France from Spain and northern Italy, and from the Low Countries (the largely Catholic southern portion, now known as Belgium, that had not gained independence from Madrid in the early part of the seventeenth century). Also exposed, from France's point of view, would be the lengthy course of the river Rhine, where the increasingly assertive German princes, technically owing allegiance to the Holy Roman Empire (an institution neither holy, Roman, or an empire, as it has been wittily described), could manoeuvre to imperil the recently established, and yet to be properly strengthened, eastern border of France. That the attention of Vienna would be permanently diverted to the south and east by unrest in Hungary and, more perilous perhaps, the growth of Ottoman aggression, was not yet recognized, and so the potential danger to France of renewed Habsburg encirclement, although in reality a shadowy myth, was not seen as such in Fontainebleau and Versailles.

The dilemma for all concerned was real enough; Carlos II was fading fast. A neat solution was found, with King Louis XIV of France and Emperor Leopold I of Austria agreeing that an acceptable choice, one that should avoid conflict between the two, would be for Joseph-Ferdinand, the young son of the Elector of Bavaria, to succeed to the Spanish throne once it became vacant. His mother, the now-deceased first wife of the elector, was the daughter of the emperor in Vienna, and so the young man had as good a claim as could be desired. Although little attention seems to have been paid to the wishes of the Spanish nobility and people over the matter, this was a sensible and pragmatic solution to a difficult problem. In the meantime, the most recent of the wars fought by France against its near neighbours, the Nine Years War (also known as the War of the League of Augsburg), had come to a gradual and weary end in 1697 with the Treaty of Ryswick. This agreement contained solemn undertakings on many counts, including providing the United Provinces of Holland with a secure barrier of fortress towns across the Southern Netherlands to deter any future French aggression, and an acknowledgement of William III as the rightful King of England and Scotland. This important provision entailed the abandonment by France of support for a Stuart restoration on behalf of the exiled King James II, who would, however, remain with his wife and young son as honoured guests of the French monarch at St Germain.

Unfortunately and inconveniently, Prince Joseph-Ferdinand of Bavaria died suddenly of smallpox in June 1699, and the careful arrangement reached by France and Austria to dispose safely of the soon to be vacant Spanish throne came to nothing. No fresh agreement could be reached, although France and England entered an amendment to the Treaty of Ryswick such that, when Carlos II died, Archduke Charles of Austria, Emperor Leopold I's youngest son, should succeed to the Spanish throne, in return for territorial concessions to France by way of recompense. Early in November 1700 Carlos II, who had never enjoyed good health as a consequence of Habsburg inbreeding, at last lay on his death-bed. In the late king's will, which had been amended shortly before his death, the throne of Spain was offered to Louis XIV's young second grandson Philippe, Duc d'Anjou, who would as a result, become Philip (Felipe) V of Spain. The news of this glittering offer reached the French court at Fontainebleau on 8 November, and Louis XIV was faced with a difficult decision. If the offer was accepted, solemn treaty obligations were to be disregarded and fears of a massive increase in French power and influence would cause alarm through the rest of western Europe. Reassurances could be offered, but renewed war might well result, and the French Treasury was sorely depleted from the years of conflict which had marked the final decade of the previous century. However, if the throne was refused by the French prince, then the same offer would immediately be made to Austrian Archduke Charles, and the old sensitivity to Habsburg encroachment and encirclement of France would reawaken.

In this dilemma, the stakes were incredibly high, and so too were the risks. Louis XIV was certainly well aware of this, but his own son, the Grand Dauphin, urged that the Duc d'Anjou be permitted to accept the offered throne. The king was persuaded, and the Duc de St Simon remembered that, on 16 November 1700:

> The King, contrary to all custom, opened the two folding doors of his cabinet [private chambers], and commanded everyone to enter. It was a very full Court that day. The King, majestically turning his eyes towards the numerous company, and showing them M. Le Duc d'Anjou, said 'Gentlemen, behold, this is the King of Spain ... be a good Spaniard, that is your first duty, but remember that you are a Frenchman born.'[1]

The French king quickly took steps to assure William III of England and the States-General of Holland that their own interests would not be put at risk by this acceptance of the Spanish throne. Camille d'Hostun, Comte de Tallard, the able French ambassador to London, worked assiduously to assure William of the good intentions of the French, and it was explicitly set out that the crowns of France and Spain should always be kept separate, although how this would be enforced in practice remained shrouded in some uncertainty. Concessions were also offered to Emperor Leopold I in Vienna, to allay any concerns or outrage from that quarter, and for a time it seemed that such assurances would be sufficient, and renewed conflict could be averted with some continued neat diplomatic footwork. Surprisingly, Louis XIV, normally so precise in these matters, now fumbled the scene, and in February 1701 French troops were sent to take possession of a number of important towns in the Spanish Netherlands. To the French king this seemed no less than simple logic – the wealthy region was a part of his grandson's domains and needed to be properly secured with good French garrisons, not left in the hands of the Dutch. However, this move inevitably caused outrage in Holland, as those same towns provided the valuable and much-cherished barrier established at the Treaty of Ryswick which the Dutch relied upon to protect them from fresh French aggression. Louis XIV, it seemed, was behaving just the same way as before.

On a pragmatic level, William III was aware that the barrier towns were no more than a trip-wire and could not be sustained against any determined French policy in the region, and he had no intention of going to war to hold on to them. Instructions had already been prepared, but not yet issued, for the garrisons to withdraw to Holland. However, the French were too quick off the mark, and the Dutch garrisons were interned (at all but Maastricht, where the governor, Johan Wigand van Goor, stoutly refused to admit Louis XIV's men). The States-General had to ask for the return of their troops, which was promptly done, but the whole episode was a distinct humiliation for the proud Dutch; an apparently blunt signal had been given as to what they could expect from the French king in the future.

It seemed clear that steps had to be taken to put a check on renewed French expansion and possible aggression, and in the autumn of 1701 a Treaty of Grand Alliance was agreed between Holland, Austria and England to limit the power of France and, principally, to achieve on broadly equitable terms a division of the Spanish Empire. Neither France nor Austria should gain too great an advantage and put the interests of other nations at risk through the accession of a foreign prince to the throne in Madrid. A key aim, rather more closely linked to the financial well-being of the maritime powers, but not to Austria, was to obtain more favourable trading terms for England and Holland in the Spanish territories in the Americas. There was no explicit requirement, at the time, that the Austrian Archduke Charles should have the Spanish throne as had been, perhaps optimistically, intended once young Joseph-Ferdinand died, but that demand, flawed and fatal, would come soon enough. Although William III negotiated the terms of the alliance with the Dutch, to whom he was obviously very well known (although often absent), John Churchill, now the Earl of Marlborough, played an active part in the discussions, and on 7 September 1701 he signed the treaty on behalf of the king.[2] Louis XIV was very soon apprised of the exact details by the Swedish ambassador to Versailles.

Louis XIV, having outraged the Dutch with his unwise, and probably unnecessary, occupation of the barrier towns in the Spanish Netherlands, made matters even worse a week after the Treaty of Grand Alliance was concluded. He went to St Germain and acknowledged to his dying friend, the exiled King James II, that his own young son, James (known to the French as the Chevalier de St George), was regarded by France as the true successor to the English throne, to be restored as King James III. This was an unguarded comment and contrary to the advice of the king's council, but was yet another infringement of the Treaty of Ryswick. Although it was generally understood that the French king had spoken incautiously and in the emotion of the moment, great offence was taken by some in London, where it seemed clear that once more solemn treaty obligations – and perhaps more tellingly an understood but unwritten agreement that France would not interfere with the orderly succession to the English crown – were of little account to Louis XIV. Tempers flared, firm action was resolved on and additional war supplies were promptly voted by Parliament. However, William III, staunch opponent of the French king and his ambitions, did not live to fight another war; he died on 8 March 1702, a fortnight or so after falling from his favourite horse, Sorrel, and breaking his collar bone.

Princess Anne, youngest daughter of James II, succeeded her Dutch brother-in-law to the throne in London (the crowns of England and Scotland still being separate until the Act of Union in 1707). The Earl of Marlborough, the new queen's close friend, was sent to Holland to affirm to the Dutch that she was resolute in support of the Grand Alliance and the overall aim to limit surging French power. Reassurances also went to the many smaller German princes and electors whose support in the effort against France would be of such value in the years to come. The queen wrote on 17 March 1702, with timely reassurances and a reminder of the growing peril, to the Electors of the Circle of the Upper Rhine. After lamenting the sudden death of William III:

> We now devote ourselves, the more especially, that We may imitate
> so excellent an example, and so far as is possible, may carry on most

accurately his great designs for promoting the Public Good, and chiefly in that watchful vigilance by which he had a care for the Holy Roman Empire and especially the well-being of the illustrious Circles adjacent to the River Rhine ... Doubtless, very well known to your Highness and Your Highness Elect is the ancient and insatiable desire of the French King to dominate; notorious are the wrongs, the cunning and the fraud by which he is scheming to aggrandize the limits of his Empire until satiated ... With the power of France increased by Spain, he will at length attain the summit of his power; so that in a short time he will easily subdue the rest of Europe to his domination.

The Queen was, understandably, overstating things a little, as Louis XIV, despite miscalculations and untypical diplomatic clumsiness, certainly wanted to avoid war (and hoped to get his own way in the process), but the concern was real enough, and now she came to the main point:

Therefore in a very friendly manner we ask and invite Your Highness and Your Highness-Elect, according to the 13th Article of the Treaty (of Grand Alliance), to enter the same Alliance, and to add strength and endurance by our accession. By which act, you will be joining with His Imperial Majesty, with the most high estates of the Dutch Allies, who are very jealous of the Public Good, and especially with Ourselves, who have now solely turned Our attentions, and are about to turn all Our energies, to the end that We may vindicate the common liberty of Europe against the immoderate power of the French.[3]

The various parties to the Grand Alliance proved firm of purpose, and on 15 May 1702 war was simultaneously declared on France and Spain (in the shape of the French claimant, the Duc d'Anjou) in London, The Hague and Vienna. In time, Portugal and the Duchy of Savoy would also, for very different and differing reasons, join the Grand Alliance, and Denmark and many German electorates and principalities – most notably Prussia and Hanover – would also take an active part in the hostilities against Louis XIV and his grandson.[4]

France at this time was the most populous country in western Europe, and Louis XIV had devoted much thought, care and expense to developing his army into an effective fighting instrument, outshining anything else that could be put in the field. French marshals of renown, men such as Turenne, Luxembourg and Condé, had carried out ruthlessly effective campaigns to push the border of the king's realm out to a comforting degree in the closing decades of the previous century. These great commanders had now gone, age and the perils of the battlefield having winnowed them away, and rather lesser men now led French armies, but in the main they were capable enough, as events would prove. Additionally, France had one notably significant advantage at the opening of the War of the Spanish Succession in 1702 – that of a central position from which the king could choose to strike at his opponents wherever it seemed likely to achieve the best effect. As tensions rose over the question of the throne in Madrid, and the prospect of renewed war became more likely, the French armies had been augmented with newly raised regiments and existing units had been strengthened to war establishment. This work had proceeded at a better rate than in the Grand Alliance, so that in the opening weeks of the war, as the Allies gradually gathered their strength, the French commanders struck in the north. The plain intention was to cripple the Anglo-Dutch army that had the task of guarding the borders of southern Holland. By defeating them, and perhaps invading the republic once more, France would surely force the States-General in The Hague to seek terms and so break apart the Grand Alliance before it could get into its stride. The plan was simple, obvious and, unless something quite unexpected happened, very likely to succeed.

The death of William III had left the States-General in something of disarray, as there was no obvious single natural leader to replace him. Each of the Dutch states had its own competing preferences, ambitions and grudges, and while a number of prominent men might consider themselves suitable – one of whom was Queen Anne's honest but uninspiring husband, Prince George of Denmark – there was unlikely to be a general agreement on any one person in the short term. John Friso, the nephew of the recently deceased king, who would become the Prince of Orange and prove himself to be a capable field commander in time, was only 14 years old in 1702, and therefore could not be considered. On the other hand, the Earl of Marlborough was appointed to be Captain-General and commander-in-chief of the army to be deployed by England in the Low Countries. Despite his lack of battle experience compared to many of their own veteran generals, the States-General of Holland were prepared to accept him in command when the combined Anglo-Dutch forces were in the field. Adam Cardonnel, Marlborough's secretary, commented on 1 June 1702 that 'The States have given directions to all their generals and other officers to obey my Lord Marlborough as their general.'[5] Simultaneous campaigns would be undertaken in Spain to consolidate the grip of the French prince on the throne, in northern Italy and the Tyrol, and in southern Germany, where the Elector of Bavaria chose to ally himself to

Louis XIV and threatened to attack Vienna. It was in the north, though, that the main French blow was initially struck, with veteran Marshal Boufflers leading 60,000 troops in a confident advance against the still-incomplete Anglo-Dutch forces under the rather hesitant command of Godert Rede van Ginkel, the Earl of Athlone, who was soon manoeuvred back against the lower Maas River at Cleves. After a good start and rapid early success, Boufflers' campaign then began to flag, as his lines of communication and supply were uncomfortably long and an unexpected but fairly minor Dutch offensive in Flanders – intended as much as anything to be a raid to gather forage and supplies – led to French troops being diverted to counter that move. A frustrating pause in Boufflers' operations, seemingly of little significance but in fact of enormous value to the Allies, then took place.

On 2 June, the earl took over the command of the Allied troops, and the Anglo-Dutch army became Marlborough's army; this would in time become his war machine. He was Queen Anne's Captain-General – that was his formal appointment – and the troops in Her Majesty's pay had to comply as a matter of simple military discipline to his orders. Marlborough had no such specific authority over the Dutch troops. In order that the affairs of the Grand Alliance should proceed, that authority is what Marlborough had in practice: he could request that things be done and those requests were to be complied with, but only while the troops were actively on campaign. The Earl of Athlone, who had a good record as one of the late William III's better generals, would have liked to have the appointment for himself, but although he was at first inclined to be resentful of Marlborough, he would feel able to write late in 1702 that 'The success of this campaign is solely due to this incomparable Commander-in-Chief.'[6]

The army that Marlborough would lead was, of course, a confederate army comprising troops not only from Holland and England but from many other sources. The Dutch had for many years recruited foreign troops into their service, usually to campaign against the French, and the Scots Brigade in Dutch service, for example, had a long and illustrious history. Now, the mighty military effort that was required to put a curb on French expansionism, as it was widely seen, required the placing in the field of large numbers of troops, in such strength that mercenary soldiers from across north-western Europe were brought into the service of the maritime powers – England and Holland. In the early summer of 1702, when Marlborough took the field in the Low Countries at the head of the army, he had under command some 60,000 troops, but only about a quarter of these were subjects of Queen Anne; the remainder, in addition to the Dutch, were drawn from the Protestant states of western Europe, hired out to the service of the Grand Alliance in return for ready cash. Much of the funding for the war had to come from London, where the recent establishment of the Bank of England and the working of the national debt enabled large sums of money to be raised and dispensed to recruit, equip and maintain the armies of the Grand Alliance. In time, London became the paymaster of the Alliance, and British influence, and the wishes of Queen Anne and her ministers, carried a weight that duly reflected that fact. The demands on her Treasury were frequent and huge, and not simply to do with raising armies and actively fighting the French. The queen had on one occasion to write in a slightly barbed tone to the Habsburg claimant, the Archduke Charles (Carlos III):

> You ask me for another advance of money, beyond the 40,000 sterling which I gave orders to be given to you immediately, in case Spain's decision in your favour, which we eagerly expect, is delayed and our activities are protracted over another campaign; you cannot doubt that I will do my best to help you in the most effective manner, to put you on the Throne of your ancestors.[7]

Providing finance for the war aside, simple campaigning in the Low Countries proved to be slow work for Marlborough in the opening years of the war. The Dutch, not yet wholly convinced of his abilities, and with so much at stake, were inclined to be cautious and noticeably reluctant to take risks, and this imposed a degree of drag upon the campaigns. On at least one occasion late in 1702, on the Heaths of Peer, the French army under Marshal Boufflers escaped a mauling because Marlborough was unable to persuade his Dutch allies to participate in an attack. He did, though, take their commanders to a vantage point, where they could see the disordered French soldiers hurry past with their flank woefully exposed. Colonel Daniel Parke paid the Dutch a rather backhanded compliment when he wrote, 'They are like rats if you surround them and leave them no way of escape, then they all fight like devils.'[8] Marlborough, soon to be made a duke in recognition for his efforts, went on to lay siege successfully to a number of important towns, amongst them Bonn, Ruremond, Huy, Limburg and Liège, but an attempt against Antwerp in 1703 miscarried, when the Dutch General Opdham was surprised at the village of Eckeren, his army badly battered by the French and forced to withdraw in unseemly haste and confusion. Marlborough's frustration was clear, as he could see that the way to win the war was to beat the

French field army in open battle, and Antwerp, unlike Eckeren, really would have been worth fighting for. After the narrow escape for his allies from this near disaster, he went forward to see if anything could even then still be attempted:

> I went with 4,000 Horse to see the [French] Lines. They let us come so near, that we beat their out-guard home to their barrier, which gave us an opportunity of seeing the lines; which had a fosse of twenty-seven feet broad before them, and the water in it nine feet deep; so that it is resolved that the army return to the Meuse, and in the first place take Huy. Upon the whole matter, if we cannot bring the French to a battle we shall not do anything.[9]

It was all very vexing, although the Dutch minted a medal for Marlborough inscribed 'Victorious without Slaughter'. The compliment was well meant, but missed the point; this was no way to win a war when an opponent was gaining ground elsewhere. Despite such limited success for Marlborough, the French had certainly had the worst of things in the Low Countries in these early years, and the borders of Holland were made fairly secure. The affairs of the Grand Alliance failed to prosper elsewhere as Philip V proved to be popular in much of Spain, and Maximilien-Emmanuel Wittelsbach the Elector of Bavaria, having combined forces with the French, moved on to threaten Vienna. If this threat became reality, and Vienna should be occupied, even for a short time, then the Grand Alliance would almost certainly fall apart.

Early in 1704, Queen Anne gave her consent to a plan hatched by Marlborough and the Austrian ambassador, Count Wratislaw, to go to the aid of the emperor. In effect, Marlborough would take those troops in the queen's pay up the course of the river Rhine to combine with the Imperial troops in southern Germany and confront the elector to remove the threat to Vienna. For Marlborough, this offered the chance to be free of the constraints imposed on him by the Dutch, while countering one of Louis XIV's main strategic initiatives, that of driving Austria out of the war. The southern frontier of Holland would be exposed by such a movement, but the Dutch troops in Marlborough's army would remain on guard there, under the reliable command of Veldt-Marshal Overkirk. The duke could see, and managed to persuade his Dutch colleagues of the fact, that if he marched south, the French would be unable to ignore the strategic rebalancing that was being made in the Allies' war effort and would have to follow, so that the immediate threat to Holland would subside.

Speed was of the essence in order that the French should remain off-balance. The remarkable march of Marlborough's army in the early summer of 1704, from the Low Counties up the course of the Rhine and then across the passes of the Swabian Jura mountains, is well known, a major switch in the emphasis of the efforts of the Grand Alliance from northern to southern Europe. The dramatic change went virtually unchallenged while it was in progress; Louis XIV was taken by surprise at such an audacious move, and his army in Bavaria, under the command of the recently promoted Marshal Ferdinand Marsin was soon under threat. The countermove by the king was to hurriedly send a fresh French army, commanded by Marshal Tallard, through the Black Forest passes to go to the support of Marsin and the Elector of Bavaria. In the meantime, dictating the pace of the campaign and always one step ahead, Marlborough had joined Prince Eugene of Savoy, the president of the Imperial War Council, and the Margrave of Baden, the Imperial field commander, and agreed with them a joint strategy to deal with the threat to Vienna. In short, Eugene would go to hold the upper Rhine secure, while Marlborough and Baden combined forces to engage Marsin and the elector on the Danube.

First of all, Marlborough had to get his army across the river Danube and interpose it between Vienna and the French and Bavarian forces. This he did in emphatic style on 2 July 1704, by seizing the partly fortified Schellenberg hill above the small town of Donauwörth at the junction of the Wornitz River with the Danube, and he destroyed Count d'Arco's Franco-Bavarian force there in the process. Marlborough now had a secure crossing to the southern bank of the Danube. Having placed his army between Vienna and the French and Bavarians, his principal objective in the campaign, he could operate almost at will in the region. On the other hand, of course, Marsin and the elector might come out of their defences to fight, although news of the approach of a fresh French army under Tallard was soon received in the Allied camp, and it seemed almost certain that nothing would be attempted until Tallard's arrival in Bavaria. Meanwhile, in an effort to prise the elector away from the French, the duke embarked on a ruthless campaign of destruction in Bavaria, but the elector was not to be moved from his own set course and clung to his alliance with Louis XIV, despite the urging of his wife. By late summer there was something of a stalemate in southern Germany; Marlborough could not winter his army south of the Danube, at least partly because the region had been devastated by his own cavalry and dragoons. The alternative was to withdraw along his own newly established supply lines towards Nuremburg in central Germany, but this would be a tacit admission of failure, and whether the campaign in the south could be renewed in 1705, with the Dutch growing more anxious at the duke's continued absence, was very much in doubt. Also in doubt would be Marlborough's reputation as a commanding general who could deliver real success, particularly as many politicians in London were far from convinced that their troops should be so far away at all, on what might prove to be a fool's errand.

On 13 August 1704 all such misgivings were set to rest. Marlborough had joined forces with Prince Eugene and attacked and defeated the French and Bavarian armies on the plain of Höchstädt, in the battle that became known as Blenheim (from the nearby village of Blindheim, into which Marshal Tallard's French infantry were pointlessly packed and then herded away as prisoners of war). 'We took them all prisoners,' Donald McBane, serving with Orkney's Regiment, wrote, 'they laid down their arms and marched a mile to the right of our army, we took a great many of their head officers, with the standards, tents, and their whole Train and ammunition.'[10] In the aftermath of utter defeat, Marshal Marsin and the elector conducted a withdrawal to the Rhine with their own battered forces, and the closing months of the year saw a series of hard-fought rearguard actions and sieges of such places as Landau in Alsace and Trarbach on the Moselle. This dogged resistance, conducted in part by François de Neufville, Marshal Villeroi, a close friend of Louis XIV, slowed the Allied progress and prevented Marlborough from making the most of his astonishingly successful campaign that summer. Despite this, the French king had lost the ability to win the war on that terrible day in August; the complete destruction of one of his main field armies was a blow that could not easily be set right. 'The loss of France could not be measured by men or fortresses. A hundred victories since Rocroi had taught the world to regard the French army as invincible, when Blenheim, and the surrender of the flower of French soldiery, broke the spell.'[11] All this might be so, but Louis XIV had not yet lost the war – it remained to be seen whether the Grand Alliance could make the most of this turn of events and prudently achieve an advantageous peace for themselves.

The victory at Blenheim, so unexpected and so complete, was greeted with relief and jubilation across the Alliance. Marlborough was the hero of the hour, seen to be clearly one of the great captains of all time, a true 'master of the field'. Honours flowed to him and his commanders. Eugene had his share of glory, of course, although the Margrave of Baden had gone to lay siege to the Bavarian-held fortress of Ingolstadt early in

August and had not, to his regret, been present on the day of victory. Making the most of this success, however, was not that simple, and the duke found that he was unavoidably drawn back into the Low Countries to campaign in 1705. His overall plan for the year, almost certainly too ambitious and optimistic, was to take his troops to combine with the Imperial army under Baden to sweep through the Moselle valley into the heart of northern France, while Veldt-Marshal Overkirk held the line with a Dutch corps in the Southern Netherlands. Nothing went well – the weather was bad, the Margrave was delayed (partly due to still convalescing from a wound to his foot suffered at the Schellenberg). The duke, Captain Robert Parker wrote, 'was greatly chagrined at the disappointment, as he had conceived great hopes of penetrating France that way ... had the prince [Baden] joined him according to their agreement, the French must have drawn from the Netherlands a good part of their troops.'[12] It would, though, not have been quite so simple as the good captain suggests, for the formidable Marshal Villars, always a sound tactician, held strong defensive positions along the line of the Moselle. In addition, Emperor Leopold had died in Vienna that May, adding uncertainty to the Alliance. To complicate all this, the contractor who was supposed to be gathering stores in Trier embezzled the funds and defected to the French instead. Marlborough's troops were out of position and short of supplies: 'We camped on a hill called Hungry Hill,' Donald McBane remembered ruefully.[13]

Matters turned worse on 10 June, when Marshal Villeroi seized the town of Huy on the Meuse River, and Overkirk, thoroughly alarmed at the sudden French move, urgently sent word for Marlborough to return as soon as he could. The duke had little option but to abandon his already faltering Moselle campaign and force march his troops back to the Low Countries, where Huy was soon recovered and Villeroi forced back behind his defences. These works, known as the Lines of Brabant, stretched in a huge arc some 60 miles long, from Antwerp in the north down to Namur on the Meuse, and shielded the French field army as it manoeuvred to counter whatever Marlborough and Overkirk might attempt. On 17 July 1705 Marlborough forced his way through the lines at Elixheim on the Gheete stream and drove off the French and Bavarian detachment he met there with heavy losses. Villeroi fell back behind the shelter of the Lys River to cover Louvain, but a move by the duke to confront him there was frustrated by Dutch reluctance to move quickly enough once an initial crossing of the river had been accomplished. A month later, in mid-August, an attempt by the duke to overwhelm a French force under the

Marquis de Grimaldi on the Yssche River to the south of Brussels failed because the Dutch generals and their field deputies were unwilling to undertake what they, quite understandably in fact, foresaw would be an expensive engagement.[14] The duke might invite his allies to come to a ball, but he could not, yet, be sure that they would dance.

For his part, Marlborough declared that he would no longer work under such restrictions. The States-General, tacitly acknowledging that the campaign had stalled at least in part due to the restrictions under which he had to operate, quietly transferred elsewhere the more obstinate and short-sighted of their generals and field deputies and assured the duke of full cooperation in future. 'If he would continue at the head of the army on their frontier ... they would readily comply withal.'[15] To a large degree, they proved to be as good as their word in the years that followed. Difficulties did persist, however, over the precise terms of service and prompt payments of subsidies with some of the Protestant leaders who provided such excellent troops for the Alliance, a number of whom, welcome and gifted with military expertise or otherwise, wished to take the field in person.

Louis XIV had taken heart from the relative lack of success for the Allies throughout 1705, a time when his grandson was gradually consolidating his position across much of Spain. It was tempting to believe that Marlborough's success the previous year had been due to good fortune, and to the presence of Prince Eugene, rather than to his own skill. The king was eager to achieve a peace, however, as his Treasury was under strain, and orders went out to all the French field commanders that they should assume the offensive in 1706, to demonstrate to the Grand Alliance the vitality of the French war effort, and in that way encourage them to come at once to the conference table. So it was that Marshal Villeroi, urged on by Versailles, took the field in May with a well-equipped 60,000-strong army. He moved southwards from his concentration area near to Louvain to interpose himself between the fortress of Namur on the Meuse, and Marlborough's own army, which was then still assembling at Tongres just to the south-west of Maastricht.

Marlborough was both surprised and pleased to find that the French commander had come out from behind the lines of defence that had served so well the previous year and was apparently offering to fight in the open. Marlborough's army was not yet fully mustered, with many officers still on leave and the Hanoverian, Prussian and Danish contingents not ready to march as their terms of service for the year and arrears of pay had yet to be settled.[15] Despite this, on 19 May 1706 the duke set his troops marching without delay, moving southwards to take possession of the watershed between the Mehaine and Gheete streams, on the high ground near the small villages of Ramillies and Offus. Once there, he would be ready to move forward and confront Villeroi before he could, perhaps, think better of things and fall back behind his defences. An urgent message was sent to bring forward the Danish troops and, on Saturday 22 May, John Deane, serving with the 1st English Foot Guards, recalled that 'The Danish troops came up with our rear this evening, and encamped at a small distance from us.'[16] The very next day, Whit Sunday, Marlborough found that Villeroi had taken up position on the high ground first and was settling his troops into a decent defensive position around Ramillies to face the approaching 62,000-strong Allied army.

Marlborough did not hesitate and promptly pushed forward to fix Villeroi in position. As afternoon came on he attacked the French, first unhinging the line on their right flank at the hamlets of Franquenay and Taviers, and then driving British, German and Danish infantry forward against Ramillies and Offus on their left. A huge cavalry battle erupted on the open plain to the south of Ramillies, and by evening, Veldt-Marshal Overkirk's Dutch and Danish horsemen had lapped around the French right flank and, in a huge and carefully controlled advance, proceeded to roll up Villeroi's fine army from right to left. Nothing that the marshal could do at this stage would save things, and his broken troops fled in disorder, abandoning all their guns and equipment and looking only to find shelter behind the river Dyle.

This was complete victory – unqualified, unlike Blenheim – with the only field army that the French had in the Southern Netherlands left in tatters. Marlborough's victorious troops surged forwards in headlong pursuit. It was, an observer wrote, as if the duke's troops had thrown their weight against an unlatched door, and simply fallen through. The Allied army quickly seized such important places as Louvain, Brussels, Antwerp (where the Spanish governor changed his allegiance remarkably promptly), Ghent, Bruges and Ostend. John Deane also remembered that at that important port:

> Our heavy cannon having come up from Sas van Ghent and other garrisons adjacent, and our batteries being made ready by the 23rd of June, we began to let the town know it; firing our guns and bombs into it which struck terror into the heart of the inhabitants. But the Governor [Comte de la Motte, who had distinguished himself at Ramillies], stood it out manfully, and got what guns he could out of

the ships in that harbour and planted them where he thought he might prejudice the besiegers.[17]

A campaign that might rightly have called for years of hard fighting was concluded in just a few short glorious weeks; Marlborough's troops soon stood on the very borders of northern France, and the Grand Alliance, it seemed, had triumphed. These were heady and exciting times, but it would be too simple to say that that the French had just given up; hard fighting certainly took place at Ath and Dendermonde, while Deane remembered that some 1,400 casualties were suffered in a rather premature attempt to storm the covered way at the fortress of Menin, a hasty tactical miscalculation that could and should have been avoided.

A peace treaty, judiciously negotiated, should now have given the Allies all that was sought, but they miscalculated and became greedy with the success handed to them. Additional demands were made, for now it was thought that the French king could hardly refuse, with his borders exposed and in such peril. This was a huge miscalculation, and Louis XIV typically proved robust and resilient in the face of the catastrophe in the north. A new commander was appointed, the bruisingly confident Duc de Vendôme, and given the daunting task of gathering together the remnants of the defeated French army, drawing out garrisons from fortresses for service in the field, and filling up the depleted ranks with fresh recruits. Most of all, Vendôme was to avoid engaging in an open battle with Marlborough, and in that way to wear the Allied effort down while an acceptable diplomatic resolution was found. Marlborough found that, for all the successes of 1706, with Prince Eugene achieving a victory at Turin in northern Italy that September, and killing Marshal Marsin in the process, the following year was just one more of frustration and disappointment.

Throughout 1707, Vendôme skilfully used the fortress belt constructed along the French border region by Marshal Vauban in the latter part of the previous century to shield his weakened army and frustrate Marlborough's efforts to pin him down long enough to fight a general action. Elsewhere, the Allied cause languished, with continued lack of success in Spain, a failed attempt by Prince Eugene and the Duke of Savoy to seize the French naval base of Toulon, and eventually French support for a fresh Jacobite rising in Scotland and the north of England. Marlborough must have viewed the coming campaign in 1708 with little enthusiasm: his political support in London was beginning to wane, heavy taxation to fund a seemingly unwinnable war was causing discontent, Philip V was gradually consolidating his position in Spain and Vendôme and his army continued to be elusive. Unless something new was attempted, it seemed that what had become a stalemate must continue, but in the meantime political pressure in London had caused a new demand to take shape, that the war could only be concluded with the removal of the French claimant from the throne in Madrid. 'That no peace could be safe or honourable for Her Majesty and her allies, if Spain and the Spanish West Indies were suffered to continue in the power of the House of Bourbon.'[18] This was clearly a considerable extension of war aims, not a requirement of the Grand Alliance when it was formed, and proved to be ill judged in the extreme.

In an effort to break the deadlock in the north, Marlborough agreed with Eugene that the prince should bring his Imperial troops northwards from the Moselle valley, to combine with the duke's army and, having superiority in numbers, confront and defeat Vendôme before he, in turn, could be reinforced. Complex plans are prone to miscarry, and with political uncertainty in the empire, Eugene was delayed. Meanwhile, Vendôme sprang a surprise of his own, reaching out to retake the strategically important towns of Ghent and Bruges. Marlborough had plainly been wrong-footed by the French commander, and his gains of 1706 were now put in jeopardy, with the French army sitting uncomfortably close to his own lines of supply and communication, not only his lines northwards into Holland, but also those through Ostend to southern England. The waterways of the region, so valuable in the movement of materiel and supplies, were also now in French hands, and their loss would increasingly impose a drag on Marlborough's operations. The duke was downcast by Vendôme's success, but Eugene, riding ahead of his own marching troops, arrived at the duke's camp on 8 July, and the two friends promptly formed a plan to regain the initiative.

Vendôme, taken up with the cleverness of his own success, found on 11 July 1708 that Marlborough was fast bearing down on him, as the French army made its own unhurried way across the river Scheldt a few miles below the fortress of Oudenarde, held by the Allies. Vendôme had to share the command of his troops with the Duc de Bourgogne, the king's eldest grandson, which divided and complicated the French arrangements. In a surprisingly inept display the two men allowed themselves to be pulled into an unplanned and unwanted infantry battle in the highly cultivated country alongside the river. By that evening, the right wing of the French army had been encircled and broken by the superior tactics and fluid command procedures displayed by Marlborough and Eugene.

The remaining portion of the French army, most of which had not been engaged at all in the battle, withdrew in some dismay northwards to take up a hasty defensive position behind the Ghent–Bruges canal.

After such unexpected success, and with the French army once more battered and dispirited, Marlborough formed a plan to thrust deep into northern France to force a battle in the open, well away from the fortress belt. His commanders, Prince Eugene included, were not in favour of such a risky enterprise, dependent as they would be either on long and vulnerable lines of supply and communication stretching back into the Low Countries, or on ships lying off the Normandy coast. Given this reluctance, Marlborough did not insist and turned instead to lay siege of the great fortress of Lille. This was a vast and complex operation, with the reinforced French army seeking to interrupt and disrupt the siege, and cutting off or threatening the Allied lines of supply at every opportunity. The Comte de la Motte, the French governor of Bruges, attacked the long and unwieldy convoys by road, leading to a particularly spirited action at Wynendael in late September, and then Vendôme seized the crossings over the river Scheldt, threatening to sever Allied communications with Holland. Marlborough's engineers had under-estimated the scale of the task, and the work in the trenches went on slowly, with Eugene amongst those wounded in one of several premature and abortive attacks. Despite everything, long-delayed success came at last, with Marshal Boufflers giving up the citadel in December 1708, after a valiant four-month defence. Louis XIV regretted the loss of Lille, but Marlborough's briefly sparkling campaign that year had been pulled to a halt. He was still faced with the bulk of the French fortress belt to deal with, but did go on and regain Ghent and Bruges before his shivering soldiers went off to their winter quarters. It was not a moment too soon; had the French held out for a few days longer, the duke would have failed in the attempt, for early in January 1709 there was 'A most violent frost which continued the longer of any in the memory of man. It was rarely possible to keep the soldiers alive even in their quarters, so they must have perished if they had not broke up the campaign before this hard season.'[19]

Negotiations between French and Allied plenipotentiaries for an agreed peace had been underway for some time, and they appeared to make promising progress. With repeated military setbacks, an almost empty Treasury despite ruinous levels of taxation, and extremely foul winter weather and failed harvests in France, Louis XIV earnestly needed to bring the war to a close. Largely courtesy of the efforts of Marlborough's army, the Grand Alliance had achieved almost all it sought, but their representatives at the discussions now clumsily mishandled things and tried to impose unacceptably harsh terms on the French king. 'You are', Queen Anne wrote to Marlborough, 'to insist that the towns and forts of Furnes, Knoque, Ypres, Menin, Lille, Tournai, Conde, Valenciennes and Mauberge be at a Treaty of Peace yielded up and delivered by France ... there shall be no cessation of arms till the Allies be fully satisfied.'[20] More dramatically, the demand was that the king would have to ensure, by force of French arms if necessary, that his grandson vacated the throne in Madrid, and as surety for this, to give up other key fortresses to the Allies until it was done. The war, pointless and unaffordable for all concerned, had, it seemed, to go on.

The campaign in 1709 started late, partly due to the wet spring, but also to the lateness of bringing the previous year's campaign to a halt. Hopes for peace had been high, of course, with a general assumption that hostilities would not have to recommence, and preparations were made at one overly confident point to disband the Allied armies. All this came to nothing, but Marlborough had taken care to see that his troops remained in a state of readiness through the whole period of the negotiations. Now, he had to see what could be done with the few months suitable for campaigning that remained before the fresh onset of bad weather. Looking to erode the French defences further, the duke settled on a siege of the fortress of Tournai, a particularly strong place of Vauban's intricate design. The siege was carried on in the face of a gallant French resistance and was not concluded until the first week in September. Marlborough then moved swiftly against Mons, the seizure of which should have exposed the French defensive posture to attack in the coming year. Louis XIV was alert to the fresh danger, sending instructions to his newly appointed army commander, Marshal Villars, that Mons was to be saved: 'You are by every means in your power to relieve the garrison, the cost is not to be considered.'[21]

In a bloody and untidy battle on 11 September 1709, the French army was driven from a position in the woods near to the hamlet of Malplaquet, on the border between France and the Southern Netherlands, The fortress of Mons, for the security of which the battle was fought by Villars, fell just six weeks later. This was an undeniable Allied success but the heavy cost of the battle shocked Europe and attracted a great deal of criticism to the duke – where, it was asked were inexpensive and glorious victories such as that seen at Ramillies three years earlier? Secretary of State Robert Harley, no soldier but a brilliant and devious politician, wrote: 'The Dutch murmur that their troops are ruined; and what is worst, the French have recovered their reputation, not only amongst themselves, but also with the allies, and it is very dangerous thing to have a good opinion of the courage of an enemy.'[22] In fact, the Dutch retained their faith in Marlborough's abilities to a remarkable degree, despite the dreadful losses in their own regiments, but with political influence fading in London, the duke was gradually pushed to the margin of things, to the extent that when fresh attempts were made to negotiate a peace with France, he was not even consulted. Marlborough's repeated attempts to bolster his position by being appointed Captain-General for life were refused by Queen Anne, which weakened him further as those requests and their refusal were soon common knowledge and gossiped about. In 1710, leading his faithful army into the field once more, the duke found that the French were reinvigorated, aware, it seemed, that the Grand Alliance had missed its chance for outright success, and that the elusive fortunes of war were perhaps on the turn.

The strategy of Marshal Villars was now once again to avoid battle, and to try and wear down the Allied effort in northern France by relying on the fortresses in the region to take the brunt of Marlborough's efforts. As a result, 1710 saw a series of hard-fought Allied sieges to capture Douai, Bethune, St Venant and Aire sur la Lys, and in each case Marlborough was successful, but at a coldly measured pace – taking time that the duke could ill afford to see pass as his influence melted away. The French fought well: 'This defence was the best,' he commented ruefully of their defence of Aire in particular.[23] The weather grew progressively worse, with the troops in the siege works suffering with the wet and cold, and with the inevitable casualties and numerous sick it seemed that the shining keenness of Marlborough's army, that fine fighting instrument seen to its best effect at Ramillies and Oudenarde, was in the process of being blunted. Although it was argued that the French fortress belt was progressively being prised apart, when the duke returned to London at the end of the year, he met a cool welcome; unlike previous campaigns no vote of thanks was offered by Parliament for his efforts.

Captain-General no longer, with regimental colonelcies being granted without reference to him, and just in command of the Allied army when on campaign, Marlborough took the field once again in 1711 with little prospect of great success. Despite troubles at home, he crucially retained the confidence of the States-General at The Hague, and that of his soldiers, although numbers of senior officers, some self-seeking and some who were sincere, increasingly looked to their own careers and allied themselves with his critics. Prominent amongst these was that fine soldier 'Red

John', the Second Duke of Argyll, who was as busy in London under-mining the duke's support as he was on campaign in Flanders and France. Marshal Villars, meanwhile, was seemingly secure in his newly con-structed lines of defence – the reputedly impregnable 'Lines of Non Plus Ultra' – behind which he could shelter his army while the war took its weary course and Marlborough's time in command ran out. In what became the last of the duke's campaigns, he tricked the French com-mander into reinforcing his left flank around Arras, while the Allied army marched in the opposite direction through a long August night to pierce the French lines at Arleux and went on to lay siege to Bouchain on the river Lys. Villars could put more troops in the field than Marlborough, as Prince Eugene was absent on the Rhine with his army, but, try as he might, the marshal failed to break Marlborough's determined grip on Bouchain, and the garrison was forced to submit as prisoners at discretion on 12 September 1711.

On the last day of the year, Marlborough's opponents got their way and he was dismissed from all his offices and posts by the queen. Before long, he went into voluntary exile on the Continent, where he was every-where warmly received. With the removal of the duke, and his replace-ment by the lacklustre Duke of Ormonde, Marshal Villars took advantage of the emerging split in the Alliance to reinvigorate his campaign in 1712 and overwhelmed an exposed detachment commanded by the Earl of Albemarle at Denain. He went on to recover several of the major fortresses that Marlborough's army had taken at such cost over the previous years. Meanwhile, Philip V was secure on the throne of Spain, with only Catalonia holding out against him, while the Austrian claimant, Charles, became emperor in Vienna on the death of his older brother. The war had run its course anyway, and this was at last apparent to all. Hostilities were formally brought to a tired end with the treaties of Utrecht in 1713, Rastadt and Baden in 1714, and Madrid in 1715.[24] Sergeant John Wilson, veteran of Marlborough's campaigns, wrote:

> There was an end put to the most destructive and bloody war as ever had been in Europe, which had reigned and predominated for the space of thirteen years. In which there had been the greatest con-sumption of treasure, as also of effusion of blood that ever was known or can be read of in history to have been amongst the European Princes.[25]

Chapter 2

Finding an Army

All regular armies until comparatively recent times comprised five basic components – the Horse (cavalry), the Foot (infantry), the gunners (artillery) and the engineers. It is perhaps fair to say that these roles are clearly understood, even though weapons and tactics in the 'teeth arms', and crucially the increased importance of swift and reliable signals, have changed a great deal over the years. Then that which is sometimes derisively known as the 'tail' (logistics, support and administration), without which the rest of the army cannot function properly has to be considered – the gathering together of many thousands of men, clothing and equipping them for war, ensuring that they are fed, paid, housed and trained, always. This is an enormous and demanding undertaking, and unless it is accomplished every day, now, tomorrow, and for the foreseeable future and without a pause, all else will fall to pieces no matter what tactical brilliance and valour may be on display.[1]

The greatest initial challenge was always to get the men themselves into service in the ranks. With professional soldiers this was a relatively simple undertaking. Those who were inclined towards a soldier's life and attracted perhaps by the thought of adventure, making one's fortune in the profession of arms, readily came forward and generally proved very well suited to the role with all its various challenges, vicissitudes and rewards. In the eighteenth century, and later, bounties were commonly paid for voluntary enlistment, the well-known 'king's shilling' or its Continental equivalent being employed, and this induced many young men to step forward, particularly at times of hardship. Not unknown were enterprising 'bounty jumpers' who, having taken one bounty, promptly made off to another recruiting party to take another. Penalties for such barefaced duplicity were understandably severe, although one spirited French girl, Marie Mouron, having enlisted in two regiments, escaped the noose for her escapades on the fine legal point that, as a female, neither recruiter should have accepted her anyway.

With a natural liking for the very strange way of life that is soldiering, these professionals and volunteers often provided the best material for employment on the decisive day of battle. They were also very useful as trainers for, and examples to, the less soldierly inclined who somewhat reluctantly found themselves in the ranks because of poverty, impressment or indebtedness, or as a result of the duplicity of the recruiting officer who would promise much but deliver something rather different. With the onset of any war came a pressing need to fill up the ranks, and in the natural order of things, therefore, many of those in Marlborough's army served not for the love of soldiering, or any particular love of their country, but because it was a trade which paid and fed them and to which, for a variety of reasons, they had been called, enticed or pushed. Except in those Continental countries where conscription was practised, all armies had this difficulty with finding enough men. Still, the raw material, however dubiously obtained was sound enough, and Marlborough was able write to his wife, Sarah, in May 1704 on the eve of setting out for the adventure on the Danube, 'We shall have good success for the troops I carry with me are very good, and will do whatever I will have them.'[2]

Absolute rulers such as Louis XIV of France and the King of Prussia (who was previously the Elector of Brandenburg, having gained his royal status in return for his support for the Grand Alliance) were able simply to conscript men into the ranks, although there were still firm rules about how this should be done. The French would, in the closing years of the War of the Spanish Succession, have to resort to extending the ballot by which young men from a particular region, city or town were chosen for the army, to simply enlisting the ballot-raised militia into the army, when the militia's real purpose was supposed to be that of local security and defence. For the Dutch and the British, simple impressments, or selection of recruits by ballot, was not immediately available, and the enlistment bounty, the appeal to patriotic feelings, and the ability to force criminals, debtors and vagrants into the ranks had to suffice. The size of the armies raised in this way was inevitably rather limited. The reputation of England as a military power was still lacking, with a consequent drag upon recruitment, the lure of a red coat remaining for the time being fairly elusive. The Dutch, with their history of long resistance to Spain and recurring wars with France, were generally on a more military footing than their allies, and ahead of the game when filling their regiments ready for war and recruiting foreign soldiers into their service.

The corresponding recruiting for the renewed French war effort followed a similar pattern. In addition to his own regiments, Louis XIV had in service German and Swiss troops, usually Catholics, in addition to émigré Irish and Scots soldiers who were barred from enlisting under

Queen Anne by virtue of their Roman Catholic faith. Many of these had followed King James II into exile after the defeats for the Jacobite cause at the Boyne and Aughrim in 1689 and 1690. Notable amongst these Catholics who fought overseas and for a foreign ruler was James FitzJames, the Duke of Berwick, illegitimate son of Marlborough's elder sister Arabella when she was the mistress of the Duke of York (subsequently James II). Berwick proved himself to be a formidable campaigner and, uniquely for an English-born man, became a Marshal of France. Uncle and nephew never met on a field of battle, although they came close to it on several occasions, but they continued to correspond with each other in an amicable way, despite the demands of campaigning. The laws preventing men from enlisting on account of their religious persuasions were technically absolute, but inconvenient in practice as they shrank the pool from which suitable and willing recruits could be drawn. Some effort was made to lessen the effect, so that much-needed talent should not be cast aside lightly when it could be avoided. This can be seen in a letter from Queen Anne to Archduke Charles (Carlos III) in June 1704 as the campaign in southern Germany was getting into its stride, concerning a certain 'Henry Nugent, one of my subjects who cannot, by English law, be employed among my troops, on account of his religion. I hope you will soon be in a position to compensate him proportionably to his merits.'[3]

Spain, although no longer a major military power, fielded significant numbers of troops, and those recruited from the Spanish (Southern) Netherlands not only enjoyed a good reputation for their fine fighting qualities, but were subject more than most to the varying stresses of war, as success and failure in the Low Countries followed the fortunes of the rivals for the throne in Madrid. A good example of this can be seen in the caustically witty Flemish nobleman, the Comte de Merode-Westerloo, who left entertaining memoirs of his military service. He accompanied Marshal Tallard to Bavaria in 1704, and viewed the unexpected deployment of the Allied army onto the plain of Höchstädt from his campbed that fateful morning in August and took part in the hectic flight before nightfall. Shortly before the Allied victory at Ramillies in 1706, the comte changed his allegiance to Archduke Charles, a perfectly legitimate and acceptable practice at the time as long as it was done openly and properly recorded, although Marlborough never seemed to place very much trust in him. For Merode-Westerloo's part, he clearly had a very well-developed sense of his own worth, and was offended that Marlborough did not take him further into his confidence, or pay much attention to his advice.

In the wider sense, of course, Marlborough had command of not one army, but two. As Queen Anne's Captain-General, he commanded her forces in the Low Countries, whether they were recruited from the British Isles or hired out from the Danish king and German princes and electors. Crucially, the duke also had command over the Dutch troops and those foreign units in the pay of the States-General while their army was in the field and actively campaigning. The ability of the military forces of two of the main parties to the Grand Alliance to operate under the hand of one dynamic commander was of the utmost importance and value, 'acting like a single compact force'. This command was naturally subject to certain conditions and restrictions, as with all coalition armies, and it proved not to be at all uncommon for Marlborough to have to turn aside from actively pursuing a campaign, mid-stride as it were, to try and smooth the feelings of some German nobleman or cajole a Dutch field deputy who thought that he had been offended or snubbed in some way. The remarkable victory at Blenheim silenced many hitherto critical voices within the Grand Alliance, for everything was now different for the duke and his army.

Although their bravery was seldom in doubt, the reluctance of some Dutch field commanders to engage the French at times remained a notice-able factor, imposing a continued drag on Marlborough's efforts, as at the Yssche River to the south of Brussels in 1705. Things were all rather dif-ferent after the striking success at Ramillies the following year. A general who could deliver such additional success so soon after the glories of 1704, and at such relatively light cost, could really be refused very little, and everyone wanted to be associated with Marlborough and gain a reflected share of the glory to be had. As a consequence, throughout the Grand Alliance, the duke's authority was such that he had the command, in effect, of the armies of Great Britain, Holland and Austria, for, when they were on campaign together, Prince Eugene, the Imperial field com-mander, chose as a matter of *realpolitik* to defer to the duke as the de facto commander-in-chief of the Allied armies. The corresponding difficulty was that, with so much success, the Grand Alliance widened its aspira-tions and demands to an unrealistic degree, so that the task of Marl-borough and his generals, by direct virtue of their own efforts, became that much harder.

By the terms of the Treaty of Grand Alliance, Austria was to put 82,000 men into the field, Holland 102,000, and England 40,000 (some 7,000 Horse and dragoons, and 33,000 Foot, in addition to an artillery train and engineer park). Parliament in London initially only granted William III this number of men, as long as no more than 18,000 were recruited for the English, Irish and Scottish establishments; the remainder were to be foreign enlisted, but further progressive augmentations in strength would soon follow.[4] To achieve this, all existing regiments were to be brought up to a war strength, and fifteen new regiments raised. This overall massive tally of fighting troops for the Alliance could in any case only be achieved by the hiring of considerable numbers of foreign troops into the service of England and Holland. The Protestant states of western Europe – principally Denmark, Brandenburg and Hanover – with their own interests in many ways synonymous with those of the Alliance, readily provided these excellent troops in return for annual payments, as did smaller German principalities and electorates and the Protestant cantons of Switzerland.

The Dutch army at the outset of the hostilities was, on paper at least, an experienced and formidable instrument of war, comprising twenty-seven regiments of Horse and four regiments of dragoons. Their infantry comprised forty-eight regiments of Foot and two independent guard companies (Nos 1–51 on the army establishment list). The Dutch also had a Swedish regiment (No. 52 on the army establishment), a Prussian-recruited regiment (No. 53), three émigré Huguenot regiments (Nos 54–6), the six regiments of the Scots Brigade (Nos 57–62, augmented by three additional battalions on the outbreak of the war – the Duke of Argyll being in command) and the seven regiments of Protestant Swiss (Nos 63–9). Holland had for many years recruited Scottish, Swiss and Swedish troops into its service; in some respects this was a legacy of the republic's long war for independence from Spain. Exiled French Huguenots, who had been forced to flee their homeland when Louis XIV revoked the Edict of Nantes in 1685, also provided a ready source of good recruits. In addition, the hired foreign contingents in Dutch pay comprised 15,000 Danish and Prussian troops, while the Palatinate provided 4,000 Horse and Foot, Hanover 2,000 Horse and dragoons and 4,500 Foot. Hesse-Cassell recruited 1,500 Foot, with a single 500-strong battalion coming from Mecklenburg, and the Bishopric of Munster providing 1,200 troops. To this formidable array could be added the 9,000 troops in Anglo-Dutch service paid for jointly by the two countries, with Holland picking up the cost of two squadrons of Horse and four squadrons of dragoons.[5] The small Duchy of Holstein-Gottrup provided one regiment of Horse (for the Imperial service), two regiments of dragoons (one each for England and Holland) and two infantry battalions (England and Holland), with another battalion for Dutch service later in the war. A further increase in bayonet strength was approved in 1703, but despite the obvious attractions of large subsidies being offered by England and Holland, the more minor rulers could not always easily accede to the requests made for additional troops. In that year, the bishoprics of Munster, Osnabruck and Liège, the duchies of Saxe-Gotha, Holstein-Gottrup, Ost-Friese, Hesse-Cassell, and the Elector of the Palatinate managed to supply just 14,613 men, rather than the 20,000 which were sought.[6] The soldiers recruited in the Spanish Netherlands occasionally found themselves in a quandary, as the region was simultaneously claimed by two princes – Frenchman Philip V and Austrian Charles III. At the commencement of the war, French troops and influence were paramount in the area, and accordingly Walloon regiments, tough and well trained, fought for the French claimant, although the loyalties of certain individuals lay with the Austrian. Much of this changed with the crushing defeat suffered by Villeroi at Ramillies in May 1706, and increasing numbers of highly regarded Walloon troops in their green coats could be counted as a part of the Allied order of battle.[7]

This impressive number of troops in the service of the States-General contrasted sharply with the smaller numbers that Queen Anne could put into the field, although her Treasury had the ability to pay for considerable drafts of troops hired into Allied service from across north-western Europe. There had been for many years an aversion in England to the maintenance of a large standing army, as the bleak experience of the English Civil War and Cromwell's protectorate cast a long shadow. William III found that, with the peace achieved at the Treaty of Ryswick in 1697, Parliament in London insisted that the army be all but disbanded to save money, but also to remove this perceived potential threat to the wider civic liberty by a monarch having too large an armed force at ready disposal. The army was reduced that year from 87,000 troops to a mere 18,000, although some regiments were quietly transferred to the Irish army establishment, where the rates of pay were lower and therefore they cost less and were, presumably, out of sight of Parliament and therefore out of mind. A number of Dutch units which had been on the English establishment were transferred to the service of the States-General for the same reasons; William III lost the service of his cherished Blue Guards in the process. The departure of these lusty soldiers from London was apparently regretted by many fashionable ladies, although the men's habit of heavy pipe smoking had, it seems, caused some discomfort to feminine nostrils. A witty doggerel rhyme was abroad in London at the time:

Must we, the battalion of bold Dutch skaters, be drove by law from your wives and your daughters, and kicked from the Crown like a band of traitors? Oh England, Oh England, 'tis very hard measure, and things done in haste are often repented at leisure.[8]

Other regiments had been reduced to cadres, with the officers retained in service on half-pay and therefore able to be remustered fairly quickly when war came again in 1702. Those soldiers who were discharged had, in many cases, been reduced to idleness or begging on the streets as a reward for their past services, but were also eager and willing for re-enlistment when the army was increased once more. When Marlborough took the field as Captain-General in 1702 of the 'British' regiments (drawn as they were from the English, Scots and Irish army establishments), he had under command five regiments of Horse (Lumley's, Wood's, Cadogan's, Wyndham's and Schomberg's), two regiments of dragoons (Hay's and Ross's), and twelve regiments of Foot (the 1st Foot Guards, Orkney's, [Charles] Churchill's, Webb's, North and Grey's, Howe's, Derby's, Blood's, Hamilton's, Rowe's, Ingoldsby's and [John] Churchill's) (see Appendix B). This tally does not include, of course, those other units on home duties or the large contingent sent to fight in Spain and Portugal, and eventually across the Atlantic in North America.[9] Such was the demand of the war, and the gradual and repeated augmentation in bayonet strength that, by 1709, the long red wall that was Queen Anne's army would include no fewer than seventy-five infantry battalions, some 58,000 foot soldiers in total, in addition to the foreign troops in the service of the Grand Alliance who were paid with British gold.[10]

The ability of England to raise and finance large numbers of troops for the Allied cause was a significant asset, but persuasion and reassurance were needed at times, as the stress and strains of war took their toll. Queen Anne wrote to her brother-in-law the King of Denmark in April 1706, as Marlborough's army gathered ready for the campaign that would lead within a few weeks to the triumph at Ramillies, an action in which Danish troops would have a key role:

My Captain-General, the Duke of Marlborough, is projecting an important undertaking against the enemy, and the friendship which I have for you making me rely on your own, I hope that you will allow Your Majesty's troops now under the said General's command, to march wherever he thinks best for the good of the Service ... I have only to assure you that I will look on your consent in this matter as a particular mark of your friendship.[11]

There had been difficulties over arrears of the soldier's pay and the precise terms of their service. When Marlborough took the field against

Marshal Villeroi on 19 May the Danish troops had yet to join him, but in response to his urgent summons they came up faithfully (and yet without proper authority), in time to fight to very good effect on the day of battle.

Strictly speaking, an officer's commission was granted by the sovereign, or in the case of the Dutch Republic, by the States-General. In practice, most commissions in the army were obtained by 'purchase', a system that was, in essence, the same in both the British and Dutch establishments, although there were some differences in detail and application. The remainder of commissions, where not had by purchase, were obtained by patronage and the favour of influential men, and by virtue of seniority and meritorious service in action. Appointment as an officer, and promotion, had yet to depend upon ability, experience and worthy performance – although good service did have its rewards. Although seeming to be complex, the purchase system was quite straight-forward. An aspiring young man with a taste for the military life, or one whose family was keen to get him out of the house and making his own way in the world, would buy (usually with parental funds) a post as cornet (in the Horse) or ensign (in the Foot, the alternative title of second lieutenant being introduced in 1702). Successive steps upwards could then be obtained when vacancies occurred – leap-frogging in rank would later be forbidden – and payment for the advancement at the approved rate was made to the government. These funds were then devoted to obtaining fresh recruits for the army – at least that was the theory. In addition to the approved rate, there was a premium to be paid to the officer selling the commission, although this was unofficial and not formally approved. Officers selling out in a 'good' regiment could expect to get a better price than those from a unit whose reputation, for some reason, was not so admirable. The value and vested interest amongst officers to maintain the reputation of the regiment in which they served was obvious and had a distinct and directly connected military value. Regimental pride was a matter not simply of personal satisfaction and sense of duty performed, but of proven financial advantage when it came to selling a commission. The sum received on selling out would, again in theory, enable the retired officer to purchase a pension for himself – an important consideration because pensions from government were hard to obtain and even when granted subject to curtailment if the government changed.

At first glance, the system seems corrupt and open to abuse, but it was one which had vocal advocates as it was believed that to require an officer to buy his way upwards (at least in regimental circles, and only up to lieutenant colonel – ranks above that could not be purchased) ensured that the army was officered by 'Men of fortune and character, men who have some connection with the interests and fortunes of the country ... three quarters receive but little for their services beside the honour of serving.'[12] Whether that was the case or not, the system had developed and become part of the way the army was to a large degree manned. However, 'Constrained, as it was, by "a range of laws, warrants, orders, rules, customs and connived at abuses," the sale and concommitant pur-chase of commissions was, in fact, contrary to the law at the time.'[13] The Mutiny Act of 1695 required an oath to be sworn that no payment had been made to obtain a commission, but despite this inconvenience, the practice was widespread and officially winked at, if not openly approved. Still, in 1702, just as Marlborough set out on the campaign trail as Captain-General for the first time, a subaltern attempted to avoid an agreed pay-ment for a commission on the grounds that such a payment would be unlawful. The Court of Chancery directed that he should make the pay-ment all the same.[14] In effect, as they were granted under the hand of the sovereign to an individual, commissions were acknowledged to be per-sonal property, held only as a consequence of continued good conduct and faithful service, and capable, as a result, of being sold to another suitably qualified individual. This is evidenced by the fact that the com-missions of officers who died in action could not be sold; the investment died with them.

Eventually, bowing to the powerful vested interests in the army over the ownership and value of commissions, a scale of prices to be paid was regulated by royal warrant in 1720. Amongst other things, this stipulated that an officer could only sell his commission to another immediately junior in rank to himself, thereby preventing any egregious leap-frogging. Richard Pope of Schomberg's Horse frequently comments in his letters on the few chances for promotion and advancement, as he saw things, noting with a certain grim relish officers who fell on the field of battle and thus opened up fresh vacancies that had to be filled: 'Major Creed being killed in the action (at Blenheim), Mr Cardonnel and Colonel Sibourg tell me I may depend upon having a Troop; but they have not yet settled the majority being unwilling to give it to [Captain] Prime for some good reasons.'[15]

That there had been oddities and abuses in the purchase of commis-sions was undeniable, and the god-daughter of William III was granted a commission as captain in Hamilton's Regiment and drew the pay that went with it for over twenty years. A rather more worthy appointment was perhaps that of the infant son of Brigadier General Archibald Rowe, who was killed at Blindheim village. The lad was granted a commission a few weeks after his father's death, apparently as a kind of act of charity for the orphaned boy, but the Duke of Marlborough had to intervene in 1714, having been reappointed as Captain-General by King George I, to prevent the further granting of juvenile commissions. This was none too soon, for as late as 1713 Stair's Dragoons (Royal Scots Greys) had a 3-year-old cornet on its muster rolls: 'A child who could scarcely manage a rocking horse.'[16] Not until the time of the much (unfairly) maligned Duke of York, was a minimum age of 16 years put on the first step of purchasing or being granted a commission. For all its ills and oddities, the system for the purchase and sale of commissions – something with a tangible cash value – helped to ensure good behaviour. A commission could also be forfeited for personal misbehaviour: Lieutenant Colonel George MacArtney, 'a brave experienced officer', was cashiered for 'dishonourable conduct' towards an old woman, the precise details of which are not clear but may be imagined. He was refused the opportunity to sell his commission on account of his actions, and had to serve on as an unpaid volunteer hoping to regain his reputation, rank and fortune by his gallantry in the field. This he eventually achieved in marked fashion by his bravery under fire, in the teeming woods at Malplaquet in the autumn of 1709.[17]

The granting of brevet rank was at first widespread; it was a process that was in the gift of an army commander, not requiring the specific sanction of the sovereign. It allowed an officer to hold a temporary uplift in unpaid rank when called on to undertake a task or series of tasks requiring the necessary authority to command others and accomplish what was necessary. A major might therefore find himself appointed to take forward an attack with two battalions of Foot, with the brevet rank of colonel enabling him to give orders to the unit commanders. Marlborough granted dozens of brevets between 1702 and 1707 but they did cause some difficulty and occasional friction with those not holding a brevet, especially when the particular operation was over and the officer concerned had returned to regimental duty, perhaps having acquired certain airs and graces in the meantime. An indication of the difficulties that might occur was an order requiring officers to do duty in their regiments in the rank for which they were paid, once the active role requiring the brevet had expired, and Marlborough had to write to Robert Walpole in June 1708 that 'Colonel Hollins having a commission of Brigadier, does no wise exempt him from his duty as major.'[18] Given the problems that arose, the granting of brevet rank was no longer formally sanctioned, and although occasionally used (by Marlborough and others), the practice died away for the time being.

It is worth pausing for a moment to consider how the various officers from many different nationalities and states, both large and small, conversed. The common soldiers had less of a problem as the opportunities or necessity to converse outside their own unit were relatively limited, and if in doubt they could, in the time-honoured fashion, always resort to raising their voices and gesticulating. For commanders, things were more tricky and a Danish officer might well ride side by side in an advance with a Hessian or a Brunswicker and have to give a shouted warning in passing to the commander of a Dutch battery. The difficulty was no less for the men who served Louis XIV, as a French commander might have a Bavarian, Irishman or a Walloon (not a particular problem there, of course) at his side. So, when having to converse with someone who was not that familiar with one's own language, the answer was that the *lingua franca* (no pun intended) of both the rival armies was French, and this seemed to work remarkably well. Marlborough spoke and read French, just about, although his accent was apparently not that impressive, but he could not write in French, so all his many letters and dispatches were usually drafted in English and then translated as required. Quartermaster-General William Cadogan had an advantage when dealing with Dutch officers as he spoke their language, having married a girl from Holland, and presumably had learned to do so in agreeable circumstances.

Considerable numbers of new recruits were required with the renewed onset of war; that was inevitable, but calls to patriotic duty in an age without means of ready mass communication had little effect outside the hearing of a beating drum and the encouraging words of a recruiting officer and his roving party. As always, some likely lads, yearning for adventure, excitement and fortune, perhaps as a way to escape the plough, the apprentice's bench or a prospective father-in-law, would be inclined to step up to the officer at the table and accept the proffered shilling, pistole or guilder to enlist. However, the new demand for manpower was such that no fewer than nine recruiting acts were passed by the English Parliament between 1702 and 1711, which allowed, amongst other things, the impressment of men with 'No lawful calling or visible means of support'.[19] Vagrants, the unemployed, debtors (who would be released from their obligations by accepting enlistment) and prisoners who in many cases might otherwise have swung on the gallows were in consequence recruited into the ranks of the army. A distinguished

Huguenot officer once wrote, rather over-dismissively perhaps given their subsequent performance on blood-strewn battlefields, that Marlborough's men comprised 'Sore-footed troops ... a motley crowd of rough labourers and artisans, old soldiers, and the riff-raff of the English towns'.[20] Conscription by destitution was in force, in effect, but what were sometimes regarded as the sweepings of society could by this means be induced, with varying degrees of reluctance, to don a red coat and shoulder a musket for the queen. Despite such unpromising starts, on the whole these men did very well in their new calling.

The effectiveness of the recruiting methods varied widely from parish to parish, and there was certainly a measure of reluctance amongst English magistrates to enforce the measures fully; the rate-payers of the district would be obliged to maintain the otherwise destitute families of absent soldiers who would very possibly never return. In addition, some groups of workers whose services were deemed essential, such as farm labourers at harvest time, were kept exempt from impressments into either military or naval service. The varying fortunes of war, at least where the success or failure of campaigns was reported at home, had their inevitable effect on recruiting. As the war went on and casualty lists lengthened, whatever enthusiasm had met triumphs such as Blenheim and Ramillies, the remorseless task to fill and refill the ranks became ever more challenging. Recruiting parties were regularly sent out to try and find young men to enlist, perhaps by plying them with drink in an effort to induce them to 'list for a soldier' while inebriated. These things were not simple, and the recruit, once sober again, was quite likely to slip away if he was not carefully watched and guarded, and might even make off to muster into another regiment for yet another bounty. For all the talk of taking the shilling on enlistment, the actual bounty for an English recruit in Marlborough's day was no less than £2 – a huge sum to a labourer or apprentice, and a powerful if transitory inducement to enlist.

The trickery by which recruits were sometimes persuaded to come forward was varied, but not everyone was inclined towards or adept at these underhand practices. John Blackader, a rather severe and straight-laced officer serving in the Cameronians, wrote that 'This vexing trade of recruiting depresses my mind ... I see the greatest rakes are the best recruiters. I cannot ramble, and rove, and drink, and tell stories, and wheedle and insinuate, if my life were lying at stake.'[21] Nor was it at all useful or effective for a recruiting party to get a lad of good family drunk and then try to insist that he had enlisted voluntarily, as was seen when the Middlesex justices of the peace determined that the only son of a gentleman of property, Mr William Hall, should be set at liberty by recruiters from Ingoldsby's Regiment.[22] The often-told, but highly unlikely, tale of a shilling being quietly placed in the bottom of a glass of beer so that the imbiber could unwittingly have been said to enlist is well known, but it is just a tale. 'Bringers' (later notorious as 'crimps') were also active – they would try and persuade prospective and possibly gullible recruits of the attractions of the military life and then be rewarded for finding such promising material for the recruiting party.

Money was voted by Parliament to raise troops for specific campaigns, most notably those in Flanders and Spain in Marlborough's day, but it was not uncommon for a regiment on the 'Spain Establishment' to be found serving in Flanders, and in 1703 Raby's (the Royal) Dragoons were sent from the Low Countries to campaign in the Iberian Peninsula. On the other hand, Hill's Regiment (later the Devons), although intended for Spain, fought with some distinction at the siege of Mons in 1709. The demands of the service plainly came first, and if troops were needed in one theatre of war, that was where they were sent, at least for a limited period while Marlborough's influence on such matters lasted. As the duke's fortunes and influence waned, others would make demands which he could not resist, as with the futile expedition to North America that drew troops away from Flanders in 1710, despite his protests. Unsurprisingly, this posting of regiments between various establishments caused some bureaucratic upset, with scope for double counting and over-payments, and Paymaster-General James Brydges gave evidence to a Parliamentary inquiry in 1713 that:

> Some regiments have been placed on several establishments at the same time, Farrington's, for instance, on three, viz, Flanders, Spain and Portugal; Mordaunt's and Macartney's, in the same manner; Hill's and Hotham's were put in both estimates [for Spain and Portugal], and twice provided for by parliament ... Other regiments have been paid different from their respective establishments.[23]

Pay was drawn for at least one regiment that did not even exist, other than on paper, so bureaucratic mismanagement and uncertainty on the one hand, and corruption on the other, were jogging each other's elbows. Such irregularities seem to have been more prevalent in the Iberian Peninsula than in Flanders, where Marlborough was able to keep a keen eye on things, but, as Brydges points out, there were some exceptions and highly suspect-looking anomalies that struggled to find an explanation.

Regiments of Horse or the Foot in the duke's army were rarely all of the same size at any given time – the varying fortunes of recruiters, the incidence of casualties, malingerers and the sick, and drafts and cross-posting having to be made to bring other units up to strength did not make for such uniform neatness. The Horse had six Troops in each regiment in 1702 (although the Queen's Regiment of Horse had nine Troops), which gave a muster roll of some 400 officers and men. Dragoon regiments also had six Troops each, which was increased for Stair's Dragoons and Ross's Dragoons to nine Troops in 1708–9. Thirteen companies was the war establishment for regiments of Foot serving in Flanders from 1703 onwards, and this gave a theoretical bayonet strength of 876 officers and men, with each company finding three sergeants, three corporals, two drummers and fifty-six men in addition to the officers. Units raised for service elsewhere – Spain or the West Indies, for example – had a different established strength. The Foot Guards were also different, not being on any specific establishment, with the 1st Foot Guards having twenty-eight companies each of sixty men (seventy from 1705 onwards), and the Coldstream Guards having fourteen companies.[24] On the Act of Union in 1707 the Scots Guards were augmented to seventeen companies, each of seventy men, but this distinguished regiment did not serve with Marlborough.

Once properly enlisted and mustered into the ranks, the recruit could expect to be issued, at his colonel's expense (a cost sometimes applied so sparingly that he turned a nice profit on the transaction), with uniform, weapon and accoutrements, and to be instructed and drilled in their use. Queen Anne's soldiers commonly wore collarless single-breasted red coats reaching well down towards the knee and were instantly recognizable. Waistcoats were made up from the previous year's worn-out coat with the sleeves cut off. The gunners and engineers wore red coats with blue cuffs, and only be dressed in blue coats from the end of the war onwards.[25] Legs were clad in close-fitting kersey or shag breeches, and greatcoats were issued in foul weather while on campaign. A deserter from Cadogan's Horse was described in the *London Gazette* in 1711 as wearing a 'Red coat with green [facings] broad silver lace on the sleeves and pockets bound with narrow silver lace, green waistcoat, shag breeches, silver laced hat, brown wig/hair with black bag'.[26] Charles Colville, joining up in 1710 as a gentleman volunteer in hopes of gaining a commission, recalled that he was issued with a soldier's coat of scarlet cloth, waistcoat, linen shirt and neckcloth, and a laced hat adorned with (as a nice touch) a blue feather. He was pleased also to receive as his personal weapon a fusee (a light form of musket often carried by officers) rather than the standard musket, which was a weighty 12lb 42-inch-barrelled flintlock musket tipped with a sharp 18-inch steel socket bayonet for good measure. This concession for Colville was in itself unusual, and may have reflected the young man's position as an aspirant officer with well-placed friends.[27] He would also have been provided with a buff leather cross-belt and cartridge pouch, and a short sword of doubtful usefulness known as a hanger. It is worth remembering that a foot soldier in Marlborough's army usually carried about 50lb of equipment when on the march – knapsack, tent portion, cooking pot and so on – in addition to his arms, ammunition and accoutrements. Louis XIV's soldiers were probably encumbered in the same way.

The Dutch troops wore grey coats, although the guards wore blue (hence the term the Blue Guards), with varying facing colours. The many foreign troops in the service of the States-General wore a variety of colours – red for the Scots and the Swiss, green for Walloons. A soldier in the Regiment du Suisse d'Albemarle in 1701, one of those excellent units recruited from the Protestant cantons, typically wore a blue coat with red cuffs, blue waistcoat, buff or yellow breeches and grey stockings.[28] The Prussian and Hessian troops also wore blue with red stockings for the former, while Hanoverian Foot soldiers wore red, and their horse troopers were clad in white, all with regimental colour facings. The troops provided by Denmark had double-breasted grey coats with contrasting linings, collar and cuffs, although the gunners had red coats with blue cuffs and facings. It was common for drummers to wear reversed colours, with their coats being the same hue as the facing colours of their regiment. The lower legs of all ranks in Foot regiments were clad in stout woollen stockings or gaiters, although the men of the Horse and dragoon regiments wore long boots, turned down at the knee to protect the joint with a double fold of leather.

The colourful picture this suggests would probably not have lasted long, with the inevitable wear and tear of marching and fighting through a strenuous campaign, and the general lack of opportunity for washing and laundering clothes, or making good damage and deficiencies. Careful administrative arrangements, such as those enjoyed in Marlborough's army, would have catered for some of this difficulty, and during the long march to the Danube in 1704 fresh supplies of necessaries, particularly shoes, awaited the troops at regular intervals on the route taken. However, this attention to speedy replenishment and resupply was still uncommon enough to excite comment from several observers, and armies would have very soon acquired the appearance of shabby, if swaggering and raffish, vagabonds in need of a good bath and shave. In this respect, however, they were probably little different from their contemporaries in civilian life, which in many respects was rough and ready; soldiers could, at least, depend on being fed regularly.

The felt hat, common in both civilian and military wear, and turned up into the familiar tricorn shape, was worn by all ranks, although the quality of both material and embellishments would naturally improve in line with the more elevated rank of the wearer. The sergeants in Erle's Regiment in 1709 had silver lace adorning their tricorns; they were not unusual in this, as could be seen with Charles Colville's fitting-out for service with the Cameronians. The exception to the near-universal tricorn hat was the wearing of fur caps for pioneers, and the tall grenadier cap, which were originally simple and practically comfortable affairs which allowed the swinging arm when hurling a grenade not to brush the brim of the felt hat. The bombs were, in fact, usually bowled under-arm to prevent such a mishap with the hat and to avoid straining the arm during constant use. Over time, the grenadier cap became a mark of honour and was made still taller and more ornate, taking on the distinctive and easily recognized mitre shape, the mark of the grenadiers in an army. The additional height of the cap added to the imposing appearance of the grenadiers, who were generally drawn from the tallest and strongest men in a battalion and were in consequence an elite force often grouped together for a particularly hazardous task. Grenadier-type caps were also worn by Stair's Dragoons (Scots Greys) and Ross's Dragoons (Royal Irish), in recognition of their overthrow of the renowned Régiment du Roi at Ramillies in 1706.

French troops at this time wore coats of light grey, sometimes described as white, a colour thought to encourage cleanliness, and therefore healthfulness. This happy state would again not last very long once out on campaign. Some foreign regiments in French service, such as the troops from Alsace and the Catholic cantons of Switzerland, wore blue and red coats, and the Gens d'Armes of Louis XIV's Household Cavalry also wore red. Bavarian soldiers wore blue, while those recruited in the Spanish Netherlands, whether they served the French or the Austrian claimant to the throne, had green coats, so the chances for misunderstandings and firing on one's friends were quite common. As a matter of course, there was plenty of opportunity for confusion and mistaken identity, particularly in the smoke and noise of a pitched battle, and not a great deal changed in that regard over the centuries. The Comte de Maffei, commanding a German brigade in French service as part of the garrison of Ramillies village, rode over to some horsemen nearby to give them instructions, only to find that he was abruptly taken prisoner at pistol point, not having noticed that they were Dutch troopers and not Walloons as he had thought. Temporary field symbols to aid recognition, such as wearing a bunch of freshly picked leaves in the hat, were commonly used, but, as Maffei clearly found, it was still easy to get things wrong.

Complete uniformity within an army, or even within a regiment, was not always to be had, and the quality and cut of cloth would vary, both with the material purchased (colonels did not usually wish to spend any more than necessary) and the variable skill of the regimental tailor. Even to have a set pattern for the cloth in use was a fairly recent innovation. Some years before the outbreak of the War of the Spanish Succession, the Austrian General Gallas placed an order for 600 new uniforms for his regiment and attached with that order a sample of the precise light grey cloth to be obtained, an act which was unusual enough to attract wide comment.[29] The clothing regulations for Queen Anne's soldiers, issued in January 1707, set out again, and so that there should be no lingering room for doubt, the essential requirement that a colonel provide for his soldiers' dress. 'The sole responsibility of the Colonel for the Pay and Equipment of his Regiment, is the principle of Military Finances, who is held responsible in his fortune and in his character for the discharge of his duty in providing the supplies of his Regiment.'[30] That many colonels were attentive to their obligations in this respect, but that some others took a lesser interest and pride in their regiments was unavoidable, with varying practical results for the appearance and comfort of the humble soldier.

Officers, who often had the means and inclination to please themselves, had a degree of latitude in what they wore, but this could go too far and verge on the unmilitary. The most senior officers could fairly well wear what they wanted on campaign. Marlborough's orders for 1710, given under an anonymous hand, laid down that clothing should be uniformly made, with little irregularity in the dress of officers, other than that resulting from the superior type of cloth used:

> For the better ordering Her Majesty's Foot, His Grace the Duke of Marlborough has thought fit I should give the following orders, viz;-
> 'Tis ordered that all the clothing for the Foot be in readiness to embark the 1st day of March next, and that the whole be perfectly

uniform in the make and looping, the colour of the lining, facing and looping excepted, according to the pattern approved of by me. That the officers be all clothed in red, plain and uniform, which is expected they shall wear on all marches and other duties as well as days of Review, and that no officer be on duty without his regimental scarf [sash] and spontoon, 'tis ordered that all provide spontoons according to the pattern which I have given to Major-General Sabine. 'Tis ordered that the Foot be provided with white gaiters, both officers and soldiers, whereas several regiments have no swords, 'tis expressly ordered that the soldiers be provided with them against [before] taking the field.

The set badge of rank for regimental officers of the Foot was the gorget, worn around the neck on a silk ribbon, and the last vestige of the use of body armour. It was impractical, though, for mounted officers to wear such a device.[31] Some officers, such as the Duke of Marlborough, who might be expected to wear fine boots, instead favoured the buttoned linen gaiters mentioned in the order, and the flexibility these lightweight garments gave stood him in good stead when he was unhorsed and running to escape pursuing French cavalry outside Ramillies village. The duke, always careful with his pennies, was at pains to ensure that his servant did not tear the garments when removing them at the end of a particularly tiring day. A well-known depiction of the 1st English Foot Guards struggling across the Nebel stream on the day of battle at Blenheim clearly shows the men to be wearing gaiters.

Hair was usually worn fairly long towards the shoulder, rough cut for most men, better barbered for officers, and gathered and tied at the nape of the neck with a ribbon. The more senior officers tended to wear the full-bottom wig, the ends of which might be plaited together for neatness. Although hot to wear and hard to keep clean, these affairs had the added advantage for a mounted man of affording some of protection for the face and head against sword slashes. Beards were not commonly worn, nor, in the service of Queen Anne, were moustaches, although they were more popular in Continental armies. All units would have men with some skill at shaving and hair-cutting, but a general lack of such regular opportunities on campaign must have resulted in many bristling chins, cheeks and upper lips.

Soldiers have a way of making do and getting on with things, as their resolute performance throughout Marlborough's long campaigns demonstrates. Donald McBane, serving with Orkney's Regiment in southern

Holland in 1702, remembered a heavy snowfall in March which was still lying thickly on the ground the following month. He and his comrades were not that concerned as 'The Genever [gin] being plenty we regarded not the cold.'[32] Hard living and hard lying was their lot, with cheerful indifference to discomfort; it does not change much over the years, and shabby uniforms, scuffed shoes (boots not being in general use for foot soldiers), grubby shirts and waistcoats, worn equipment and unshaven chins do not necessarily indicate poor training, a lack of a skill or low morale. 'That lively air I see,' as Prince Eugene of Savoy commented when reviewing Marlborough's cavalry, is the same air, the same confident, even cocky, attitude that commanders down the ages hope to see in their soldiers. If it looks right it usually is right, and spit and polish does not have to be there to make it so, nor will such burnishing alone make it right. That off-handed confidence amongst troops would only stem from a belief that they knew their deadly trade and that the commanders they looked to for orders understood what they were about, and that, for all the hazards and brutality of the battlefield, their lives would not be wasted. Marlborough's arrangements for the well-being of his soldiers went well beyond the obvious practical necessity of ensuring that each man was fed, watered, clothed, equipped, armed, trained, readied to fight and brought in good time to the right place and faced in the right direction to do so. Such arrangements, seemingly mundane and far removed from dash and glory, were nevertheless essential preliminaries for military endeavour; much of the duke's success stemmed not just from his own skill and that of his commanders, but from the care he gave to the administration and ordering of his troops.

Human nature being what it is, for a variety of reasons a man might choose to seek his fortune elsewhere, by absenting himself from the ranks to mingle with the local populace, perhaps with the aid of local damsel with whom a liaison had been formed, or to try and find a way home. A more extreme course would be to go over the fields and take service with the opposing army, an option that was fraught with risk. Donald McBane, who served with Orkney's Regiment, recalled that in 1702, 'A great many of our men deserted to the French, but as soon as we catched them they were hanged.'[33] Matters were not always so clear cut, and there was a fair element of chance about such a thing. Desertion to the enemy, or in the face of the enemy during battle, was naturally a grave military offence, but to be absent without leave – which might be construed as desertion of a kind – was sometime regarded with a degree of leniency. John Muddey, a private 'centinelle' in the 1st English Foot Guards was excused from punishment as 'He went from his post without leave, with intent only to visit an acquaintance in Major-General Murray's Regiment, but was stopped on the way, and his officer affirming that he is a weak and silly man.'[34]

Soldiers who had the misfortune to be taken prisoner could usually expect to be exchanged at a fairly early point for a like number of their opponent's troops who were being held as prisoners. There was a well-developed and widely observed system for paroles and exchanges, and amongst the obvious benefits was not having to house and feed (to a limited degree) large numbers of men who had been captured. Some Allied soldiers taken prisoner at the defeat at Almanza in Spain in 1707 were then induced to enlist for the French claimant to the throne. Thirty of these men were taken prisoner again, perhaps because they were not that devoted to their new calling, this time by the Allies at the Battle of Oudenarde the next year. Surprisingly, they were permitted to return to their true allegiance without too close a questioning, twenty of them being sent to Stair's Dragoons and ten going to Ross's Dragoons – after all, trained soldiers were valuable assets and were clearly not to be lightly wasted.[35] The loss of such men was always to be regretted, if for no finer reason than that they would have to be replaced by the laborious and time-consuming process of recruiting and training. On another occasion, two British regiments (Stewart's and Stanhope's) were taken prisoner in Spain when their Portuguese comrades insisted on surrendering the fortress in which they formed part of the garrison. The captive troops were then marched to Bordeaux, where they were exchanged for French soldiers taken prisoner at Blenheim. They were eventually shipped back to England, where some resentment was caused when the stocks of wine bought by the released officers while in Bordeaux was promptly impounded, as no excise duty had been paid.[36]

An enemy soldier who surrendered 'on giving his parole' was generally one who was held to have behaved well and was, in consequence, deserving of considerate treatment. Officers usually gave their parole both on their own behalf and that of their men; once paroled 'on terms' in this way, the captured troops would be released, often still in possession of their arms and equipment, and allowed to go to some local town, on the strict understanding that they would not actively serve again, but wait for an agreed exchange for a similar number of their enemy's men also on parole. This system was mutually convenient, and it seems little abused – to break one's parole was deemed to be a highly dishonourable thing, and if apprehended under arms such an errant soldier could expect little sympathy. On the other hand, men who were held not to have behaved that valiantly or well when under fire and were forced to surrender would usually do so 'at discretion' and were, in effect, prisoners of war and not eligible for any special treatment other than what their captors chose to give them. Generally speaking, however, there was little ill-treatment of prisoners, at least in western Europe, as that would lay the way open for reprisals. Conditions for prisoners of war were, though, basic at the very least, and an English dragoon who served in Spain and was taken at Brihuega in 1710 remembered that he and his fellows were treated worse than dogs by their captors. Inevitably there were occasions when there was doubt or dispute over whether men had yielded 'on terms' (eligible for parole) or 'at discretion' (as prisoners of war). This was not unimportant: quite apart from the difference in treatment to be expected, the professional reputation of officers, in particular, was at stake – a commander at whatever level who had to yield at discretion was clearly assumed not to have done his utmost. In the summer of 1702 the small Allied garrison at Tongres was overwhelmed after a hard-fought defence by a French attack, but despite their undeniably tough resistance the garrison were not offered terms by the French. Samuel Noyes wrote of how this affected the conduct of the subsequent siege of Huy on the Meuse River: 'My Lord Marlborough refusing them any conditions but to be prisoners at discretion (which he does to get again the two regiments taken at Tongres), the castle only won't yet submit, so our guns play again very smartly and we don't doubt will bring down their stomachs [courage].'[37]

As with much in warfare, things were not always clear cut, and an opponent who had fought to the last ditch and inflicted heavy loss in the process could arguably not expect the best treatment on at last having to yield – 'Too late, chum', might be the thought in the mind of the victor as he closed in with musket butt and bayonet. Nine years after the affair at Tongres, when Marlborough had forced a submission from the garrison in the fortress of Bouchain on the Lys River, the French commander, the Marquis de Ravignan, protested that he had yielded on the promise of good terms and the garrison were therefore eligible to be paroled. The duke insisted that this was not so, as the marquis had been forced to submit at discretion to avoid a further bombardment and storming of his breached defences. The affair was sufficiently sensitive for the French army commander Marshal Villars to protest, and for Louis XIV to get involved, writing to Marlborough to insist that, as a matter of honour, the terms of the surrender be properly observed. After making careful inquiries of those of his officers who had arranged the details of the garrison's submission, the duke was able to reply to the king that, good terms not having been offered or implied, he would not change his mind, and the garrison would remain as his prisoners of war for the time being.

These matters were not a case of simply good form; on occasions the lives of captured soldiers were at stake, if it were suspected that they had deserted their colours and illicitly taken up arms with their late opponents. Donald McBane's comments on hanging deserters in 1702 set out the standard practice for such things, although the dragoons allowed to return to Allied service after Oudenarde shows the other side of the picture. The previous year, the Comte de Merode-Westerloo, by then in the service of the Habsburg claimant to the throne, had to intervene to save some of his men who had fallen into French hands:

> The enemy wanted to hang two of my dragoons that they had taken prisoner, as sometime soldiers in the Spanish Army. I at once sent off a trumpet [messenger under a flag of truce] to claim their release on the grounds that they had changed their allegiance by due form of law ... A few days before we had captured a Cornet of Horse and two troopers, and I said to him very gravely that I regretted that I had some bad news for him. I was going to have him hanged on the morrow.[38]

The comte's threat, which was probably quite sincerely meant, had the desired effect, and the French quickly agreed to exchange the prisoners without doing anything more drastic.

Discipline lies at the heart of good military practice and was at the root of much of Marlborough's success, but this was thoughtfully and sensibly applied, firmly enough to be effective but not brutal and unthinking. It was remarked that:

> His camps were like a well governed city and much more mannerly ... Divine Service was regularly performed and a high standard of discipline was maintained. The poor soldiers who were, many of them, the refuse and dregs of the nation became after one or two campaigns by the care of their officers and by good order and discipline, tractable, civil, orderly, sensible and clean.[39]

Duties within the camp included finding guards and pickets to prevent soldiers from wandering off and unauthorized persons from entering – perhaps to illicitly sell food or other comforts, or to gain information – and of course to deter any surprise approach by an enemy raiding party. The number of men allotted for such duties was strictly in accordance with the number of individual contingents present – British, Dutch, Danish and so on – so that no one group was disadvantaged or given more than its fair share of duties. Escorts had to be found for supply wagons, and to provide protection for foraging parties that might otherwise fall prey to enemy cavalry or, occasionally, bands of aggrieved locals. The cleanliness of the camp was seen to be very important, with latrines set up (and to be used), butchered offal and dead horses to be burned or buried at a decent distance and rubbish properly disposed of. There were also firm rules on the security of weapons, to avoid loss or damage and against these being discharged negligently within the crowded confines of a camp. Particular care had to be taken of the powder store, which would be kept at a safe distance from the main camp, to both prevent accidents and acts of sabotage.

It is well not to linger too long on this happy picture of regularity and order, for there were always exceptions. As already noted, colonels of regiments would often pare back the quality and quantity of the uniforms issued to their men so that they could comfortably pocket the difference, while contractors supplying provisions might try and send stale or rotten goods. Soldiers were not permitted to leave their camp without permission, and regular roll calls would be held to enforce this. Donald McBane's reminiscences, however, indicate that this was a rule that was difficult to enforce, or was not enforced that carefully. Plundering and looting was forbidden, and officers were required to search their men's tents for booty. The renowned female soldier Christian (Kit) Davies, enterprising as ever and serving as a sutleress after the discovery of her deception, found that her own pony had been stolen, and so she illicitly obtained another:

> Which I did from a huzzar, who, as I apprehended, had stolen it from a boor [peasant]. This latter found her in my possession, though I had docked, trimmed and endeavoured to disguise her; but to no purpose, the peasant was not to be deceived; he knew and claimed his beast.[40]

Severe penalties for looting were threatened and occasionally enacted, including 'running the gauntlet', as happened during the march up the Rhine in 1704 – even the death penalty was imposed for severe infringements of this rule. Two dragoons, sentenced to die for plundering, asked to be shot like soldiers, rather than be hanged like felons. Whether their request was granted is uncertain.[41]

A casual kind of bravery, a disregard for personal safety, was as a matter of course expected to be shown by officers, but not all could meet the requirement. Charles Colville recalled with disapproval that, while fighting in the woods at Wynendael in the autumn of 1708, he noted, 'During the action [Ensign] Sinclair had bowed himself towards the ground for a considerable time together.'[42] Samuel Noyes recalled that nearly a third of chaplain posts in the army were vacant at any one time, with the regimental colonels apparently keeping for themselves the pay saved in this way. Despite such laxness, the officers as a body, both regimental and on the staff, by and large set the example expected. Occasionally officers were drunken and dissolute louts who ill treated and abused their men, but they were the exception and not tolerated for long – if the system did not see them off, there were other more direct methods. In the closing moments of the fighting for Blindheim village in August 1704, an unpopular and callous officer, who clearly for all his other faults did not lack bravery, stepped forward through the drifting smoke to exhort his men to one final effort to secure the village. He turned towards the defenders and was promptly shot dead, but not, it seemed, by a Frenchman.

All this may indicate good management, sound discipline, and a striving for a sense of *esprit de corps*. However, it was well known in Marlborough's Anglo-Dutch army that other commanders led men who were poorly clothed and equipped, and Prince Eugene's troops in northern Italy in the opening years of the war more closely resembled a gang of tattered vagabonds and beggars than a military formation ready for war. The medical supplies for his whole army at the time were woefully inadequate and took space on no more than two small carts. The French march in 1704 through the Black Forest on the road which led to the disaster at Blenheim was marked by wholesale plundering of villages, confiscation and requisitioning of supplies of every kind on the way. The effect was, inevitably, that the passage of the army had to be forced, with each road barred by desperate villagers, and stragglers and foragers were picked off and murdered at every opportunity. In this case the army's behaviour was born of simple military necessity, as the French quartermasters had not been required to ensure that their troops be fed and supplied on their march. Living off the land and the local population was nothing new in warfare, and such frightfulness had an effect in cowing the population in an area and enforcing a kind of bitter, begrudging compliance, but there was an obvious price to be paid in practical terms. Generally, it made sense to pay for the goods taken, and to make sure that the troops behaved themselves and kept their hands off the farmers' daughters in the process. But such efficient procedures depended inevitably upon the ability of the commanders to pay for their supplies, and in that respect Marlborough had an advantage: 'His Grace', Francis Hare wrote approvingly, 'was not unmindful to provide money and order regular payments for everything that was brought into the camp.'[43]

Not that things were always sweetness and harmony with local people, even when there was no conscious attempt to impose on or intimidate them. Quite apart from a natural inclination amongst many soldiers to help themselves when they could, despite stringent measures to prevent this, to campaign over a region was to ruin it, with damage and deprivation inflicted upon the civilian population. Sometimes this destruction was a deliberate act; it had been adopted as policy by French commanders 'eating up the country' in the closing decades of the previous century. They were not alone in this ruthless way of waging war, for Marlborough devastated Bavaria in July 1704. Even when careful instructions were given to avoid damage, as was done by the duke in the Low Countries, harm could not realistically be avoided, and there was inevitable retribution. 'They nailed his hands across each other up against a tree and left him standing to look at them, and a corporal of the Hannovers they hanged up dead in a tree,' John Deane wrote in 1709. 'Several others was found with their heads cut off from their bodies in the same field.'[44]

To take part in any pitched battle was likely to be a testing and grim experience, quite unlike anything to be found even in the rough and tumble of civilian life in the early eighteenth century. There are plenty of anecdotes to show that the soldiers actually relished the experience, for all the hazards and dangers involved in the line of battle, once they had become accustomed to the novelty of the event. The daring exploits in 1708 of Sergeant William Littler of Godfrey's Regiment, swimming without orders across the flooded ditch in front of Lille under heavy French fire to hack down the supports holding up a drawbridge, are well known. The gallant sergeant, who can hardly have expected to walk away unscathed that night, was granted a commission as reward; the incident was remarkable but not unique. Life on campaign, with hard marching in heat, rain and cold, living on short rations inadequately cooked up in heavy iron kettles or pots, sleeping in the open or in rudimentary tents and shelters in all weathers both fair and foul, could be trying, but also soon encouraged a kind of swaggering acceptance. Hard campaigning toughens a man, physically and mentally, and he is in consequence a better soldier for it.

Not all conditions could be met with insouciance: 'We left camp at three o'clock in the afternoon', Lieutenant Colonel Blackader wrote of one approach to battle, 'and marched all night, a tedious and fatiguing march ... It poured down in heavy rain, and the cavalry had so broken up the ways, that the men marched in clay and dirt to the knees almost the whole day.'[45] Then, on another occasion, when Marlborough's army was foot-slogging its way back to Flanders from the Moselle valley, 'Marching all day. Uneasy with hot weather. A soldier's life is an odd, unaccountable way of living. One day too much heat, another too cold. Sometimes we want sleep, meat and drink.'[46] Even when in camp for a brief spell, the trials of a soldier's life were ever present, as John Deane describes during the frustratingly unproductive campaign in 1707:

> On June 4th (O.S.) about seven o'clock in the evening there happened a very terrible storm of wind, rain and hail, to that degree that it did great damage in our camp, especially in the line, blowing down and tearing to pieces the officers and sutlers tents, driving their beds and bedding, clothes and other effects about the streets.[47]

Still, there will always be men who relish this odd life, for all its attendant trials. Civilian life at the time was rigorous enough, with daily labour in all weathers and a poor diet the common experience, which must have coloured the view of many. Over the years soldiers become used to receiving inexplicable orders, and soon afterwards counter-orders, with all the frustration and inconvenience that goes with them. Nothing in that respect is new, and John Deane recalled that in 1708, during the manoeuvring in the early stages of the siege of Lille:

> The 25 (August) we struck tents again and lay on our arms again for some hours, waiting the enemy's motions. And so we wait till Doomsday. However we had orders to pitch our camp again which was no sooner up but another false alarm came that the enemy was just at hand, advancing upon us in all haste, which caused us to strike our tents again; which in the end proved to be some of our own forces.[48]

The robustness of the common soldier in Marlborough's army, and the powers of endurance and patience that were commonly displayed, can be seen late in 1708. After the fall of Lille that December, the weather turned bitterly cold, but there was business yet to be finished with the recapture of the French-held towns in northern Flanders; only then could the troops be sent off to their winter quarters. The duke wrote to Foreign Secretary Sidney Godolphin on 13 December of the operations against Ghent:

> Till this frost breaks, we can neither break ground for our batteries, nor open our trenches; and which is yet worse, if this weather continues, all the canals will be frozen, so that we shall not be able to get forage from Holland ... The soldiers as well as the officers are convinced of the necessity of having this town.[49]

There was certainly another side to enlisting for service, quite apart from the novel opportunity to exercise some legally sanctioned unbridled violence every now and then, for which young Englishmen have long had a marked prediliction. Life as a soldier was rough and ready, within certain strict boundaries, but men with enterprising natures could and would make the best of things, and find ways to secure what comfort and pleasure was to be had, even in the most unpromising circumstances. As soldiers across the ages know well, any fool can be uncomfortable, and – while never volunteering for a task – old soldiers will take every opportunity, and even contrive to make those same opportunities, for enjoyment, ease and comfort of a rudimentary kind. When a little spare money was available to Marlborough's soldiers, recreation could be sought in the tents of the many sutlers, such as that managed by Kit Davies, who were permitted to accompany the army both in quarters and on campaign; there, food, drink and convivial company were to be had. 'The army was ordered into winter quarters,' Davies recalled as the long campaign of 1708 drew to a shivering close in the bitter weather, 'our regiment stayed in Ghent, where I got a comfortable living by cooking for, and selling beer to, the soldiers.'[50]

Camp regulations required that new recruits should receive instruction in the use of their arms and the basic drills to be followed and the drum rolls to be harkened to and obeyed. Those recruits joining a regiment while it was on campaign – battlefield casualty replacements, as they would become known – may have had fairly basic, even rushed, education in such matters, but they would tend to be the exception, as losses would usually be made good once the campaign for the year was called to a halt with the onset of bad autumnal weather. When in camp and not out on campaign, the soldier's day was not particularly long or that arduous, allowing for routine parades, drills and duties, depending very much upon the zeal or otherwise of junior officers. Some of these would be thrusters eager to make a name for themselves, but many were not and, outside the season for campaigning, absenteeism amongst officers was rife, albeit usually with permission. There would be also be fatigue and guard duties, for that is the soldiers lot, but a man would often find that, with a little careful management, a second, more congenial, occupation could be pursued alongside the profession of arms. Helping local farmers to bring in the harvest was popular, in return for a good meal and draught of locally brewed beer or cider, and this came easily to men who, in many cases, had grown up on the land. Those who were enterprising enough, and sufficiently handy with fist or cudgel to see off competitors, could seek to profit by the human weakness of their comrades. Donald McBane graphically illustrated the seamy side of camp life – gambling, whoring and duelling – in his salty and revealing memoirs, which were published in 1729. Gambling with card and dice was common place, and card-sharping was just as common, while a few, such as McBane, ran one of those ever-popular establishments, a brothel, apparently having endless trouble keeping his 'lassies' under control. Such comforts that were provided were sometimes attended with risk, of course, as Kit Davies remembered when, in 1708, some soldiers relaxing after a spell in the siege trenches before Lille spent a convivial evening at 'a house of civil conversation, where one of them was received with so warm an affection, that he must be ungrateful if he ever forgets it, for the favour she bestowed on him was of a lasting sort.'[51]

Marlborough's army may have been a polyglot arrangement, with a mix of regular troops and hired regiments owing allegiance to foreign rulers, and in consequence drawn from many different quarters, but his faith in them and their abilities, and in return their own trust and affection for the duke, was quite profound. On both sides this was justified, and well rewarded with success. Although the Grand Alliance fought the War of the Spanish Succession on many fronts, it was Marlborough's army, whether in southern Germany or in the Low Countries, that was the main spring of the Allied war effort. If the duke succeeded, so too would the Alliance, given some judicious negotiation. If, on the other hand, Marlborough failed, then all was lost, and nothing that happened elsewhere mattered very much.

Chapter 3

The Commanders

The General, one of those brave old commanders
Who served through all the wars in Flanders'[1]

It is necessary to review the career and character of **John Churchill, First Duke of Marlborough (1650–1722)**, as a preliminary to any consideration of his commanders and the soldiers they led. Born in June 1650 in the West Country of England into a family ruined by its adherence to the Royalist cause in the English Civil War, young John Churchill was taken as a page into the court of King Charles II on the Restoration of that monarch to the throne in 1660. He served with an English regiment in Tangier, and with troops loaned out to Louis XIV in the wars with the Dutch, where he proved himself to be a gallant and capable, if not outstanding, soldier. Introduced to the French king, he left a good impression although Louis XIV seemed to doubt that he would ever achieve anything, as he was too much given to the exotic and enticing pleasures to be found at the English court. Churchill declined an offer of a commission in the French army, and by 1675 he held the rank of lieutenant colonel in the Duke of York's Regiment of Foot. Alliances were shifting, and three years later the young officer was sent with Sidney Godolphin to The Hague to discuss with William of Orange, the Dutch Stadtholder, ways to limit the growing power of France. In 1682 he became Baron Churchill of Aymouth, in the Scottish peerage, a decided mark of growing influence and royal approval at the time. When Charles II died in 1685, Churchill was sent as envoy to Versailles with the news, a mark of his growing stature as someone of importance. At the Battle of Sedgemoor in July of that year, he had command of the Royalist infantry in the fighting that brought to ruin the young Duke of Monmouth's brief and futile rebellion against his uncle, the newly enthroned James II.

Churchill continued to rise with the favour of the new king and was made major general in 1688, but he switched his allegiance to William of Orange during the Glorious Revolution of that year, a move that did much to undermine James II's position within the army. Churchill was made Earl of Marlborough, but the newly installed Dutch king seemed hesitant to trust him too much. Also, his fiery-tempered wife, Sarah, was a close confidante of Anne, youngest daughter of James II. Moreover, the earl remained in correspondence with the exiled king in France, and perhaps, having hurriedly left the service of one king, he might be inclined at some future point do so again. Once war with France came, Marlborough was also suspected – almost certainly wrongly – of incautiously passing information that led to a military defeat for Dutch and English troops at Camaret Bay in Brittany, and for a brief time he was detained in the Tower of London, although this seems to have been to serve as a warning, a signal not to be too pushy and over-ambitious, rather than anything more serious.

Despite the reserve with which William III regarded Marlborough, the earl steadily regained his position and influence, particularly after 1695, when Queen Mary, William III's wife, died of smallpox. Her younger sister, the Princess Anne, was now heir to the throne when the king died (unless there was to be a restoration of James II or his young son which, given their close adherence to the Roman Catholic faith, seemed to be very improbable). At the turn of the century, as renewed war with France became likely over the disputed succession to the Spanish throne, Marlborough, who was by now a general, was appointed by William III to be ambassador-extraordinary and plenipotentiary to the States-General of Holland. He accompanied the king on a visit to The Hague to negotiate the terms of the Grand Alliance and in this way, the Dutch came to know Marlborough better, and they found that they liked him and trusted his judgement. So, when the moment came to choose an overall commander for the Anglo-Dutch forces, Marlborough was, despite the competing claims of other more experienced generals, not a surprising choice.

Above all else, Marlborough became the commander, the leader and the driving force in the huge struggle waged by the Grand Alliance to limit the power of France and achieve an equitable division of the moribund Spanish Empire. As Queen Anne's Captain-General, and commander of the Anglo-Dutch forces in the field, Marlborough's influence was arguably greater than any other individual during the war, and he demonstrably gained the most remarkable and oft-repeated military successes. At the same time, Marlborough conducted, almost single-handedly, the foreign affairs of England (Great Britain from 1707 onwards). The power and influence that he could wield were due in part to the close relationship that William III had developed between England and Holland in the years before his death, so that the aims and interests of the two countries, who had in the past been such rivals and occasionally enemies, were at length seen to be the same where the perennial threat from France was concerned. To this must be added the abilities of the duke himself, the trust that was placed in him by Queen Anne, and his harmonious relationships with the key figures in the Grand Alliance, whether they were princes, dukes, electors, counts, generals, deputies or politicians.[2] These were men, and occasionally women, who recognized and acknowledged the influence that Marlborough wielded as a friend and confidant of Queen Anne. Furthermore, his repeated military successes in the field added significantly to his influence within the Grand Alliance, and with a commander who could achieve such astonishing results, particularly in 1704 at Blenheim and 1706 at Ramillies, there was no other of comparable stature who could lead the Allied armies on to ultimate victory. When he left the scene at the end of 1711, so too was the mainspring of the Alliance dislocated, and failure and disappointment soon followed.

Once appointed as Captain-General and to the command of the Anglo-Dutch forces, the Duke of Marlborough was the supreme commander both of that army, and also in a wider sense of the forces of the Grand Alliance. A concern at the start of the War of the Spanish Succession was that his reputation as a field commander had yet to be fully established, as had the military prowess of England itself; it says much for Marlborough's own charm and tact, and also for the persuasive effect of English financial subsidies to the other partners in the Alliance, that he should have been so well and so readily accepted. His early tactical successes against the doughty veteran Marshal Boufflers and his French troops, limited though they were, did much to strengthen his position as commander of the army. His authority and reputation became such that other men, each of considerable military prowess and renown, greater experience, and of equal standing in a wider sense, such as Prince Eugene of Savoy and Henry of Nassau, Veldt-Marshal Overkirk, deferred to the duke and his judgement, and in large measure they took their orders from him. With the Imperial commander Eugene, of course, such orders were couched as polite requests, as was warranted by his rank and standing with Emperor Leopold or his sons in Vienna, but these requests were to be acted upon nonetheless, and that was understood. Although the Dutch field deputies who were appointed by the States-General to accompany the Anglo-Dutch army proved on several occasions to be reluctant and obstructive, in the main the duke's authority was implicitly acknowledged and accepted by them with good grace. When this proved not to be so, his powers of persuasion were formidable, or he managed to have the more awkward of the generals and field deputies posted somewhere else.

It was of the greatest importance that there should be one guiding hand in the overall military effort of the Grand Alliance. The operations of the Allied armies, both the Anglo-Dutch forces and those of Imperial Austria operating alongside them, were a huge collaborative effort with all the difficulties, friction and scope for misunderstandings or ill-feeling that often attend such efforts. The fate of nations, and that of carefully crafted military reputations, could turn upon a single decision. That Marlborough enjoyed the trust of so many senior officers and so many skilful and diversely talented subordinate commanders speaks volumes for his abilities and skill. This is not to say that Marlborough's commanders slavishly obeyed his every word and whim; they were almost all strong-willed characters, often gifted soldiers with firm opinions of their own and judiciously honed reputations long and laborious in the making to protect. These same commanders were also often subject to the wishes and instructions of their own prince or elector – men who would carefully watch for any breach or infringement of the terms of service of the troops they had hired out to fight the French. The Danish troops commanded by the Duke of Wurttemburg, for example, were under firm orders not to take the field in the spring of 1706, until outstanding arrears of pay were settled. That Marlborough's urgent summons to battle on the Ramillies–Offuz ridgeline that Sunday in May was heeded all the same says much for Wurttemburg's strength of character, as he was in fact acting in defiance of his own instructions. It also speaks very well for the high regard in which he held Marlborough, and the clear importance of the message he had received, which could not be lightly ignored. Marlborough also gave assurances that the arrears of pay for the Danish troops would be forthcoming, even if he had to provide the money himself, which undoubtedly helped matters. The Hanoverian troops did not appear at all that day, as the terms of their service were still under discussion, and the elector, George (who one day would be George I of Great Britain), was being difficult.[3]

While the authority of the Duke of Marlborough was widely acknowledged, his subordinates were never slow to express their opinions either to him, each other in the field, or in letters of complaint, protest or self-justification to politicians and friends in London, The Hague, Hanover, Copenhagen, Berlin or whatever other court or capital city was most appropriate. This tendency to gossip and politic was common at the time, and was not seen as insubordination, as it would to a later generation. This activity noticeably increased as the war went on, as taxation, expense and casualties were incurred for apparently little return, and the duke's influence visibly flagged in London. Marlborough, a determined man who was rarely seen to lose his temper, did not and could not demand blind obedience, and he would often take pains to take a commander to one side to explain things and persuade. His early life as a courtier, and later experience as an urbane and persuasive diplomat when negotiating with the Dutch the terms of the Grand Alliance, stood him in good stead on that score: 'He could refuse more gracefully than others could grant, and those who went from him the most dissatisfied as to the substance of their business, were yet charmed by his manner.'[4] A clear example of this approach may be seen in the duke's intentions after the victory at Oudenarde in July 1708, when he planned to press on past the fortress belt deep into northern France and by so doing to try and force the French field army to fight a final and decisive battle in the open. His commanders were almost all set against such a daring plan – even intrepid Prince Eugene was not convinced. Marlborough did not insist or try to cajole or browbeat, but turned instead to lay siege to Lille, an important operation with a potentially valuable prize, but one that ate up four precious months of campaign time and, arguably, negated the success that had so daringly been snatched in open battle. Louis XIV naturally regretted the loss of Lille when it fell, but appreciated the value of the delay that the prolonged siege had imposed on Marlborough and Eugene.[5]

On occasions, Marlborough could not hide his exasperation with commanders who failed to share his clarity of vision and sense of what could be achieved with a little daring and urgency. This was illustrated quite starkly in the summer of 1705, after the abandonment of the duke's campaign in the Moselle valley and the subsequent breaching of the Lines of Brabant at Elixheim. On two occasions shortly afterwards, at the Yser River and the Yssche stream, the duke's plans to advance and confront the French army were foiled by his Dutch commanders and the field deputies, who had achieved much in that campaign but were reluctant to risk more. Accused of wishing to endanger his troops' lives in a rash attack that August, the duke declared to the Dutch officers clustered around him, 'I disdain to send troops to dangers which I will not myself encounter. I will lead them where the peril is most imminent.'[5] It was of no use: they had decided against taking action, and a promising opportunity to damage the French was allowed to slip by.

This was a turning point, for Marlborough declared that he would no longer operate under such restrictions, and wrote to Queen Anne that he might even retire from active campaigning. The States-General, to their credit, understood what a damaging move this would be for the Grand

Alliance and took him at his word. The more uncooperative of the Dutch officers and field deputies, few of whom lacked skill or energy, but who clearly failed to grasp the essentials of Marlborough's manner of campaigning – that of decisively forcing action in the French – were quietly transferred elsewhere. Marlborough was assured of full cooperation from then on, and as a result, the following spring he could lead the reinvigorated Anglo-Dutch army, flushed with confidence, to a remarkable success at Ramillies. Even then, the duke had to turn an occasional deaf ear to helpful words of caution he was given that misty May morning, as Field Deputy Sicco van Goslinga recounted in his memoirs:

> When the Duke advanced towards the enemy for the reconnaissance, he was accompanied by the [Veldt-]Marshal Overkirk, Generals Dopff, Cadogan, Chanclos, the Captains of Cavalry Tryse, Walon and myself. The last two, who had served under the Spanish, and understood the terrain, stressed hard and positively to the Duke, that the left of the enemy did not offer the chance of success; it had hedges, ditches and the marsh [of the Petite Gheete Stream], which they depended on against attack; but they did not provide enough to arrange in battle-line to attack our right; they in accordance set three or four lines; they were on a plain without roads or obstacles. The Duke listened calmly, but still did not say anything, he declared the battle-line such, which had in fact with an equality of cavalry on both Wings.[6]

What the bold field deputy did not mention, although he should have been aware of it, was that Marlborough was quite well acquainted with the lie of the land on the Ramillies–Offuz ridgeline. The previous year, after the disappointment of not being able to press home the advantage on the Yssche, the duke had his set his troops to level the French lines of defence in Brabant, and meanwhile took the chance to scout thoroughly for himself the area over which his army was now advancing to attack Marshal Villeroi.[7] Accordingly, for all the well-intentioned comments of the two Walloon cavalry officers, and their advice against pressing on, Marlborough was confident of the soundness of his outline plan and was soon proved right in unmistakable fashion.

It is easy to blame the Dutch for what appears to be a lack of vigour or vision, but they were certainly men of energy and courage in the normal course of events, and we can remember Dan Parke's comment that they would fight like devils if cornered, but they were perhaps too aware of what Holland had to lose by failure. Memories were long, and it was not so many years since the States-General had to breach the sea-dykes and flood their crops, herds and land, sooner than submit to Louis XIV and his armies. Having gained much, the stout Dutch feared to lose much, for if Marlborough should ever meet with a serious defeat, he and Queen Anne's troops could always go back across the Channel to England; their Allies, however, could not so this, and might be left alone once more to face the might of France. Given what would eventually take place in 1712, when parties on all sides had thoroughly tired of the war and the Grand Alliance sundered itself, this concern was not without at least some degree of foundation.

That lay in the future and could not be foreseen, and it says a great deal for Marlborough and his commanders that, despite the stress and uncertainty of war, the Anglo-Dutch army and that of their Imperial Austrian comrades worked together so well. The capabilities and reputation of Marlborough were the talk of Europe, and professional soldiers sought to join his army on campaign and to have their share in the associated glory. The success could not be Marlborough's alone, as whatever was achieved was a collaborative effort at all levels of the army and on an increasingly large and complex scale – in 1704 at Blenheim, Marlborough and Eugene had 52,000 troops under command, but five years later at Malplaquet they led over 120,000 men. This way of making war was a joint enterprise, and much of the success depended upon the subordinate commanders who received, trusted and readily executed Marlborough's orders and directions with such skill and flare. It might, nonetheless be asked whether such a huge army as in 1709 could fully be controlled and commanded with the relatively unsophisticated methods available at that time. The bloody fighting at Malplaquet, with losses that caused consternation and attracted to Marlborough a good deal of sharp criticism, resulted to a marked degree from an inability in Marlborough and Eugene to exert their full authority and influence uniformly across the field. This was seen most obviously on the left of the Allied line that grim day, where the Prince of Orange gallantly but unwisely pressed on with expensive attacks well past the point when there was any real chance of success.

By the time Marlborough took command of the Anglo-Dutch army he was, at 52 years of age, an old man by the standards of his day. His prodigious energy and application to duty, and the dynamic way he approached his campaigning have to be seen in the knowledge not just of his advancing years, but in his increasing physical infirmity with severe headaches and occasional dizziness (foreshadowing, perhaps, the series of strokes that he suffered from 1716 onwards). The duke also had trouble with his eyesight, writing in 1703, shortly after the frustrating failure of an attempt to seize Antwerp, 'My letter ... was writ by candlelight, as this; and my eyes are so bad that I do not see what I do, so that I hope you will excuse me that I do not answer all in your two letters.'[8] That he then campaigned with such success for another eight years, despite these infirmities, is not the least of any number of astonishing things about his military career. The duke certainly had a tremendous capacity for hard work, despite this indifferent health, and he had a good memory – essential when working with a remarkably small staff, as he was. These men were well known to him and were tried in adversity, and so they were trusted. It was a trust that was well repaid; certainly, some who had profited by their association with Marlborough in happy times turned against him as self-interest and political winds and alliances shifted, but these were few. His attention to detail, on both a very large and a very small scale, can be seen his letters written in April 1709, when hopes for a peace after the calamity for France in the previous year had not yet faded entirely. The King of Prussia, who provided such excellent troops for Marlborough's army, had taken offence at not being complimented, unlike the Elector of Hanover, in the address given by Parliament in London on the satisfactory outcome of the 1708 campaign. There were also arrears of pay for the regiments sent for Imperial service, but given the poor state of the finances in Vienna this was not that unusual.

To smooth things, Marlborough sent Lieutenant General Grumbkow to Berlin to reassure the king. Grumbkow was able to arrange that, in return for additional subsidies, a remittance of the Captain-General's customary deductions from sums paid to Prussia (legitimate and acknowledged, but subsequently the cause of much difficulty) and additional money for better subsistence of Prussian officers when on campaign, the additional troops required for the coming campaign would be forthcoming. Writing to Marlborough with further details of how the agreement was struck, Grumbkow explained that the king had felt that his contribution to the Allied cause was undervalued, and:

> When it was considered that we sent all our best and finest troops, and that the King paid for the regiment of Mecklenburg entirely, and added two squadrons more, he was very well assured that Your Highness would make no difficulty, since the maintenance of fourteen squadrons, of which the King received [money] for only twelve, cost him, beside the subsidy, three hundred thousand francs ... He [Marlborough] must own that he does not find among other princes

so much facility and so much good faith as with us ... I [the King] will pledge my word that the troops shall be on the Meuse the 1st of May.[9]

To his trusty quartermaster-general, William Cadogan, Marlborough wrote of the movement of Allied reinforcements, should active hostilities have to resume. Careful not to jeopardize the negotiations then still underway for an agreed peace, he still had to prepare for war:

> The troops in Brabant and Flanders must be kept in readiness for any emergency; otherwise they must wait the motions of the rest ... The other generals assure us if the Horse on the Meuse marched out as soon as was intended, they would be soon entirely out of condition of serving the rest of the campaign, so I pray you will form a new scheme of the whole, putting the march backward ten days ... The English regiments at Antwerp must not march for Lille till those of the garrisons are ready to go into the field.[10]

Two days later the duke wrote to his chief of engineers, Colonel John Armstrong, with a sharp codicil to those instructions for restraint in preparations for ready deployment: 'The backwardness of the season obliges us to defer the opening of the campaign eight days later than was intended.' A postscript was added: ' Notwithstanding this delay, the troops must be always ready to march at an hour's warning if the service should require it.'[11]

Clearly, Marlborough, for all his admirable staff work when in head-quarters and energetic attention to the welfare of his soldiers, could not be everywhere, and the method of receiving information and passing instructions to subordinates in a timely fashion was at the time slow and, to a degree, unreliable. The shot and shell that swept a typical battlefield would scythe down staff officers just as readily as cavalry troopers and their horses or foot soldiers standing in line. An officer sent galloping off with an order might very well never be seen alive again, with no clear assurance that the message itself had been received or acted on. In the meantime, moves would be made in anticipation that those same orders had indeed been received, understood and were in process of timely execution. Confidence and trust between the duke and his senior com-manders was therefore of prime importance. A clear understanding of Marlborough's mode of operating on the field of battle was vital, and this enabled his generals to operate as they saw fit, to achieve the subordinate tasks that they were given, under the overall directions of what was known to be the duke's aim. This foreshadowed very well the modern concept of 'mission command' and can be seen on frequent occasions, as with Prince Eugene's brutally effective attacks from the Allied right at Blenheim, Veldt-Marshal Overkirk's very capable handling of the Dutch and Danish cavalry two years later at Ramillies, and Eugene (again) in the teeming woods of the Bois de Sars at Malplaquet. On the other hand, Marlborough would at times have to spell things out in the plainest terms to his commanders to ensure adequate compliance with his own evolving plans in fast-moving situations. He had to send William Cadogan to the Earl of Orkney with firm orders not to press on with the English infantry attacks at Ramillies, to leave the fighting on the Ghent road and ride to assist Veldt-Marshal Overkirk to get his Dutch and Danish troops into place on the Boser Couter hill at Oudenarde two years later, and then to gallop across the shot-swept battlefield to instruct the Prince of Orange not to persist with his failing attacks at Malplaquet in 1709.

Marlborough was a tactical innovator, but his overall method was similar in all his major battles – to strike hard at an opponent's flanks to force the early commitment of scarce reserves and then to break through at a weakened point. The duke always took careful account of the topography of the battlefield, however, and interspersed his Horse and Foot for mutual support, something which his opponents often struggled to do – this was clear at both Blenheim and Ramillies. At Oudenarde, where the employment of cavalry en masse was difficult due to the close nature of the country, he used the squadrons of British and Dutch cavalry on the Ghent road to intimidate the French commanders and draw attention away from the deadly turning movement by Overkirk around their right flank. Given the impromptu nature of the engagement, with outnumbered Allied troops marching straight into battle from the forced line of march, this was confident employment of troops of a high degree. The following year at Malplaquet the thick woods on either flank made the deployment of horsemen impractical other than in the centre, and briefly on the French left near to La Folie Farm. However, the large uncommitted reserves of cavalry that Marlborough maintained enabled him to follow through the breaching of the weakened centre of the position and then to force the French cavalry, for all their valour but fighting without adequate infantry support, from the field. These things do not happen by chance, and although the French commanders certainly studied the duke's methods and to a certain extent learned from them, the high degree of both innovation and organization that he displayed on the field is evident.

In spite of his efforts and achievements, and those of his troops, on 31 December 1711 the Duke of Marlborough was removed from his appointments by Queen Anne and was, in effect, cast out of public life. He wrote in reply to her hand-written letter of dismissal in sombre terms, 'I wish your Majesty may never find the want of so faithful a servant as I have always endeavoured to approve myself to you.'[12] After such a record of unbroken success, repeated if clearly slowing in the achieving, this was a harsh reward. Allegations of corruption in the financing of the army during his campaigns were made by the duke's vociferous opponents, particularly with regard to a percentage taken over the contracts to supply bread, and there was the threat to Marlborough of impeachment. Commissioners appointed to inquire into this matter found that he had received large sums of money, over 330,000 guilders, from Sir Solomon Medina, the contractor to supply bread to the armies in the Low Countries between 1707 and 1711. The fact that such practices were commonplace and sanctioned was found not to matter, although Marlborough pointed out in a letter dated 10 November 1711 that the money had been devoted in large part to providing secret intelligence for military purposes by way of bribes and inducements (and for which he held a warrant from the Queen, dating from July 1706). 'Whatever sums have been received on this account have been constantly employed in procuring intelligence, in keeping correspondence, and other secret services.'[13] In fact, Marlborough's successor did exactly the same, but that appeared not to count for very much as he was still in favour with Queen Anne and her ministers.

The duke and his wife, together with a few close friends, including William Cadogan, went to live abroad, while the command of the British troops in the Low Countries was given to the Second Duke of Ormonde. He was capable enough, although undoubtedly lacking Marlborough's deft touch, but within a fortnight was constrained by confidential orders from London not to engage the French too closely. In fact, Great Britain was negotiating its way out of the war and Queen Anne's troops left the field in 1712. It is necessary to relate that the generally good discipline and administration amongst the British troops while under Marlborough's supervision did not long survive his departure, with food being provided of deteriorating quality, growing arrears of pay, looting on a widening scale, and occasional outrages against French civilians. An attempted mutiny by troops in Ghent was put down severely. 'What can be the meaning that all our garrisons are disturbed in this manner?' Corporal Matthew Bishop asked an officer, 'It is an instance that never happened during the time of the Duke of Marlborough.'[14]

With the accession to the throne in London of King George I in 1714, Marlborough returned to England and was restored to all his offices and appointments. He was active in preventing too drastic a reduction in the army now that the war had at last come to an end, and in this he was undoubtedly helped by the Jacobite rising of 1715 which, while inept and futile, required to be put down with some firmness. The duke was not very close to the new king, who perhaps remembered being snubbed by him and Eugene over the plans for the 1708 campaign. Marlborough suffered increasing ill-health, suffering the first of several strokes in 1716, and he grew to be frail and gradually had to retire from public life. He gave up the post of Captain-General in 1721 and died at Windsor Lodge in June the following year.

To appreciate Marlborough and his achievements properly, we should turn our attention to **Prince François-Eugene (Eugen) of Savoy-Carignac (1663–1736)**, who must be counted, first and foremost and by a wide margin, amongst the duke's fellow commanders. Usually known as Prince Eugene, and born in Paris the son of the Comte de Soissons, his Italian-born mother was a niece of Cardinal Mazarin, and the young man had been intended by Louis XIV for a career in the Church. Instead, Eugene took himself off in July 1683, without royal permission it should be said – a kind of *lésse majesté* – and offered his service as a soldier to Emperor Leopold, who was residing at the time in Passau (Vienna having been evacuated for the time being on the approach of the Ottoman army). The fact that Eugene was the second cousin to the Duke of Savoy made him particularly welcome, as Leopold hoped to detach that duchy from its friendship with France. Eugene's assertion of his future loyalty to the House of Habsburg was honest and striking, with him declaring that he had:

> Reached this decision only after having tried to follow my ancestor's example of serving my country and the Bourbon Court with all my heart, and only after having in vain sought service many times under the French Crown ... I assure you, most merciful Emperor of my constant loyalty and that I will devote all my strength.[15]

Rising to be a major general in 1685 and fighting at the famous siege of Vienna in that year, he was lieutenant general 1687 and became a general in 1690. Appointed to be the Imperial commander in Hungary, Eugene established a fine reputation as a dashing commander in the many campaigns Austria waged in eastern Europe. He was well known to dislike ostentation or finery, although certainly not averse to good living, and was once described rather unkindly by his mother as 'Small and ugly in appearance, with an upturned nose, extended nostrils, and an upper lip so narrow as to prevent him ever shutting his mouth'.[16] Eugene achieved a notable victory over an Ottoman army at Zenta in 1697 and became commander-in-chief in Italy 1701, and president of the Imperial War Council two years later. The prince's great partnership with Marlborough began with the campaign on the Danube in 1704, which, despite Eugene's inability to hold Marshal Tallard on the Rhine, led to their triumph at Blenheim and a warm friendship that lasted to the end of the duke's life.

With an aggressive instinct and boundless courage, Eugene's skills proved to be the perfect complement to the Captain-General's calm but decisive manner, and the accession in 1705 of the young Emperor Joseph, an ardent supporter of Eugene, strengthened the prince's energetic influence over the somewhat uneven Imperial war effort. At Oudenarde three years later, although Eugene's troops were not present on the field, he was given command of the scrambled fighting along the Ghent road on the right of the Allied line, while Marlborough arranged the huge turning movement by Dutch and Danish troops around the open flank of the hastily deploying French army. In 1711, as Marlborough's influence waned and dismissal grew near, Eugene came to London to express his support for his friend and comrade, but despite the high regard in which he was held this was all to no avail. Appointed governor general of the Austrian Netherlands (previously a Spanish possession) between 1716 and 1724, Prince Eugene remained a bachelor, although he undoubtedly had a fondness for female company and continued to campaign in Imperial service well into old age. He died in Vienna, heavily laden with honours, at the good age for a warrior of 73.

With the maintenance of good relations between Great Britain and Holland so critical for the success of the Grand Alliance, and with Marlborough the field commander of the Anglo-Dutch armies, the senior Dutch generals with whom he had to work were vital to this enterprise. Marlborough was fortunate that for much of the war he had the support and cooperation of **Hendrik van Nassau, Count Overkirk (1641–1708)**, who was descended from an illegitimate line of the House of Orange, and as such was a cousin of King William III. Becoming major general in 1683, lieutenant general (in the English army) in 1689, lieutenant general (Dutch army) two years later, and general in 1701 as preparations for renewed war gathered pace, Overkirk was the veldt-marshal and commander of the Dutch forces at the time of Marlborough's appointment. Almost alone amongst Dutch generals, Overkirk saw, as Marlborough did, the pressing need to force the French army out into the field where they could be confronted and defeated in open battle. For all his valour, Overkirk was beset with understandable concern at what might befall Holland, should things go badly wrong, and came to rely on Marlborough's calming presence, imploring the duke to suspend the march to the Danube in 1704. He failed to hold Marshal Villeroi in check in 1705 when Huy was lost for a time, while the duke was attempting an advance along the line of the Moselle valley. He then proved reluctant to support Marlborough when pressing the merits of an attack on the exposed French detachment commanded by the Marquis de Grimaldi at the river Yssche that August. The veteran Dutch soldier even took the chance to have a quite nap in his coach during a heated debate over whether to proceed with the attack – a sign, perhaps, of his increasing years and the oppressive heat of the summer afternoon. Nonetheless, Overkirk at his best was skilful and courageous, and his handling of the Dutch and Danish cavalry at Ramillies was exemplary, conserving their strength and good order when under heavy and persistent pressure from the very able French cavalry commander, General de Guiscard. This fine display of tactical robustness, ensuring the security of the left wing of the Allied army at critical moments, and then striking with deadly effect at just the right time, did much to secure the startling victory for the Allies that Sunday.

The way in which Marlborough and Overkirk worked so well together was notable, and an essential ingredient for the good of the combined Allied effort. With so many Dutch troops effectively under command of the Englishman, the confidence that Overkirk showed in the duke's competence and skilful direction of campaigns was essential for the cohesion of the Alliance. The cautious States-General in The Hague, who had so much at stake in the war and to whom Overkirk ultimately had to answer for his conduct and that of his troops, were reassured by this evident harmony. Some Dutch officers held a lingering sense of regret that the duke had been appointed to the command of the Anglo-Dutch army at all, and their cooperation was at times grudging, but the generally close accord between Marlborough and Overkirk was an example of how things should be done. Despite this, Overkirk's late arrival in position at Oudenarde in July 1708, although apparently caused by the congested passage his troops had to take through that fortified town, probably cost Marlborough a complete victory. The duke was obliged to leave the fighting on the right of the Allied forces in the capable hands of Prince Eugene while he went to oversee the veldt-marshal's belated deployment on the Boser Couter hill. The Dutch soldier was plainly ailing, and he travelled now in his coach even on the battlefield. His exertions at the subsequent siege of Lille, at a time of clearly faltering health which led to his death in

September, represented nothing short of dogged devotion to the Allied cause.

Marlborough's right-hand man at the head of the Allied army was undoubtedly his quartermaster-general, **William, First Earl Cadogan (1671–1726)**, whose grandfather had moved to Ireland in the 1630s and became secretary to the ill-fated Earl of Strafford. Intended for the law, and studying at Trinity College in Dublin, at the age of 17 he became a cornet in Wynne's Regiment of Dragoons in William III's army, fighting at the Battle of the Boyne in 1689 against James II when that exiled king attempted to regain his throne. Cadogan also served at the Battle of Aughrim in 1690 and the subsequent capture of Cork and Kinsale, meeting the Earl of Marlborough (who was present on the instructions of Queen Mary, who was acting as regent in her husband's absence from London on campaign) for the first time. By 1694, Cadogan was a lieutenant in Erle's Regiment of Foot, campaigning in the Low Countries against France, and taking part in the famous siege of Namur the following year, when Marshal Boufflers was obliged to yield the fortress – the first time a Marshal of France had ever done so. In August 1698, Cadogan managed to secure an appointment as major and quartermaster in Ross's Dragoons and returned with that regiment to Ireland on the temporary peace that had come with the Treaty of Ryswick. Marlborough appreciated Cadogan's good qualities and capacity for hard work, and in June 1701 he had the young man promoted to lieutenant colonel.

Once active campaigning in the Low Countries began in 1702, Cadogan fulfilled the additional function of chief of staff for Marlborough and proved to be a first-class soldier with a good eye for ground, enormous energy and a fine capability both as a tactician and as a staff officer. He had an exuberant and boisterous manner, however, which occasionally gave offence, but Cadogan's close friendship with Marlborough, and the way in which the duke could depend upon him, almost without question – as chief of staff, quartermaster-general and unofficial director of military intelligence – was a marked feature of the many campaigns that the two men shared during the war. This bond was widely acknowledged to a rather surprising degree, as when Cadogan was taken prisoner in 1706. The newly appointed French army commander, the Duc de Vendôme, arranged his early release, in exchange for a senior officer in Allied hands, as he knew how much Marlborough valued Cadogan's services. Such consideration reads rather oddly today, but seems to have attracted little comment at the time. Marlborough did indeed value Cadogan's grasp of terrain and the vital elements of time and space in which to achieve

things, and the quartermaster-general's temporary absence from the
Allied camp in the summer of 1708 is sometimes given as the main reason
for Marlborough being caught out by the sudden French offensive to take
Ghent and Bruges. Francis Hare certainly thought so, and wrote of
Cadogan at that time, 'He would have known the difference between their
coming to us and marching by us and would have given His Grace better
intelligence.'[17]

Cadogan had been made Colonel of the 6th Regiment of Horse in 1703,
a prestigious appointment, and the next year his skills were put to the test
on the long march from the Low Countries to the Danube. The logistical
challenge was enormous, but Cadogan carried out his tasks to Marlborough's complete satisfaction. The army's financial agent in Frankfurt
ensured that sufficient funds were made available at all stages of the
famous march so that supplies and necessaries of all kinds were readily
available – food for the men, fodder for the horses, shoes, horseshoes,
quarters and camping grounds – nothing was seized, everything was paid
for. 'Surely,' wrote Captain Robert Parker of the Royal Irish Regiment,
'never was such a march carried on with more order and regularity.'[18]
Cadogan's duties did not keep him out of the line of fire, and he was
injured and had his horse killed under him at the storm of the Schellenberg in July 1704. He led his own regiment to the charge at the Elixheim
fight in 1705 and was in command of the Allied vanguard on the approach
to Ramillies the next year, being the first to see the unexpected French
deployment around that village. He led the advanced guard on the forced
march from Lessines to the river Scheldt prior to the Oudenarde battle in
July 1708, and his competent handling of the fighting for the Allied
bridgehead across the river contributed greatly to Marlborough's success
that day. In January 1709 Cadogan was made lieutenant general, and
when he was wounded during the siege of Mons in the autumn, Marlborough wrote to his wife expressing keen concern for the swift recovery
of his close friend. The two men certainly had found that they thought and
acted in accord, and while preparing for a siege and riding on a scouting
expedition, Marlborough dropped his glove, as if by accident, and asked
Cadogan to recover it for him. This was done, and that evening the duke
asked if he remembered the spot and, if so, to have a battery emplaced
there; the quartermaster-general was able to respond that he had already
given the necessary orders for this to be done.

When Marlborough was dismissed at the end of 1711, Cadogan's star
fell too, and he accompanied the duke into temporary exile on the Continent. Cadogan also had to relinquish all his offices and appointments

but returned shortly before the accession of George I to the throne in London in 1714, at which point he was reinstated in his appointments. He became Colonel of the 2nd English Foot Guards (the Coldstream) in October that year and was employed on diplomatic duties at The Hague, a role for which he showed great aptitude, despite his hectoring manners, assisted, no doubt, by his ability to converse in the language. One of Cadogan's more questionable actions was to have the tails of all horses in Queen Anne's regiments docked, as they looked 'neater' that way – a strange custom that would persist for many years. During the 1715 Jacobite rebellion, Cadogan was appointed to replace the Duke of Argyll as commander in Scotland, a rather unnecessary move as Campbell had already asked to be recalled to London. Created Baron Cadogan of Reading in 1716, his later career was not without controversy or mishap, and he became embroiled in a lengthy and regrettable argument with Sarah, Duchess of Marlborough, over a large sum of money which she had asked him to invest safely. Instead he placed the funds in more speculative investments, hoping perhaps to reap the difference in anticipated return as his own profit, but then lost heavily and eventually had to repay the sum to the duchess. Cadogan had been Member of Parliament for Woodstock, near to Blenheim Palace in Oxfordshire, for many years, but when he attempted to be elected as Member of Parliament for Reading in Berkshire, the liquid inducements offered to persuade voters flowed a little too freely and a sprawling riot broke out in the market square. In 1717, Cadogan was appointed to be general of all the Foot forces (infantry) of the crown, as Marlborough's health was fast failing, and that same year he signed the Treaty of Triple Alliance with Holland and France, on behalf of the king. He became an earl in May 1718, was made the Captain-General in 1721, and on Marlborough's death the following year appointed to succeed him as Master-General of the Ordnance and Colonel of the 1st English Foot Guards. Cadogan died at his Kensington home on 17 July 1726.

Arnold Joost van Keppel, First Earl of Albemarle (1669–1718), was born in Gelderland, and began his career as a favourite of King William III. His good looks and easy charm, together with the favour shown to him by the king, aroused some jealous and malicious allegations as to the precise nature of the relationship, but this was without real foundation. Keppel was a clear admirer of women, but gossip being what it is, the slights and allegations left a mark that never quite faded. As William III lay dying early in 1702, he handed the young man the keys of his private cabinet and whispered, 'You know what to do with them.' As a commander of

Dutch cavalry, Keppel became Earl of Albemarle and major general in 1697, and lieutenant general in 1701, A trusted confidant of the Duke of Marlborough, when out on campaign Keppel proved himself to be a leader of considerable tactical skill and someone who could safely be entrusted with difficult tasks. His operation to cover the movement of the vast convoys of guns and siege materiel being brought forward to the siege of Lille in 1708 was a notable example of his competent handling of cavalry in a complex and critical operation. The closing campaigns in 1711, shortly before Marlborough's dismissal as Captain-General, saw Albemarle successfully conduct cavalry operations against reinvigorated French commanders who could by then deploy greater numbers of troops. One of Marlborough's last letters while in command of the Anglo-Dutch army was to congratulate Albemarle on his capable handling of a cavalry operation against a superior French force. Taken prisoner by Marshal Villars at Denain in March 1712, the earl was released shortly afterwards.

Dubislaw Gneomar von Natzmer (1654–1739) was a Pomeranian by birth; he took service with the Dutch army in 1672 at a time of high tension between the republic and the French king. He subsequently entered the Brandenburg army, serving with the elite Eskadron-Dragonen, and then as an adjutant to Georg von Derfflinger. He established a good reputation as a dashing leader of cavalry and went on to fight against the Ottoman forces in Hungary in 1685. Natzmer was in command of the Prussian cavalry, seconded to the Dutch service, during the Danube campaign in 1704 and was wounded and taken prisoner at the battle of Blenheim. This was the third time he had been captured by the French, and Marlborough had sought his advice on the terrain on the plain of Höchstädt, as he had been beaten there with Count von Styrum the previous year. Natzmer fought at Oudenarde, where his timely but costly charge late in the day kept the French attention away from Overkirk's delayed deployment to turn their right flank, and he was also at Malplaquet. After the conclusion of the war for Spain, Natzmer served on in the Brandenburg service, was made general of cavalry and became field marshal in 1728.

George Hamilton, First Earl of Orkney (1666–1737), was born in 1666, the fifth son of the Third Duchess of Hamilton and William Douglas, Earl of Selkirk. At the age of 18, he was made a captain in the Royal Scots (a unit commanded by his uncle, the Earl of Dumbarton, and which became famous as Orkney's own regiment in later years) and soon established a reputation as a bruisingly confident and aggressively competent field commander, fighting through all the major campaigns of King

William III's turbulent reign, being at the battles of the Boyne, Aughrim, Steenkirk and Landen. He was also wounded at the siege of Namur in 1695. That same year, Hamilton was made brigadier general, and married his distant cousin, Elizabeth Villiers (rather unkindly known as 'Squinting Betty' on account of the cast in one eye), who had been one of the king's mistresses, the illicit liaison clearly doing her prospects in the marriage field no harm. Created Earl of Orkney, Viscount Kirkwall and Baron Dechamont in 1696, he was made major general in 1702, and lieutenant general in 1704, when he commanded Marlborough's infantry at the Schellenberg and Blenheim. At Ramillies two years later, his forceful attacks with British and Danish infantry almost pierced the French and Bavarian line, and Orkney had to be recalled by William Cadogan as he was going on too far and too fast for his local success to be properly supported. '"What's this?" said my Lord Orkney,' according to Tom Kitcher. 'He had no mind to give ground when we were giving no quarter, nor we hadn't either, being up to our necks in deadliness and noise.'[19] Orkney commanded a brigade of troops covering Brussels during the campaign that led to the victory at Oudenarde in 1708, but at the Battle of Malplaquet his British and Prussian infantry forced a passage through the French centre, laying open the way for the Allied cavalry to move through. Orkney became a privy councillor in 1710 and was made general of infantry that same year; he was also appointed to be governor of Virginia, an apparent sinecure with few real duties, as he never took the trouble to go there; Alexander Spotswood, deputy quartermaster-general in the 1704 campaign, was the lieutenant governor in residence. Orkney campaigned in Flanders until the end of the war and lived long enough to be made the British army's first field marshal in 1736, before dying at his apartments in London in January 1737. 'As a second in command he was a most dependable and successful commander. He saw an immense deal of active service, and he won his high rank and position by his sterling qualities and personal bravery.'[20]

Known as 'Red John' amongst his troops, **John Campbell, Second Duke of Argyll and First Duke of Greenwich (1678–1743)**, was both a valiant soldier and a gifted politician. Born the eldest son of the Earl of Argyll, Campbell was granted a commission at the tender age of 14 by King William III, as colonel of his father's own regiment, and also made captain of a company (such double commissions not being unusual at the time). Lord Lorne, as the young man was then known, continued his studies while his regiment campaigned in the Low Countries during the Nine Years War, only to be 'broken', or disbanded, with the peace that came with the Treaty of Ryswick in 1697. Four years later, as preparations for the war for Spain gathered pace, Lorne was granted a fresh commission with the command of the newly raised Duke of Argyll's Regiment in the service of the States-General of Holland. Campbell first saw service at the siege of Kaiserswerth, where his natural aptitude as a soldier and indifference to enemy fire was soon noticed, and he took part in the famous and impetuous storm of the French-held Fort St Michael at Venlo soon afterwards.

In September 1703, Campbell became Duke of Argyll on the death of his father. He was appointed Colonel of the 4th (Scots) Troop of Horse Guards, and insisted that they should retain the silver lace trimmings to their uniforms, rather than adopt the gaudier gold lace of their English counterparts. Argyll was made a privy councillor to Queen Anne and, being a firm believer in the benefits of the union between England and Scotland, played an influential role in the lengthy and complex negotiations and Byzantine deal-making that led to the Act of Union in 1707. Argyll was both politician and soldier, of course, and he displayed sound tactical sense combined with ardent bravery and energy. He was at the Battle of Ramillies in May 1706, leading his Scots regiment in the Dutch service in the final storm of that village, once the French cavalry had melted away under the advance of Overkirk's massed squadrons. 'The Duke was himself the second or third man who, with his sword in hand, broke over the enemy's trenches.'[21] At Oudenarde in 1708 Argyll led twenty battalions of British and German infantry in the fiercest fighting along the Diepenbeek stream, and the following year, as a major general, he had command of a brigade of British troops in the fearfully difficult and expensive fighting in the Triangle, part of Bois de Sars on the right of the Allied attack. It was written of him there, that:

> The Duke of Argyle exposed his person in such a manner that he had several musket shots through his wig and clothes. It was not from an overheated valour which runs into all places merely to show a contempt for it, but that might animate the troops to imitate his example and to perform those miracles which, from their being put upon such an attack, seems to have been expected from them.[22]

Kit Davies recalled the incident very well in her account of the battle: 'You see,' he called to his men when he was struck by spent French musket balls in the woods at Malplaquet in 1709, 'I have no concealed armour, I am equally exposed with you.'[23] Argyll still thought that Marlborough had been wrong to fight there, and that the battle had been badly handled and unnecessarily expensive in casualties as a result. He was not slow to report his misgivings to London, where Marlborough's political enemies welcomed such ready ammunition for use in Parliament.

In 1710, Argyll was made a Knight of the Garter by Queen Anne, and his political influence continued to grow as that of Marlborough waned. The following spring he was appointed to be Her Majesty's ambassador and commander-in-chief in Spain, where he soon found mismanagement and incompetence, even having to pledge his own credit so that the soldiers could be paid, writing from Barcelona in June 1711:

> In the last six months only £71,000 has been sent here from England, which sum does not clear this establishment for one month. Judge then in what condition we must be; the privates have hitherto been subsisted by what money could be borrowed up and down this town, and in the villages where they are quartered. The officers have been reduced to the extremist misery, having scarcely clothes to their backs, and neither tents nor horses.[24]

On his eventual recall to London, Argyll continued to intrigue against Marlborough, and this had a rather inevitable outcome when, with the accession of King George I in 1714, Marlborough returned to London and was reinstated in his posts and offices. Argyll had been appointed to be commander-in-chief in the north, 'General of our Foot in Scotland', as the order from the king stated on 25 September, but early in 1716 Marlborough had him replaced by William Cadogan, on the very thin grounds that Argyll was not pursuing the Jacobite rebels under the Earl of Mar vigorously enough after the Battle of Sherriffmuir in November 1715. Argyll remained active in politics and was a firm advocate of the benefits of union between England and Scotland for the rest of his life. He was governor of Portsmouth for seven years, and became a field marshal of the British army before dying at his home in Surrey in October 1743, fortunately, perhaps, too soon to see the tragedy of the 1745–6 Jacobite rising, of which he would almost certainly have taken a dim view.

General Charles Churchill (1656–1714), younger brother of the Duke of Marlborough, saw extensive service under William III during the Nine Years War, being present at Steenkirk, Landen (where he captured his nephew, the Duke of Berwick) and Namur. A lieutenant general in 1702, he played a major role in the Danube campaign two years later, escorting the captive Marshal Tallard back to England, and then commanding Marlborough's infantry at the victory at Ramillies. Churchill became a full general in 1707, and in addition he was Member of Parliament for

Weymouth in Dorset, but suffered ill-health in 1708, and thereafter with-drew from active campaigning. He had been the lieutenant governor of the Tower of London until becoming governor of Guernsey in 1706, and on his brother's dismissal Charles was also stripped of his posts and appointments. A soldier of undoubted ability and solid loyalty to his older brother, his career was unavoidably overshadowed by that of Marlborough: 'He obeyed his brother's wishes implicitly, carried his instructions into execution, and took his place at the head of the English troops as his brother's deputy in his absence.'[25] The duke's other younger brother, George, was an admiral in the Royal Navy and he died in 1710.

John Friso (1683–1711) was the son of Henry-Casimir, Prince of Nassau-Dintz, and he assumed the title of Prince of Orange-Nassau on the death of King William III in 1702. By virtue of his rank he was a general in the Dutch army, and was a perfectly competent field commander. There was some controversy over his handling of the attack from the Allied right at Malplaquet and the startlingly heavy casualties that his regiments suffered. In 1711, as he was returning to the army, Orange drowned when his boat sank while crossing the Moerdyk at Hollands Diep. 'The Prince of Orange', Kit Davies remembered,

> quitted the army to make a tour to The Hague, to terminate the difference between His Highness and the King of Prussia ... He left us on the 11th of July N.S., but to my great sorrow for the loss of my generous benefactor, he was drowned while crossing the Moerdyk, on the 14th.[26]

Friso's son, who was born six weeks later, became in due course William III, Prince of Orange.

A Brandenburger by birth, **Karl-Philip Reichgraf von Wylich und Lottum (1650–1719)** entered Dutch service to fight in the republic's war with the French in 1668. A colonel in the service of the Elector of Brandenburg by the time the War of the League of Augsburg broke out (the Nine Years War, 1688–97), Lottum was made a major general in 1694. In 1702 he was given command of the Prussian troops in Dutch service and fought with great distinction at Blenheim, Oudenarde (where his infantry held the left of the hard-pressed Allied line at a critical point) and Malplaquet. A capable and hard-fighting general, Lottum enjoyed Marl-borough's entire trust and was often tasked with the most demanding duties. In 1715, shortly after the end of the War of the Spanish Succession, Lottum was promoted to field marshal and given the command of the

Prussian army and made a member of King Frederick William I's War Council.

John Dalrymple, Second Earl of Stair (1673–1747) was born in Edinburgh and served as a volunteer with the Cameronians at Steenkirk in 1692, before studying in Germany and being appointed to the Scots Regiment of Foot Guards in 1702. After fighting with distinction at Ramillies four years later, Stair was appointed to be Colonel of the Scots Dragoons (Greys) and commanded a brigade at Oudenarde, after which he took the dispatch from Marlborough announcing the victory back to London, and was suitably rewarded by Queen Anne. Service during the siege of Lille followed, and in 1708 Stair was made major general and was present at Malplaquet. After going to Poland as Queen Anne's envoy, he became a lieutenant general early on 1710, but as a firm supporter of Marlborough he was dismissed from all appointments the following year and had to give up the colonelcy of the Greys. On the accession of King George I he was reinstated and became colonel of the 6th Dragoons in 1715, being sent as envoy to Versailles. A Scottish peer in Parliament, Stair was appointed to be governor of Minorca in 1742 and was field commander at the Battle of Dettingen in June 1743, where the presence on the field of King George II proved to be something of a hindrance. He became commander-in-chief in Great Britain in 1745, at the time of the last Jacobite rising, and died at his home in Edinburgh in May 1747.

Leopold I of Anhalt-Dessau (1676–1747) was the younger son of Prince Johan-George II of Anhalt-Dessau and Henrietta-Catherine, daughter of the Prince of Orange. With a natural liking for the military life, Leopold entered the Brandenburg service, serving as an officer in that army while being a sovereign prince in his own right. He fought throughout the Nine Years War and as a lieutenant general was present at Höchstädt in September 1703, where the Allied and Imperial forces were defeated by Marshal Villars. He took an active part the following year in the victory at Blenheim. In 1706, Leopold campaigned with Prince Eugene in Italy and was at the victory at Turin, before returning to the Low Countries and fighting at the siege of Tournai and the Battle of Malplaquet in 1709. The next summer he was appointed to the overall command of the Prussian forces, with the rank of field marshal from 1712 onwards. In later years Leopold commanded the Prussian army in the Great Northern War, defeating Charles XII of Sweden in battle at Rugen. Active in reorganizing and training the army, he was instrumental in the introduction of iron ramrods to replace wooden ones for flintlock muskets. Achieving a victory at Kesseldorf in 1745 during the First Silesian War, Leopold was a strict disciplinarian, serving with great success under Frederick the Great, who owed much of his military success to the foundations first laid by the 'Old Dessauer'.

Henry Lumley (1660–1722) was appointed to be captain in the Queen's Regiment of Horse at the age of 17 – he was a convert from Catholicism to Protestantism, otherwise he could not have held a commission in the army. Lumley served in Flanders during the Nine Years War and was promoted to be colonel of the regiment in 1692, and fought at Steenkirk, advancing to brigadier general the following year. Lumley helped to cover William III's withdrawal at the Battle of Landen when the French pressed their attacks towards the Gheete stream, and he went on to serve at the successful siege of Namur in 1695, and in 1696 was made major general. As lieutenant general he commanded the British cavalry during the 1704 Danube campaign that took him to the Schellenberg and Blenheim. Lumley led the British cavalry with great flair and distinction at Ramillies, Oudenarde and Malplaquet, and was made general of Horse in 1711. He served as Member of Parliament for Sussex and Arundel for several periods.

Born in Lubeck, **Jorgen-Rantzau (1652–1733)** was a member of a Danish noble family from Schleswig-Holstein. He entered military service in the army of the King of Denmark when very young, and by 1701 had attained the rank of brigadier general, commanding the Jydske Horse Regiment at Blenheim. The following year Rantzau was promoted to major general, having established a good reputation as a dashing yet dependable cavalry commander. He had command of the Hanoverian dragoons in Cadogan's advanced guard at Oudenarde in 1708, screening the rapid Allied approach march with skill and judgement, and leading an impetuous charge against the flank of the marching French columns. He commanded a brigade of infantry in the Allied centre at Malplaquet, and sent two battalions to assist in the unsuccessful attempt to seize Bleiron Farm. Later that year Rantzau returned to Denmark to take part in the Great Northern War against Sweden. He unfairly attracted some blame for the Danish defeat at Helsingborg in 1710, having unexpectedly been handed the command immediately before the battle commenced, and then being wounded.

Frederick, Prince of Hesse-Cassell (1676–1751), was the son of Karl I, Landgrave of Hesse-Cassell and his wife Princess Maria Amelia of Courland. As a lieutenant general commanding the Hessian troops hired to Holland, he suffered defeat at Speyerbach in 1703, but took a conspicuous part in the fighting at Blenheim the following year. Although the prince was beaten in 1706 at Castiglione, he enjoyed a good reputation and had the command of the cavalry of Allied right wing, ably supporting the Prince of Orange's Dutch infantry at Malplaquet in 1709. His timely advance that afternoon forced the French right Wing out of the Bois de la Lanières and into withdrawal. He became Prince Consort of Sweden upon his marriage to Princess Ulrika Eleonora in 1715. Five years later, on the princess abdicating her right to the throne vacated by her brother, Charles XII, Frederick was elected as King Frederick I of Sweden. The reign was . generally regarded as benevolent, although royal power was increasingly limited by the constitution, and the king's rather unfair reputation was that of an indolent and ineffective ruler who had never bothered to read a book.

'Typical of the trustworthy battle-experienced infantry brigadier on whom so much depends',[27] Irish-born **Joseph Sabine (1661–1739)** served in Ingoldsby's Regiment during the Nine Years War, fighting at the siege of Namur in 1695. Made colonel in 1703, he was present as brigade commander in the Danube campaign, and became colonel of his regiment (subsequently the Royal Welch Fusiliers) in 1705. He took part in Orkney's infantry attacks at Ramillies and commanded the British brigade in Cadogan's advanced guard in the opening phase at the Battle of Oudenarde beside the river Scheldt. A highly competent infantry commander, Sabine served at the siege of Lille, and at Malplaquet in 1709. As governor of Ghent, he put down a mutiny of the garrison with great firmness, but also exercised considerable leniency amongst those soldiers who returned to their duty willingly. Sabine became major general in 1710 and, being a close and trusted confidant of Marlborough, his career faltered on the duke's dismissal but prospered again once he had been reinstated on the accession of George I to the throne. Sabine served on Argyll's staff in Scotland during the 1715 Jacobite rising, and became commander-in-chief in Scotland in 1717, rising to lieutenant general ten years later, and general in 1730. The Member of Parliament for Berwick on Tweed, he was appointed to be governor in Gibraltar, where he died.

Johan Wigand van Goor (1647–1704) was a Dutch officer of considerable ability, and a trusted confidant of the Duke of Marlborough. He had commanded a Walloon regiment in the Dutch service in the 1680s, was put in charge of William III's artillery at the Battle of the Boyne and served as colonel of the English artillery train, where he made Marlborough's acquaintance. He was quartermaster-general in the Prince of Waldeck's army during the Nine Years War, and became governor of Maastricht, defying the French summons to submit when Louis XIV's troops occupied the Southern Netherlands in 1701. Goor was made major general in 1702, and the following year was appointed to command a corps of Dutch troops sent to support the Margrave of Baden in defending the Lines of Stollhofen on the upper Rhine. He distinguished himself in this role, largely thwarting the attempts by Marshal Villars to break through this defensive barrier. Goor was, however, unable to work harmoniously with Baden, but became master-general of the Dutch artillery with the rank of lieutenant general in 1704. He combined forces with Marlborough and Baden ready for the advance into Bavaria that summer, and while commanding the infantry assault on the Schellenberg on 2 July was shot in the eye and quickly bled to death. He was buried in Nordlingen; the loss was much regretted by Marlborough, as Goor was undoubtedly one of the most talented and aggressive of the Dutch commanders: 'A Lieutenant-General of the Hollanders,' Samuel Noyes wrote, 'the best engineer they had.'[28] That being so, it might be felt that his life and skills were wasted in the bloody assault on the hill, but officers were expected to lead by example, and Goor did not hang back for an instant.

Louis-Guillaume (Ludwig-Wilhelm), Margrave of Baden (1655–1707), born in Paris, was an Imperial field commander with a long military career and well-established reputation in fighting the Ottomans in south-eastern Europe. He earned the nickname 'Turken Louis' and won a significant victory at Slankamen in 1691. Baden captured the fortress of Landau in Alsace from the French in 1702, but was subsequently defeated at Friedlingen by Villars, a victory which earned the French commander his marshal's baton. Although overly proud and sensitive, and difficult to deal with, Baden was brave enough, and his assistance was crucial to the success of Marlborough's attack on the Schellenberg, where the Margrave was shot in the foot, a wound that refused to heal properly. His assignment in August 1704 to lay siege to Ingolstadt on the Danube excluded him from the victory at Blenheim, and it is often said that this was deliberate policy on the part of Marlborough and Eugene to keep Baden out of the way. This seems improbable as the fortress was an important place, the possession of which would have been crucial if Marlborough had not been able to bring the French and Bavarians to battle and win so decisively. Accordingly, the margrave's task was not a trivial one, and it is unlikely that Marlborough and Eugene foresaw the chance of decisive action on the plain of Höchstädt quite that clearly and so far in advance, or that they would lightly give up a numerical advantage of almost 15,000 troops in order to sideline their colleague. Baden's failure to rendezvous with Marlborough in 1705 led to the abandonment of the Moselle campaign (which was languishing anyway), but the margrave was undoubtedly a sick man, with a festering wound. His lameness, however, did not prevent his showing Marlborough around the ornate gardens of his home on one occasion. Baden died three years later, a disappointed man, snubbed and ignored by the emperor in Vienna to whose family he had rendered long and loyal service.

Born in the Spanish Netherlands, **Claude-Frederick, Comte T'Sercales de Tilly (1651–1723)**, was a Walloon officer who entered the Dutch service at the age of 21. A major general by 1691, he became lieutenant general of Horse four years later, and governor of Arnhem in 1701. One of Marlborough's most skilful and dependable cavalry commanders, with a disciplined but dashing style, Tilly was made general of Dutch cavalry in 1704, and took a prominent part in the fighting at Ramillies. Becoming veldt-marshal in 1708 on Overkirk's death, he was heavily involved in the latter stages of the fighting at Malplaquet the next year. At the close of the war Tilly became governor of Namur, and subsequently of s'Hertogenbosch and then Maastricht. Tilly's wife became unintentionally swept up in the Battle of Eckeren in 1703 when the French attacked and almost overwhelmed Opdham's Dutch corps. The Comte de Merode-Westerloo, at that time in the service of the French claimant to the throne, remembered chatting to her at the door of her coach and gallantly attempting, without much success, to assure her that she stood in no danger. The countess was a controversial figure, accompanying her husband on campaign and suspected of simultaneously engaging in indiscreet correspondence with French friends.

One of the tribulations that the Duke of Marlborough had to endure was the insistence of the States-General that field deputies appointed by the individual Dutch provinces should accompany the army on campaign, to make sure both that the duke was not exceeding his authority, and that their troops were not being ill-used, or over-used to save Queen Anne's troops. There is, in fact, no evidence that the duke ever tried to exploit the troops in this way, but the deputies were on the watch to make sure anyway, and the most well-known of these men was **Sicco van Goslinga, Bailiff of Franckeradsel (1664–1731)**. Born in Friesland, van Goslinga was an able and shrewd diplomat and politician, appointed to be a member of the Dutch Council of State. Although technically not one of Marlborough's commanders, as a senior Dutch field deputy, he accompanied the duke on many of his campaigns. Obstinate and opinionated, he had undoubted energy and bravery and in turn gradually came to appreciate the duke's many good qualities. His caustic and questioning comments, which might at times seem to be overly negative or timid, appeared to act as a useful caution on some of Marlborough's more overly ambitious plans, and it is only fair to say that the field deputy's heart was certainly in the right place. Appointed as plenipotentiary to the French court in Versailles after the 1713 Treaty of Utrecht, van Goslinga left informative and valuable memoirs of his times. Written in French in a rather charming if slightly archaic style, these were eventually published in the 1850s, and although very much slanted to portray their author's own actions and opinions in the best light, they are nonetheless very informative.

Although he was, strictly speaking, not one of Marlborough's commanders, **'Colonel' Daniel Parke** is of particular interest as one of the duke's aides de camp, as he was the galloper who brought to London the astonishing news of the great victory at Blenheim in 1704. Even in an army that was full of intriguing characters – 'Salamander' Cutts, Kit Davies, Donald MacBane, the Comte de Merode-Westerloo and others – Parke stands out as one of the most colourful and notorious. He was not really a regular officer, as he held no formal commission from Queen Anne or from any of her numerous allies, but he was a member of the colonial Virginia militia, from which convenient arrangement he claimed his rank, rightly or otherwise, as colonel. Parke abandoned his family in Virginia, going to live in London with his mistress, and after an abortive attempt to rig a by-election in England (not in itself that unusual at the time; William Cadogan did the same thing at least once), he managed to attach himself as a volunteer to Marlborough's staff for the campaign in southern Germany. In this role he clearly had some merit, being wounded in the ankle during the Schellenberg battle. Six weeks later, when Marlborough had scribbled his famous Blenheim dispatch on the back of a tavern bill that momentous Wednesday evening in August, he turned and handed it to Parke. The Virginian was clearly quite a horseman, for he flogged his steeds along and only eight days later dropped to his knee before the queen in Windsor Castle, to hand her the remarkable note. In this extraordinary way, she learned that, at her instruction, the Captain-General had achieved the unthinkable and destroyed a main French army in open battle. Parke was gratified to receive, not only a miniature portrait of the queen, which he always wore thereafter on a silk ribbon, but a purse of 1,000 guineas for bringing the good news of victory.

Parke's career was thereafter something of an anticlimax, and he failed to secure either a permanent commission in the army, or the governorship of Virginia, which had gone to the Earl of Orkney. Parke was appointed to be governor of the Leeward Islands, a post he accepted with some reluc- tance. He offended the local landowners there, however, partly because he was energetic in suppressing smuggling and shut down this illegal but lucrative trade in which they all participated, but also because of his equally energetic philandering with their wives and daughters. During a landowner-inspired riot in 1710, Parke defended himself gamely but was struck down and murdered by a mob on the steps of the governor's house in St John's, Antigua, a rather sad end to a disreputably raffish, but undeniably interesting, career. 'Thus dy'ed Colonel Parke, whose brave end shews him sufficiently deserving the commission which he bore, and by his triumphant death, acquir'd an honour to his memory.'[29]

The career of the Comte de Merode-Westerloo is full of interest and even entertainment, and illustrates rather well the complex, shifting, and volatile nature of the war and the coalition army which Marlborough commanded. **Eugene-Jean-Philippe de Merode-Westerloo (1674–1732)** was born in June 1674, his father was a Merode, his mother a Westerloo, and at the age of 18 he inherited his deceased father's large estates in the Spanish Netherlands. As a young man he travelled widely and served in north Africa at the siege of Oran, in recognition of which he was granted the prestigious Order of the Golden Fleece by King Carlos II of Spain. He was a naturally devoted servant of the Spanish king and, serving the French claimant to the throne in Madrid, Merode-Westerloo went on campaign to southern Germany with Marshal Tallard in the summer of 1704. Commenting on the devastation of the Bavarian countryside by Marlborough's cavalry, he remembered, 'We took the road to Augsburg, where the Elector was camped, in company with Marshal Marsin, watch- ing his country burn ... we saw clouds of smoke drifting to the skies.'[30] The comte left a well-known, and rather amusing, account of how he viewed the deployment of the Allied army on the plain of Höchstädt in the opening phases of the Battle of Blenheim:

> I don't believe I ever slept sounder than on that night, and the rest certainly did me good ... I slept soundly until six in the morning when I was abruptly awoken by one of my old retainers ... This fellow blurted out that the enemy were there ... the whole area appeared to be covered by enemy squadrons, I rubbed my eyes in disbelief.[31]

Merode-Westerloo survived the catastrophe to French arms and hopes that day, claiming to have organized the rearguard action to cover the withdrawal of the defeated army, while bemoaning the loss of ninety-seven of his own horses and all their harness during the campaign. He left the service of Philip V to attend to his own family affairs in 1705, and allied himself with the Austrian claimant to the Spanish throne shortly afterwards. This was all above board, and he was certainly in good company as many others switched their allegiance in the same way, particularly after the victory at Ramillies, but Marlborough seems to have treated the comte with some reserve, perhaps doubting his good intentions. The self-seeking nature of many of Merode-Westerloo's actions may have counted against him, and his previous service with the French would not have helped. Even so, the duke clearly had a marked blind spot where the comte was concerned, and when Merode-Westerloo came to him early in 1708 with a warning that a plan had been formed to surprise the Allied garrisons in Ghent and Bruges while his main army was covering Brussels and Louvain, Marlborough rebuffed him. Merode-Westerloo reported, 'I had received news from a reliable source advising me to take good care of Ghent and Bruges ... he treated my news as something of no account, telling me that it was impossible, and I could say nothing to make him change his mind.'[32]

A few weeks later the Duc de Vendôme had audaciously seized both places and was defying Marlborough to do something about it. Undervalued and ignored, as he saw it, Merode-Westerloo became increasingly critical of the duke's methods, writing of the arrangements for the siege of Lille in the autumn of 1708, 'The combination of gross faults and blind good fortune of out two generals [Marlborough and Eugene] during this campaign truly beggars belief ... they considered Lille to be a fortress of scant significance.'[33] This seems to be too partial, and demonstrates his prejudice and disappointment at a lack of advancement more than anything else. However, there is a certain degree of truth in what was said, as the arrangements for the siege were, at first, inadequate and overly optimistic, and Marlborough's campaign, particularly the bringing forward of the vast quantity of stores and equipment necessary from Brussels and Antwerp, prospered as much from the confusion in the French high command as any of his own arrangements. Mixed fortunes followed Merode-Westerloo's later career, although he was made field marshal in the Imperial service by Emperor Charles VI (who would, in other circumstances, have been King Carlos III of Spain) in 1716, although a coveted governorship of Luxembourg was awarded elsewhere. Continuing to be dissatisfied with the rewards that came his way, the comte resigned all his appointments and retired to his family estates to manage his debts, pursue local feuds and write his memoirs. These he never managed to complete, as he died while giving dictation in September 1732, dropping to the floor in mid-sentence.

John Richmond Webb (1667–1724) was a highly competent infantry officer, first commissioned at the age of 19, who served at Blenheim as brigadier general and at Ramillies as major general. He distinguished himself at Oudenarde in 1708 and fought a dogged and narrowly successful action at Wynendael against a superior force led by the Comte de la Motte that September, in order to protect one of the precious convoys bringing munitions and supplies from Ostend to the Allied army in the trenches before Lille. Affronted not to receive due credit for his success from Marlborough, Webb became a quarrelsome opponent and critic of the duke, but served on with the army and was badly wounded in the fighting at Malplaquet. Made governor of the Isle of Wight in 1710, Webb became a general in 1712, but left the army on the Hanoverian succession to the throne.

*   *   *

Any account of the work of Marlborough's army would be less than complete without at least a nod in the direction of the gallant French commanders against whom he fought. By opposing the duke, with varying degrees of success, they tested the mettle and steel of the Allied commanders and their troops. The measure of whatever were the French fortunes, limited as they were on many occasions, is conversely also the measure of the worth of Marlborough's men when tried and put to the keenest test.

First amongst these French opponents must be **Camille d'Hostun, Comte de Tallard, Marshal of France (1652–1728)**. He had been the French ambassador to London in the opening years of the eighteenth century, and his calm influence there was a great asset, but he was sent back to France by William III on the declaration by the French king that the Chevalier de St George was the rightful heir to the throne of England. Hurriedly sent in 1704 to Bavaria by Louis XIV, Tallard was outclassed by Marlborough as a field commander and allowed the Marquis de Clerambault to pack French infantry into Blindheim village, where they could not influence the unfolding battle, and his cavalry, as a consequence lacked essential support and were routed. Tallard's young son was killed during the fighting, a day of double tragedy for a decent man, who was sent as a state prisoner back to England. 'I grieve for Marshal Tallard,' Louis XIV wrote, 'and I feel deeply his pain at the loss of his son.'[34] The defeated marshal lived in comfortable confinement in Nottingham, baking bread and growing celery (a delicacy hitherto unknown to the English) and becoming very popular with the local gentry, until his return to France with the end of the war. It is pleasant to be able to say that he not in disgrace and was warmly received by his king on arrival back at Versailles on the conclusion to the war.

François de Neufville, Duc de Villeroi, Marshal of France (1644–1730) became a childhood friend of Louis XIV at a time of civil war and great uncertainty. At home in the elegant surroundings of Fontainebleau and Versailles, he was a soldier of rather modest talent and owed his position very much to his closeness to the king, who sustained him in positions for which he was, perhaps, not best suited. Campaigning in northern Italy in 1701, Villeroi was beaten by Prince Eugene at Chiari, and then surprised and taken prisoner at Cremona, although he was soon exchanged and returned to France. He shadowed Marlborough's march up the Rhine in 1704 and conducted a cautious and capable defence of Alsace in the aftermath of the French defeat at Blenheim that summer, doing much to deny the duke the ability to make the most of his great victory before winter set in. Commanding the French army in the Low Countries in 1706, and urged against his better judgement to go out and fight Marlborough, Villeroi was utterly defeated at Ramillies, and never held a field command again. Embroiled in the dispute over the succession that followed the old king's death in 1714, he was eventually appointed to be governor of Lyons, where he died in 1730.

Not a Marshal of France, although he is often referred to as such, **Louis-Joseph de Bourbon, Duc de Vendôme (1654–1712)**, was descended from an illegitimate son of King Henry IV of France. A bruising and confident field commander, his abilities led him to success in northern Italy and, for a time in the Low Countries when he was sent there by Louis XIV to stabilize things in the wake of the disaster at Ramillies. His royal lineage enabled him to outrank the Marshals of France, who did not always appreciate the fact or his boorish manner and arrogance: 'Once he has taken a decision he adheres to it, so that nothing whatever can shake him.'[35] Over-confident after the seizure of Ghent and Bruges in 1708, Vendôme grossly mishandled the fighting at Oudenarde that July and, having sent a highly misleading report to Versailles on the day's events, was dismissed by the French king shortly thereafter. He hung up his sword and went into sulking retirement, but was reinstated soon afterwards to campaign in Spain. There he had considerable success, in 1710 battering a small British army commanded by James Stanhope to defeat at Brihuega, before dying of food poisoning in 1712.

Claude-Louis-Hector, Duc de Villars, Marshal of France (1653–1734), was a Gascon with undoubted military flair. Hot tempered and impetuous, he was also very capable and much admired by his soldiers and respected by his opponents. As a young man he had taken part in the siege of Maastricht in 1672, when, with Marlborough and Monmouth at his side, they had tried to storm a Dutch outwork and seen their captain, d'Artagnan, killed in the attempt. Appointed to command the French field army in the aftermath of defeat at Oudenarde and Lille in 1708, Villars did much to restore order and morale amongst the troops and fought a good defensive battle at Malplaquet, where he was gravely wounded in the knee by a musket ball. He was unable or unwilling ever to engage Marlborough and Prince Eugene in open battle again, relying with considerable skill on the fortress belt along France's northern border to soak up the energy of the Allied campaign. In 1712, with Marlborough removed from command, Villars had a notable success against the Earl of Albemarle at Denain, and went on to recover a number of the fortresses lost by France in the preceding five years. The marshal continued to campaign, despite the intense discomfort of his mangled leg, and on hearing that the Duke of Berwick had been decapitated by a round-shot at the siege of Philipsburg in 1734, commented rather ruefully, 'He always had luck that one.'[36]

* * *

By modern standards, Marlborough conducted his campaigns with an astonishingly small staff. In addition to his indefatigable quartermaster-general, William Cadogan, the duke was served by a secretary, Adam Cardonel, his financial agent, Henry Davenant (with whom Daniel Parke maintained a lively correspondence), senior gunnery officer Colonel Holcroft Blood (until his death in 1707) and chief of engineers, Colonel John Armstrong. Francis Hare was his chaplain-general and left an intriguing account of the campaigns (although this is sometimes said to be the work of Josias Sandby – chaplains were ranked as officers, with the equivalent rate of pay as captains). For example, Marlborough's command structure and headquarters staff in the victorious campaign of 1706 comprised:

A general (his younger brother, Charles Churchill)
Three lieutenant generals

Three major generals
Seven brigadier generals
Adjutant general
Quartermaster-general (also fulfilling the modern role of chief of staff)
Secretary
Judge advocate-general
Wagon master
Surgeon
Physician
Chaplain.

Like all general officers, Marlborough was attended by his aides de camp, usually young men of good family hoping to make their fortune and reputation in the service of a great commander. For the 1704 campaign in southern Germany the duke had twenty-one aides at his headquarters, Daniel Parke being listed as having the fifth such appointment – like the ill-fated James Bringfield who was the first listed, he received a bounty of £30 for the day of victory at Blenheim.[37] Well mounted, hard riding and very often relentlessly ambitious and eager to make their way in the world, these aides performed a wide range of functions, taking important messages, riding around a battlefield to find out just what was going on and hastening back to report to Marlborough on what they had seen and learned, and ensuring that the duke's commands were both understood by subordinate commanders and being properly carried out. Amongst many instances, this can be seen clearly at the Battle of Ramillies when a series of aides were sent by the duke to call off Orkney's attacks on Offuz and Autre-Eglise. Marlborough, knowing Orkney's fiery temperament, was well aware that the earl might not heed messages brought to him by the aides, men junior to himself – no matter what authority their orders might convey – and eventually he sent William Cadogan to ensure that the orders were followed. Even then Orkney robustly argued the point with Cadogan before reluctantly complying. Being an aide to Marlborough was certainly no easy sinecure, and we have already seen that Daniel Parke, although shot through the ankle at the Schellenberg, was sent by the duke to take the famous Blenheim dispatch to London. The aides also provided a commander with an element of close protection, in addition to that of personal staff, as when Marlborough's trumpeter intervened to cut down a Bavarian assailant at Elixheim in 1705. James Bringfield was famously decapitated by a French cannonball just outside the village of Ramillies late in the afternoon on that day of battle, while holding the duke's stirrup to help him mount a fresh horse. The scene was depicted in gory detail on a set of playing cards that were very popular at the time.

When General Joachim von Grumbkow was sent as an envoy to King Charles XII of Sweden, he recounted the same exploit to that warlike monarch, as explained to Marlborough in a letter written on 11 January 1707:

> He asked me if your Highness yourself led the troops to the charge. I replied that as all the troops were animated with the same ardour for fighting your Highness was not under the necessity of leading the charge, but that you were everywhere, and always in the hottest of the action, and gave your orders with that coolness which excites general admiration. I then related to him that you had been thrown from your horse; the death of your aide-de-camp, Brinfield [sic], and many other things.[38]

Intelligence in the widest sense is always of prime importance in military operations, the ability to know in advance what your opponent intentions are, where they will appear and in what strength. In addition to the obvious methods of intelligence gathering – scouting the ground, encouraging desertion of enemy soldiers, questioning prisoners and so on – Marlborough is known to have had a confidential informant at Versailles, who from time to time provided him with letters containing gossip and background detail to what was going on at the French court. The identity of this person, who was running a quite considerable personal risk if caught in this illicit and scarcely innocent correspondence, is not known. The information imparted, given the inevitable passage of time between pen being put to paper and the arrival of the missive in the duke's hands, must nonetheless have been of a limited, although undeniably useful, nature. Like all good commanders, Marlborough took pains to keep himself informed of the state of the country and the temper of the people in the regions in which he had to campaign, and he would encourage local gentry and notables to come forward with whatever information was to hand. On 23 August 1708, as arrangements for the siege of Lille got underway and manoeuvring to cover those preparations was undertaken, he wrote to a Monsieur Cronstrom from the Allied camp near to Helchin:

> I have received your letter of the 16th and 17th of this month, and am obliged to you for the advice you give of the enemy's movements

who have passed your area. I would like you to continue to inform us of everything you learn. We are now prepared to march the moment the enemy begin any movement and pursue them tomorrow ... we know nothing of the troops who you have heard have now passed through Sedan.[39]

Such information had, as in all cases, to be carefully assessed for its worth and reliability. Informants were not always well intentioned, reliable or acting in good faith, with money often having to change hands. Marlborough occasionally 'planted' deserters amongst the French with misleading information, and it may be assumed that this was not an uncommon process, with such intelligence gathered having to be treated with caution as a result.

Marlborough also made use on campaign of 'running footmen', clad in the duke's livery with jockey-style caps, and each carrying a staff as a badge of office; their task was to scout the battlefield quickly and unobtrusively. Not being mounted, they would attract less attention and enemy fire than the aides de camp – and could then come hurrying to report back to the duke on what they had seen. On the face of it, this ability to have 'eyes on' the fighting would have been valuable in providing current information, and these footmen can be clearly seen on several of the Blenheim tapestries. However, their use does not seem to have been widely copied by other commanders, so perhaps they were not quite as effective as was hoped or intended. As an aside, their use would also have entailed the cost of recruiting, training, equipping and maintaining them, and general officers had a tendency not to be that lavish with their pennies.

*   *   *

At this time brigades were ad hoc tactical formations, just groupings of battalions brought together for a certain task or phase in a campaign, and Marlborough would commonly give orders directly to the officers appointed for the time being to command brigades. In this regard, divisions did not exist as formations in the sense of several brigades grouped together – that would have to wait until much later in the eighteenth century – but armies would usually be divided into two 'wings', a right and a left, to aid command and control. These were all-arms groupings, with Horse and Foot operating together, and each wing would be subdivided into a first and second line operating under two subordinate commanders. Again, this aided command and control, and offered a second echelon of relatively fresh troops to take forward whatever had been achieved in the opening phases of a battle. If, however, things were going badly, the first line could fall back on, and draw support from, the second line.

Not unlike a modern army corps, these wings could operate independently of each other for a limited period, and very often did manoeuvre in this way prior to coming together for a major action. Although it was not intended that the wings of an army should stand and fight alone, they were each large and powerful enough that, if challenged, they could look after themselves long enough for the other, unengaged, wing to come up in support and bring on a general action if the opponent stood his ground. Each wing would be commanded by a senior officer who would, in turn, report to the army commander, although Marlborough often had tactical command of one wing while a colleague, Veldt-Marshal Overkirk or Prince Eugene typically, would command the other. Once action was joined, however, Marlborough would exercise the overall direction of the fighting as the acknowledged commander-in-chief. At Blenheim in 1704, the duke commanded the soldiers on the left of the Allied line, while Prince Eugene commanded the Imperial troops on the right. This was, of course, an occasion when two separate armies were operating in close cooperation in action, rather than the two wings of the same army, as would be the case in later years, but the theory and practice was the same. Five years later at Malplaquet, with an army over twice the size, such a tactical arrangement would not work, and while Eugene commanded the left wing (rather confusingly situated on the Allied right), the Prince of Orange had command of the right wing (operating on the left). Marlborough exercised overall command and retained control of the reserve, the massed cavalry in the centre, but that the command and control of such a large force stretched the abilities of all concerned that day is hardly in doubt.

The mode of operation for the wings of an army can be seen very clearly in the manoeuvres that led to the fighting that fateful September day at Malplaquet. Marshal Villars had used the dense belt of woodland to the south-west of Mons to screen his own movements from the attentions of the numerically superior Allied army, as it moved into position to lay siege to that fortress. With Villars acting aggressively in this way, in accordance with his instructions from Louis XIV to save Mons, it was difficult for Marlborough to concentrate his army too soon, before the marshal's real intentions became more clear. Prince Eugene covered the gap in the

Bois de Bossu with the left wing, some 6 miles away to the north and close to the smaller French-held fortress of St Ghislain, while Marlborough stayed with the right wing to cover the Gap of Aulnois and block the direct route to Mons. A third substantial detachment, under command of Lieutenant General Henry Withers, protected the lengthy Allied trains still on the road from the recently seized fortress of Tournai. If Villars acted swiftly enough, he might isolate and overwhelm any one of the dispersed Allied formations and inflict a localized but highly damaging reverse on the Allied campaign. In the event, on 8 September, Marlborough found the French army moving forward to take up a defensive position astride the very same Gap of Aulnois that he was covering. The duke fell back with his wing of the army, while summoning Eugene to close up from the Gap of Bossu. In this way, Marshal Villars might just have been tempted to move through the wooded belt to try and savage the right wing of the Allied army before Eugene came up with the left wing in support. In such a case, Villars would have been drawn on and found himself exposed in an advanced position, with a dense woodland obstacle at his back, and every chance that Marlborough would use one wing to fix him in position and then have the other wing outflank and roll up his army. Villars was astute enough not to be caught in this way and contented himself with fortifying a strong position in the Gap of Aulnois and preparing to defy Marlborough and Eugene to attack him there.

The routine manner in which Marlborough's orders were prepared, and made known to his senior officers, was carefully regulated to avoid misunderstandings and delay in execution:

Every Day, at orderly time all the general officers (especially the Lieutenant-General, the Major-General, and Brigadier-General of the Day) assembled at the Duke's Quarters to receive Orders. The Major-General of the Day is to receive the Orders from the General in Chief; and that no Time may be lost, the Major-General is to give the Orders he received to the Brigadier-General of the Day first, then to the General of Foot, and to the Lieutenant-General of the Day. The Brigadier-General of the Day is to distribute the Orders he received immediately to the Majors of Brigade; and see that all the Details are made upon the Spot. What Orders the Major-General of the Day happens to receive at any other Time, he is to send them by his Aide de Camp to the major of Brigade of the Day; who is to lie in Camp, and always leave a Direction where he may at any time quits his Tent that he may be immediately found.[40]

Marlborough's officers, of whatever rank and whether in command of a formation, on the staff or serving with their regiment, were all expected to lead by example. This had the inevitable outcome of incurring casualties, and the numbers of fallen officers, some of senior rank, could at times be heavy. Amongst many other losses suffered at the storming of the Schellenberg in 1704 was the death of Major General van Goor and Count von Styrum, while the Margrave of Baden, whose smart flank attack won the day for the Allies, was hit in the foot by a Bavarian musket ball. It was noted that from the thirteen British infantry battalions present at Blenheim a few weeks later, three field officers (majors and above), thirteen captains, fifteen lieutenants and four ensigns were killed, while eight field officers, thirty-three captains, forty-two lieutenants and twenty-seven ensigns were wounded.[41]

The assault on Blindheim village in the opening phase of that battle was pressed forward with great determination in the face of heavy French musketry. Brigadier General Archibald Rowe led the initial British infantry attack and was almost the first to fall. A British officer wrote home:

> Betwixt twelve and one the attack began, Brigadier Rowe made the first attack on their right with his brigade and marched upon the head of his own regiment, we went through the water that was upon their front [the Nebel stream] with little opposition and took one piece of cannon. After we had made a little halt and attacked the village that was upon their right, which they had all pallisaded with planks. They received us with so hot a fire that they killed or wounded twenty officers, our Brigadier Rowe is mortally wounded and his leg broke which is regretted by the whole Army.[42]

Such losses are not easily made good, and as a result the Allied pursuit of the defeated French and Bavarians through the autumn of 1704 lacked a certain punch at times.

A common feature in armies at this time were the sons of noble families who were sent on campaign, but who had no specific regimental or staff duties. Louis XIV would insist that his grandson, the Duc de Bourgogne, who had no great talent or liking for the military life, accompanied the French army operating in the Spanish Netherlands. The divided command that this caused, with the young prince at odds with the army commander, the Duc de Vendôme, led to the mistakes and misunderstandings that caused such confusion, misunderstanding and ruin on the battlefield at Oudenarde. That same day in 1708, the impetuous charge of

Jorgen Rantzau's Hanoverian dragoons along the Ghent road early in the afternoon, routing the French Royal La Bretache Régiment in the process, saw George, the young Electoral Prince of Hanover, fall from his horse amongst the milling horsemen. He would have been cut down, never to eventually become King George II of Great Britain, had his squadron commander, Colonel Anton Losecke, not sprung from his saddle and, at the cost of his own life, helped the young nobleman to mount so that he could escape the French cavalry.

Army commanders were not immune to harm, as Marlborough's narrow escape from French horsemen at Ramillies showed, when he was 'Unhorsed and in great danger of his life.'[43] Then again, Prince Eugene was wounded in the forehead by a musket ball while leading an assault during the siege of Lille in 1708, and wounded again (this time in the neck), in the woods at Malplaquet a year later. Major General August Wackerbath, the Saxon infantry commander on that day was gravely injured in the same incident, and the Marquis of Tullibardine, eldest son of the Earl of Atholl, was killed leading his own Scots regiment in the Dutch service on the left of the field. It should also be remembered that Marshal Villars was shot and wounded nearby, and the Marquis de Chemerault was killed in the same incident, while the young Jacobite Pretender, the Chevalier de St George, was wounded by a sabre slash in the ensuing cavalry action. The fighting for the Gap of Aulnois on 11 September 1709 was, of course, a particularly bloody affair, and it is not labouring the point too much to comment on the death of the Dutch generals Dohna, Week and Spaar during the Prince of Orange's failed attacks, or that of the veteran Swedish soldier Count Oxienstern, along with many of their gallant men. As Lieutenant Colonel Blackader wrote:

> I have not seen the dead bodies lie so thick as they were in some places about the retrenchments, particularly at the battery where the Dutch Guards attacked. For a good way I could not go among them lest my horse should tread on the carcases that were lying, as it were, heaped on one another.[44]

Considering his apparent insouciance when viewing the heavy losses at the Schellenberg fight five years before – 'The carcasses were very thick strewed upon the ground ... Yet all this works no impression or refor-mation upon us, seeing the bodies of our comrades and friends laying as dung upon the face of the earth'[45] – Blackader's comments are stark indeed.

Chapter 4

The Horse

'That lively air I see'[1]

At the beginning of the eighteenth century, an army in western Europe would typically contain anything from a quarter to a third of its total strength in cavalry.[2] Any campaign would, accordingly, involve vast numbers of horsemen and their mounts, with all the associated demands of grooming, smithying and gathering forage. With a potentially deadly combination of mobility, speed and striking power, both moral and physical, well-trained and properly equipped horsemen still had the ability to dictate the pace and to force an engagement upon an opponent, and very often to determine the outcome of a pitched battle. As a result they were seen, and saw themselves, as the key battle-winning element in an army at that time. It was a simple fact, however, that for the expense of having one cavalry trooper, an army commander could have three fully trained and equipped foot soldiers, although whether or not those men could be a more effective combination on the battlefield than their mounted comrades was yet to be seen with any certainty. For the time being, the mounted arm was regarded as most effective at the crucial time, to deliver the decisive blow at the right moment in battle, but, given the natural limitations on the use of mounted troops in built-up areas and close country – marshes, woods and hedgerows proving serious impediments to ease of movement – capable and well-handled infantry would often prove of more practical use than the cavalry. Therefore, on the grounds of both cost and capability, the trend would be for a greater proportion of infantry (and dragoons as a kind of mounted infantry) than cavalry to be recruited and employed as time went on. Despite this gradual change in the composition of armies, more evident in retrospect perhaps than at the time, the power of the mounted arm when used judiciously was little questioned. The experience of such a notable battle as Ramillies in 1706, where the Dutch and Danish cavalry – after a tough struggle, certainly – swept around the French right flank to roll up Marshal Villeroi's fine army from one end to another, demonstrated in the most graphic fashion that disciplined and well-handled horsemen en masse could still be the decisive arm on the battlefield. The cost and trouble of having cavalry deployed in this way, appeared therefore to be self-evidently worthwhile.

The custom was for a cavalryman to provide his own mount on enlistment, or the not inconsiderable cost of providing the animal was deducted from the wages over a period of time. There was, though, no corresponding lessening in the overall cost to the public purse of the cavalryman, as horses were expensive to purchase and maintain, and they were large and prominent targets very prone to wounding and injury on the battlefield, and sickness in camp, however well groomed they might be. Those horses of the rank and file which were lost in action or unavoidably succumbed to disease while on campaign were replaced at the public expense, although if negligence were evident then the cost of replacing the animal was, once more, stopped from the trooper's pay. Remounts for campaign losses were not considered to be private property, unlike those horses that a soldier had brought with him on enlistment, or had paid for through deductions from pay. Officers were expected to purchase their own remounts, no matter what the circumstances of their loss, and it was noted that Conyngham's Dragoons, when en route from southern Ireland to Portugal in 1704, lost an eye-watering 141 horses during the sea voyage. At the time £15 was the remount cost for each animal, entailing a quite phenomenal financial loss, and a crippling practical one for the proper employment of the regiment on arrival in the Iberian Peninsula.[3] A later observer commented with perfect truth, 'How the armies were in the circumstances kept mounted at all, even at the excessive cost to the officers, it is barely possible at this distance of time to discover.'[4]

The ability to overwhelm an opponent decisively, however, had distinct limits as the tactics and weapons of the foot soldier became more robust. The expense of recruiting, equipping, mounting, training, maintaining and supplying these large numbers of horsemen was formidable, as could be seen with Conyngham's unfortunate regiment on its way to Spain, and ready success for cavalry was becoming less certain. This was particularly so with the introduction of the flintlock musket, the plug bayonet and its successor the socket bayonet, as well as the development of infantry drills necessary to counter the mounted attack effectively. Cavalry were noticeably losing their long-held capability to dominate infantry, even in open country. The most effective use of the cavalry gradually became to fight an opponent's mounted troops (rather in the same way that, in the twentieth century, the key role of armoured tanks, originally intended to overcome infantry defences, became instead to fight other tanks). However, well-handled cavalry could still force an engagement upon a reluctant opponent on favourable terms, dominate a decisive portion of a battlefield with a telling combination of speed and striking power, as in May 1706, or isolate and overwhelm a slow-moving infantry detachment or artillery train. The rapid deployment of cavalry could also 'fix' an opponent caught off-guard and force him to stand and fight on disadvantageous terms. There was also a persistent worry for all commanders of the perils of cavalry raiding and Marlborough wrote to William Cadogan during the preparations of the siege of Lille in August 1708, on hearing that French horsemen were on the road and looking for trouble, 'For God's sake be sure you do not risk the cannon.'[5]

Outright battles in the open were infrequent affairs, however memorable they might be – siege warfare was more common, positional and methodical and offering little obvious scope for dashing mounted action. As a result, the most frequent use for mounted troops on campaign was that of scouting and screening, in addition to providing a fast striking capability when the moment came. 'A single squadron of my regiment caused a complete panic to spread through their whole rearguard', the Comte de Merode-Westerloo recalled, 'by getting in amongst their baggage train.'[6] Much more often, though, the cavalry provided the valuable role of finding out where the enemy was and what they were doing, or providing an element of protection and forewarning to an army commander, whether in camp or on the march, to prevent a surprise by some sudden march or unexpected stroke by an opponent. This key function was of the utmost importance, for, although armies tended to move at a rather measured pace – the state of the roads at the time usually allowed for little else – on occasions such as Marlborough's sideways march to the Yssche River in August 1705, they could strike with disconcerting speed. Nonetheless, the uncertain nature of warfare meant that mishaps did occur, as when Hompesch's own cavalry detachment was surprised by the French five years later, when encamped within cannon-shot of their own garrison in Douai. Richard Pope recalled that:

> Without being so much as challenged by one sentry, they fell upon the right flank of our Horse, trampling and cutting down all before them, and had they not taken to plunder too soon, they might have driven through our whole detachment ... They suffered little or nothing, but killed and wounded many of our troopers, and carried off a considerable number of our horses.[7]

This last comment is significant, for the resupply of good horses was always a problem, and remount officers increasingly had to scour further afield, as the years of the war went on, to keep the armies adequately supplied. A lack of good horses could ruin a campaign, and they were almost more in demand than good riders, as it was found that cavalry, in general, had little problem in obtaining enough recruits, unlike the less highly regarded infantry. Marlborough was keenly concerned at the quality of the horses in his army and preferred where possible that the British horsemen should be mounted on animals obtained in England and Ireland.

The striking capability was needed when the chance came to out-manoeuvre and out-think an opponent, with the possibility to close with him, perhaps while his army was strung out on the line of march, or move with deadly effect upon some exposed detachment or flank. The alluring chance would be that of forcing the opposing commander to face a running fight on the road, which might tumble out of control, or to stand and fight an unplanned pitched battle in adverse circumstances and perhaps a poor tactical position. This can be clearly seen at Oudenarde in July 1708, when Marlborough's advanced guard, a strong mix of Jorgen Rantzau's Hanoverian dragoons and Dutch, Prussian and British infantry under William Cadogan, managed to get across the Scheldt River un-molested by the nearby French who were calmly marching along on their way to take position on high ground. The battle is rightly regarded as a largely infantry affair, but Rantzau's headlong mounted charge, expen-sive though the limited local success was for his troopers, turned the attention of the French commanders away from their purpose, that of securing a new defensive position, towards dealing with the growing but still relatively insignificant Allied bridgehead on the riverbank. The Hanoverian squadrons' role, in diverting and capturing the attention of the French commanders, was a significant factor that day – the ability to fix an opponent and force him to react to you rather than pursuing his own objectives.

Although superficially the two categories of mounted troops – the Horse and the dragoons – were very similar in appearance, their original roles were quite different. The Horse were regarded as true cavalry, well-mounted men on large horses (about 15 hands or more), armed with pistol or carbine and sword, and drilled in Marlborough's army to dictate the pace of a battle and deliver shock action in a highly disciplined way to break an opponent's formation at the right moment. In this category were the cuirassiers, who still wore armour, not unlike the well-ordered troopers of Gustavus Adolphus and Oliver Cromwell of fifty or sixty years before, but Marlborough had little time for such things, preferring speed and mobility of the more lightly equipped cavalryman to the ponderous pace of the armoured cuirassiers. The breast- and back-plates of his cavalry were put away into store in 1702, although the breast-plates were reissued a few years later, to be worn under the thick coats of the troopers. In the Imperial Austrian service, however, and that of their Bavarian opponents, the employment of the armoured cuirassiers persisted for longer, remembered as 'Riding closen, liken to a brassen wall.'[8]

Regarded as an elite, certainly by themselves, and paid and equipped accordingly, the regiments of Horse included such units on the English Establishment as the Life Guards, the Horse Grenadier Guards and eight other regiments of Horse with a strength of 350 all ranks (the Royal Horse Guards also being regarded as one such unit, and not as a part of the Household Cavalry). The Dutch Horse Establishment contained two companies of guards – the Gardes du Corps de Roy and the Gardes du Corps de Frise, with a combined total of 430 all ranks. Dutch cavalry regiments typically had an established strength of 312 all ranks. Each regiment was composed of a number of Troops, of about fifty officers and men, commanded by a captain. These Troops would in turn be grouped into either two, but sometimes three, squadrons, each with a strength on paper of some 150 officers and men. The squadron was only a tactical grouping, however, and the cavalry tended to be referred to as comprising a certain number of Troops. One of the first references to cavalry being deployed as 'squadrons' can be found in Marlborough's order of battle for the Schellenberg battle in July 1704 and these groupings of Troops from a particular regiment would not necessarily always fight alongside each other, as brigades of cavalry were made up by drawing the sub-units together as needed for the task in hand.

The French mounted arm was notable for its size and high standard of equipment and training, and it enjoyed a fine reputation for bravery, dash and skill. The quality of the horses and equipment would diminish noticeably during the long course of the War of the Spanish Succession, which had an inevitable impact upon the force's effectiveness, but the men were gallant enough, as they proved on the plain of Malplaquet in 1709. The French Household Cavalry, all of whom were required to be ranked as gentlemen, comprised the Carabiniers, the Grenadiers à Cheval, and the Musketeers (Noir and Gris). The elite Gens d'Armes also included a squadron (two companies) of émigré Scots in the French service. All other regiments of Horse were referred to as *chevaux legers* to distinguish them from the Household troops, but they were not light Horse at all; the employment of that kind of cavalry did not become common in western Europe until later in the century.

On the other hand, the dragoons in all armies were originally intended to be more like mounted infantry, ranked as Foot on the English Establishment when in garrison, but as Horse when on campaign. According to Richard Pope they were: 'Musketeers, mounted, who serve sometimes on foot, and sometimes a-horseback, being always ready upon anything'.[9] Their regimental strength on the English, Scots and Irish establishments was slightly less than that of the Horse, at about 325 all ranks, and they were grouped into companies rather than squadrons when on campaign. Dragoons were armed with a musket and bayonet – rather more effective than the horse-pistol or carbine – in addition to the sword. Each dragoon regiment had side-drummers, rather than the trumpeters employed by the Horse, but their drill was very much the same as the cavalry, alongside whom they often fought. 'When on horseback they are to fight as the Horse do,' Richard Kane wrote, but they could also deploy mounted but then dismount ready to fight.[10] The valuable speed and mobility that the horses gave was partly hampered by the need for at least one man in four to stay back as horse handlers, with consequent reduction in firepower when on the ground and in action. The men's long boots would also impede easy movement on foot, and the theoretical value of having horse-mounted infantry was one that never quite came to fruition. Still, dragoons were often employed in a dismounted role but their deployment as a cheaper kind of cavalry grew to be more common than as a less able infantry. There was also a fine judgement to be made while the dragoons were busily fighting as infantry, as to just when should they break off and remount ready for the pursuit.

Despite this, by combining mobility, speed and firepower, dragoons were a useful asset, more so as their pay was less than cavalrymen's, and the horses were smaller (at some 14 hands) and thus less expensive to purchase. The British dragoons (from Hay's and Ross's regiments) took a key role in the attack on the Schellenberg in July 1704, toiling up the long slope of the hill to bolster the infantry and then remounting to harry the defeated defenders. Marlborough noted the useful service provided by the mounted troops in a letter written the day after the battle: 'The horse and dragoons appointed to sustain the Foot standing within musket-shot of the enemy's trenches most part of the time.'[11] The close cooperation between Horse and foot soldiers that was required was plainly in evidence, although the duke did not mention that he had brought the horsemen close up behind the assaulting infantry, who were beginning to flag under the heavy fire from the hill, so that they could not fall back too far or too quickly, and so jeopardize the operation, but had instead to press forward with their attack. 'Lieutenant-General Lumley keeping close with eighteen squadrons in the first line, and Lieutenant-General Hompesch bringing up the other seventeen in the second.'[12] As the Franco-Bavarian defence of the Schellenberg fell apart, Lumley took his squadrons forward in hot pursuit across the brow of the hill, and down towards the waiting pontoon bridges laid over the Danube. 'He remounted,' Francis Hare recalled, 'and soon got over with our other squadrons, which now put the enemy to flight, and pursuing them, killed a great many, took thirteen of their colours, and drove great numbers of them into the Danube.'[13] A few weeks after the bloody assault on the hill, the same two regiments of dragoons, in the dismounted role and with their bayonets fixed once more, would play a notable part in the final assault on Blindheim village; they acquitted themselves very well. Two years later, the Dutch dragoons of Holstein's and Opdham's regiments joined in the attack on foot against the French-held hamlets of Franquenay and Taviers in the opening stages of the Battle of Ramillies. There they played a key role in that initial success in unhinging the French right flank, at least in part by driving off several squadrons of dismounted French dragoons, who were themselves attempting rather ineffectively to mount a counter-attack.

The dragoons could also perform a useful role when mounted and in close support of their cavalry comrades, such as in the closing moments of the Ramillies victory, when the British Horse routed the vaunted Bavarian cavalry on the plateau of Mont St André and almost laid hands on Marshal Villeroi and the Elector of Bavaria as they fled the field. 'Had I been so fortunate to have known', Lieutenant General Cornelius Wood remembered, 'I had strained Corialanus, on whom I rode all day, to have made them prisoners.'[14] Hay's Scots Dragoons and Ross's Irish Dragoons, having negotiated the marshy Petite Gheete stream valley, charged '*à la hussar*' and in best cavalry fashion, to utterly overwhelm two battalions of the French Régiment du Roi, which had withdrawn from the village of Autre-Eglise to try and march off the field in something approaching good order. The report in the *London Gazette* described the exploit in stirring tones: 'Our dragoons, pushing into the village of Autre-Eglise, made a terrible slaughter; the French King's own Regiment of Foot, called the Regiment du Roi, begged for quarter and delivered up their arms and colours to Lord John Hay's Dragoons (the Greys).'[15] The dragoons' success was so dashing that both regiments, Hay's and Ross's, were permitted to wear grenadier caps, in recognition of the achievement.

The lower daily rates of pay for dragoons, compared to the Horse, was also an attractive inducement to increase their numbers and employment. In 1704 a trooper in an English regiment of Horse was paid fourteen shillings a week, while a dragoon received only eight shillings and two-pence.[16] As they were so much cheaper, there was a growing and natural tendency to have more regiments of dragoons, but they were long regarded as being inferior to true regiments of cavalry, and when moves were subsequently made to convert British Horse regiments to dragoons, in order to save money, such was the outcry and resentment amongst officers and men that the title 'Guards' was added to assuage the feelings of grievance. This resulted in the designated regiments (numbered 2nd–8th, the 1st Horse being the Royal Horse Guards, the Blues) becoming 1st–7th Dragoon Guards respectively.

Horsemanship had to be learned, and the particular requirements of the tactical employment of cavalry in action had to be drilled in hard. The ability to stay in the saddle, both when moving at a gentle walk or trot, and during something more headlong and thrilling such as a charge at a brisk canter, was an essential skill for a cavalryman or dragoon. Those recruits who had grown up in the country, as many did, had a decided lead in this over their town-bred comrades, but even farm-raised boys used to handling horses needed careful instruction on just how to man-oeuvre in formation at the word or signal of command on trumpet or side-drum. This was more so as the rider would have to manage the reins with the left hand while wielding a sword or pistol with the right, in the press and haste of the charge or the deadly confusion of a cavalry mêlée. This gave rise to the tactical trick of trying to attack the opponent on his left side, where the weaker 'bridle' hand away from that wielding the sword was so much more exposed. Marshal Marsin's French cavalry were confronted by Count Fugger's Imperial cuirassiers in that precise way outside the village of Oberglau, during the Battle of Blenheim, and had to draw back from an otherwise promising opportunity to disrupt the advance of Count Averock's Dutch cavalry across the Nebel stream.

Good horsemanship also meant ensuring that the trooper's mount was properly stabled, groomed and fed before the rider could attend to such comforts for himself. Again, the country-bred lad would find that this came naturally, without the necessary goad of the barked instruction from a non-commissioned officer. On the march this care would demonstrate itself by seeing that the horses were not over-tired, with troopers walking for lengthy periods to rest their horses, rather than staying comfortably in the saddle for too long. In this respect, the French tended to be less well-disciplined, and the condition of their horses was noticed to be not as good as that of their opponents, saddle-sores being a particular problem. The degree of care shown for the animal was a simple matter of pride to a good horseman and brought with it an enthusiasm and natural feeling of *esprit de corps*. In June 1704, Prince Eugene of Savoy, on the arrival of Marlborough's cavalry and dragoons at Gross Heppach in southern Germany after their march up the Rhine from the Low Countries, commented, 'I never saw such better horses, better clothes, finer belts and accoutrements, but money, which you don't want in England, will buy clothes and fine horses, but it cannot buy that lively air I see in every one of these troopers faces.'[17]

Allowance has perhaps to be made for the diplomatic compliment that the prince was making to Marlborough, and of the fact that the Imperial commanders were always short of money and their troops presented a markedly shabby appearance as a result, but there is little doubt that the duke's cavalry arrived on the banks of the Danube in good condition after a long and tiring march in poor weather. They were fit and ready to go straight into action, which contrasts rather well with the cavalry of Marshal Tallard, which had soon afterwards to endure a forced march through the passes of the Black Forest from Alsace to reinforce the French and Bavarian armies in southern Germany. This march was an altogether less well-handled affair, with many horses suffering from sickness and a lack of decent forage; the French cavalry regiments were not in particularly good condition on arrival. The Comte de Merode-Westerloo remembered very well the outbreak of the equine disease glanders in his regiment of dragoons: 'The incurable murrain [sickness] this regiment contracted whilst sharing winter quarters with the French Sommeri Regiment had already put most of the troopers on their own two feet.'[18] It was, however, not just the Franco-Bavarian army that suffered in this way, and Lieutenant Richard Pope of Schomberg's Horse recalled that, later on in the campaign:

> There is not the least forage to be found ... our horses live upon very bad straw, and those that are too nice for that diet die daily ... We have not above twenty horses to a Troop left, and probably there will not be ten of those able to march to Holland. I have lost six of my own equipage.[19]

The latter comment was significant, representing as it did a substantial financial loss to the young officer, who had to find and pay for the remounts himself.

Little stands still for long in military matters, and cavalry tactics had evolved significantly throughout the mid- and late seventeenth century. The previously common 'reiter' tactics, derived from the sixteenth-century German and Dutch practice, had seen ranks of horsemen trotting gently forward en masse, to halt and fire their long-barrelled pistols and carbines at their opponents from a respectable distance, before turning about 'en caracolle' and making to the rear to reload their weapons and be ready to repeat the manoeuvre when their turn came. This method had evolved to enable cavalry to break up massed formations of pikemen by the use of firepower, but had then become the practice when cavalry engaged other cavalry. Such ponderous tactics had been largely, but not entirely, replaced by more dynamic methods developed during the Thirty Years War. King Gustavus Adolphus of Sweden had insisted that things change, with the employment of the massed charge at a brisk canter, intended to break through the opponents' ranks using not pistols but the sword in outstretched hand. The tactical employment of cavalry in this way in the English Civil War saw such opposing commanders as Henry Wilmott and Oliver Cromwell employ the technique to good effect, enhanced by the insistence on the good discipline and restraint of the New Model Army in particular.

The Allied commanders during the war for the Spanish throne needed little schooling in the merits of this way of soldiering, but the French, so innovative in other respects, remained wedded for the time being to the use of pistols and carbines, fired at the halt in the old manner. As a result, their employment of cavalry, at least in the early years, lacked a degree of punch, and they continued to deploy in the old style, six deep, and on a narrower frontage than the formations of their opponents. As such, they tended to be overlapped and enveloped, unable to manoeuvre swiftly and freely enough about the battlefield. Such a passive tactical approach was widely seen as outdated and overly cautious, for cavalry that received a charge when at the halt – necessary to discharge firearms – were generally expected to be overthrown and dispersed. This was noticed particularly at Blenheim, when Tallard's troopers were repeatedly driven back after halting to discharge their weapons, losing their forward impetus in the process rather than pressing home to good effect the local advantages they had gained. The French Gens d'Armes rode down Rowe's Regiment of Foot on the outskirts of Blindheim village, and Captain Robert Parker recalled the subsequent encounter between the British cavalry under the command of Colonel Palmes and the Gens d'Armes later that afternoon:

Tallard seeing Palmes advanced with his squadrons some distance from our lines, ordered out his five squadrons (some said seven), to march down and cut Palmes' squadrons to pieces, and then to retire. When the commanding officer of these squadrons had got clear of their lines, he ordered the squadron on his right, and that on his left, to edge outward, and then to march down till they came on a line with Palmes; at which time they were to wheel inward, and fall upon his flanks, while he charged him in front.

This encircling manoeuvre by the French was intelligent and, if carried out quickly, would be very dangerous for the British horsemen, but, Parker goes on:

Palmes perceiving this, ordered Major Oldfield, who commanded the squadron of the right, and Major Creed, who commanded that on his left, to wheel outward, and charge those squadrons, that were coming down on them ... When they had done that, to wheel in upon the flanks of the other squadrons that were coming upon him, while he charged them in front; and everything succeeded accordingly.[20]

The Swiss-born commander of the Gens d'Armes, Comte Beat-Jacques von Zurlauben, had once again squandered what advantage he had gained by halting his troopers to fire off their pistols, and the British cavalrymen were able to take back the initiative in emphatic style. Only perfectly drilled and well-mounted cavalry could attempt this manoeuvre with any hope of success, and the importance of the repulse to the French squadrons should not be overlooked. These were elite units, and Tallard was alarmed and unsettled by their overthrow and began to hurry about the battle-field, moving units to shore up his deteriorating dispositions, and losing both his composure and grip on the battle. Writing to Versailles to explain his defeat that day, he listed first of all, 'The Gendarmerie were not able to break the five English squadrons.'[21] Actually, Palmes had gone on to overdo things, let his troopers get out of tight control and had been driven back with some loss (Major Creed was killed), but that did not detract from his initial very neat success.

At Ramillies the French cavalry stood their ground well for a while against the Dutch and Danes who came on, 'In four dense lines like solid walls', and even drove them back on one occasion in some confusion before Marlborough's brilliant tactical shift from right to left threw every-thing in the French army into disorder. Colonel de la Colonie noticed that the Allied regiments were well closed up, unlike those of the over-extended French, who attempted in vain to cover the frontage allotted to them, and that the troopers, as a result, found themselves being attacked from the flank and occasionally from the rear. 'I now saw the enemy's cavalry squadrons advance,' he wrote. 'The Maison de Roi decided to meet them, for at such a moment those who await the shock find themselves at a disadvantage.'[22]

Firing off pistols and carbines from the halt was a tactic that was falling into gradual disuse, and cavalry was more often deployed for battle in formation designed to achieve striking power and mass effect. The squadron would draw up in two – or sometimes three – lines, each composed of a Troop, with the senior Troop commander, accompanied by his trumpeter, at the front of the formed unit. Marlborough's strong insistence on the use of the sword in a dynamic advance rather than employing relatively ineffectual firearms led to the tactical innovation of having two squadrons, each drawn up in this two-line formation, operating together in a steady resolute advance to drive their opponents back. As the moment for action grew near, the troopers would move from open order to close order, with the rear-most Troop closing up on that to their front (as a rule, deploying in open order meant that some 6-foot distance was maintained between the riders, while in close order this was reduced to just 3 foot, which close proximity added power and weight to any charge). A further refinement of this technique was to move together still further and ride *en muraille*, with the attacking troopers very well closed up, the second rank being tight up behind the first rank, and each rider's jackbooted innermost knee locked firmly behind the knee of the rider to his front – 'Not only close but even glued together'.[23]

This close order, the 'flying wedge' in which cavalry were required to manoeuvre and advance, required some degree of protection for the troopers' legs and knees, otherwise they would be crushed between the charging mounts. This was provided by the common practice of turning down a few inches of the tops of the long leather boots routinely worn by horsemen, to give a double thickness at the knee-joint. By doing this, a rider not only shielded the limb from damage in the press of a charge, but had some measure of protection also from musket and pistol shot, and sword slash, as the Comte de Merode-Westerloo found outside the village of Blindheim in 1704, when the thickness of his stockings also proved of value. His knee swelled up to an alarming degree, but no lasting damage was done when 'A bullet had been fired at me at point-blank range, it had failed to penetrate thanks to my strong thigh boots with thick flaps ... the bullet had got as far as my stockings but had penetrated no further.'[24]

In a well-ordered advance, the pace would be gentle at first, conserving both the strength of the horses and the good order of the riders, but this would steadily and progressively build from a walk, to a trot, then to a canter – rarely a gallop as this was both exhausting and too hard to control – at the moment of impact. The charge, conducted *en muraille* in this way, saw the rider lean forward over the neck of his horse, sword arm outstretched in front of him, ready for the deadly stroke against his enemy. In this highly disciplined and drilled manner, massed shock effect was achieved, albeit at the cost of having to exercise great skill, determination and horsemanship. The aim was to break an opposing cavalry formation, which would very often be deployed in equal or superior strength but might not be employing the same skilful technique. Cavalry having to meet such a charge in anything but the most resolute way would quite literally be overthrown and driven back in confusion, having to attempt to reform and recover their order as best they could under considerable pressure, if they had not been scattered completely at the first impact.

It follows that the use of pistols and carbines, underpowered and inaccurate unless used at close range, was discouraged, at least in Marlborough's army. The duke was so set against his cavalry employing these weapons – the use of which saw Tallard's squadrons squander their many advantages at Blenheim – that he only allowed his troopers to be issued with three rounds of pistol ammunition, for use when on picket duty or out foraging. Such measures were not always effective, for Captain Peter Drake wrote of the weapons discharged at him, during the cavalry mêlée in the closing stages of the battle at Malplaquet in 1709:

> His ball only grazed my shoulder, and tore the flesh a little, but the powder blew off, and burnt the breadth of an oyster shell off my coat, and the wadding which was tow, lodged between my waistcoat and shirt, setting them both on fire. Most of the front rank of the [enemy] squadron, if not all, fired a volley at the same time, so that I had eleven shot fairly marked on my cuirass, or breastplate, and two through the skirts of my coat.[25]

Again, it is clear that old habits tend to die hard, for the troopers Drake was engaged against were Germans, as the Irish soldier of fortune was in the French service at this time. The injury that he suffered was only because his opponent had actually pressed the muzzle of the pistol hard against him before firing his shot. Otherwise it seems that little harm would have been done at all. Drake, in return, had killed his man by using the same technique, but to better effect, managing to blow the top of his head off.

The lance had not made a reappearance in western Europe and, the curved sabre not yet being in general use, the long straight cavalry broadsword was the weapon to be employed in all other circumstances, and Richard Kane, an infantryman, wrote:

> It is sufficient for them to ride well, to have their horses well managed and trained up to stand fire ... That they march and wheel with a grace, and handle their swords well which is the only weapon our British Horse makes use of when they charge the enemy; more than this is superfluous.[26]

Even though this may have been so, the effect of a blow from the cavalry sword was often a nasty bruise rather than a disabling cut or slash; the thick coats and leather gauntlets worn would have afforded an element of protection, just as would the breastplates mentioned by Drake. The use of the armoured helmet was diminishing in the same way as the employment of armoured cuirassiers, but many troopers wore a metal cap beneath their cocked hat, to protect the forehead and skull from sword cuts. Despite this, dragoon officer James Campbell, a noted Scottish swordsman, employed a neat backhanded stroke with his weapon, specially sharpened for the day at Malplaquet, to decapitate a French cavalry officer. The Earl of Orkney expressed his admiration for both his horsemanship and his handling of his sword, and likened his conduct, rather incongruously given the circumstances, 'to an angel'.[27] Such an exploit was unusual enough to warrant special notice, and much would have depended upon the skill and strength of the swordsman, the angle at which the deadly blow took effect and the keenness of the blade, for it was difficult to maintain an edge with the swords in use at the time.[28]

Marlborough was careful always to hold some cavalry in reserve, no matter what local success or reverse took place in the opening and middle phases of a battle, to make the best use of a decisive breakthrough when that should happen. The holding back from the general fray of a strong mounted reserve was, on crucial occasions, regarded as the battle-winning stroke. Even though the duke's cavalry was heavily engaged for much of the afternoon's fighting at Blenheim, and also at Ramillies, the strength of both horses and their riders was conserved by careful positioning of infantry supports and reinforcements at important moments. The French and Bavarian opponents, however, struggled to provide these supports and their cavalry were allowed to wear themselves out, and as a result could not summon the strength to resist the final and most telling stroke when it came. At Oudenarde in 1708, most of the fighting was carried out by infantry as the close nature of the country constricted the easy movement of horsemen to a degree, but the fatal blow for the Duc de Vendôme was still delivered by the turning movement of the massed Dutch and Danish squadrons under command of Veldt-Marshal Overkirk and Count Tilly.

Tight discipline had to be maintained in the handling of cavalry, as headlong pursuits were discouraged because they were tiring for the horses and, with no commander able to exercise command and control properly, would jeopardize any success. At Blenheim the British cavalry went on too far in their repulse of the French Gens d'Armes and were badly cut up for their trouble. Once reordered, however, Marlborough's squadrons pushed resolutely forward and Tallard's cavalry broke and fled, and Marshal Marsin and the Elector of Bavaria had to withdraw their troops in some haste. The victorious Allied pursuit was noticeably measured, no doubt due partly to the losses suffered in the hard fighting that had taken place, but also to the tiredness of both the troopers and their horses. There was also a degree of confusion amongst the Allied commanders, right and left, as to just what was happening on the other side of the battlefield, and for all that had already been achieved, undue risks were not to be taken. With the dramatic collapse of the right flank of the French army at Ramillies, however, the enthusiasm and vigour of the triumphant Dutch and Danish troopers could hardly be contained, but the case was very different from that on the plain of Höchstädt. In May 1706 Marshal Villeroi's army was in headlong flight, abandoning everything – guns baggage, equipment and camp followers – in its desperate haste to escape, and outright pursuit was wholly appropriate to the occasion. The duke took part in the chase, which was only called to a halt with the onset of darkness, and he slept that night under a cloak on the grass, without really knowing exactly where his small party was:

> The French were hounded North-West along the roads towards Brussels and Louvain ... Guns, baggage and stragglers strewed the roads and before long their loss in prisoners alone exceeded the total Allied casualties in the battle ... It was two months before the army could be properly mobilized on a campaign footing.[29]

Such resounding victories as Blenheim and Ramillies demonstrated in dramatic fashion just what could be achieved by well-handled and disciplined cavalry. The success on each occasion, however, depended upon

n Duke of Marlbrough 1726

John Churchill, First Duke of Marlborough, by Godfrey Kneller. (*His Grace the Duke of Marlborough*)

2. The Duke of Marlborough at the Battle of Blenheim in 1704. Detail from the tapestry in Blenheim Palace. (*His Grace the Duke of Marlborough*)

Prince Eugene of Savoy. Imperial field commander and close friend and comrade of Marlborough.

4. Henry of Nassau, Veldt-Marshal Overkirk. Dutch field commander and staunch supporter of Marlborough. Died during the siege of Lille in 1708.

John Churchill, First Duke of Marlborough. Commanded the Anglo-Dutch armies 1702–1711.

6. Queen Anne of Great Britain. A staunch friend and supporter of Marlborough, but she dismissed him in 1711.

Louis XIV of France, the 'Sun King'. He allowed his grandson to accept the throne of Spain, and brought war back to Europe.

8. Louis-Guillaume, Margrave of Baden.
A brave field commander, but Marlborough
found him too obstinate.

9. Major General William Cadogan.
Marlborough's valuable chief of staff and
quartermaster-general

10. Arnold Joost van Keppel,
First Earl Albemarle. A
favourite of King William III
and a highly capable Dutch
cavalry commander, entruste
by Marlborough with compl
and demanding operations.

. Lieutenant General Charles Churchill.
arlborough's younger brother, and general of
fantry at Blenheim in 1704 and Ramillies in
'06. Retired through ill-health and died in
'14.

12. George Hamilton, First Earl Orkney.
Marlborough's aggressive infantry commander
at Blenheim, Ramillies and Malplaquet.
Became governor of Virginia.

. Claude-Louis-Hector de
illars, Marshal of France.
ormidable opponent of
arlborough between 1709 and
'11. Gravely wounded at
alplaquet.

14. Major General Joseph Sabine. Served in all of Marlborough's campaigns, and commanded the infantry of the advance guard on the march to Oudenarde in 1708.

15. Major General Lord John Cutts of Gowran Led the infantry attack on Blindheim village in August 1704. Known as 'Salamander' for liking to be in the hottest fire. Died in Ireland in 1707.

16. George, the Elector of Hanover. Firm supporter of the Grand Alliance and capable field commander. Became George I of Great Britain in 1714.

George, Electoral Prince of Hanover. Served
h the Hanoverian cavalry at Oudenarde in
8, and almost lost his life. Became George II
Great Britain in 1727.

19. Major General John Armstrong.
Marlborough's gifted chief of engineers, who
provided the Allied army with mobility.

John Campbell, 'Red John',
ond Duke of Argyll.
gressive field commander,
o became a political
ponent of Marlborough.
mmanded the Allied forces
Spain in the later part of the
r.

John Duke of Argyll &
Greenwich

20. Christian Davis (Mother Ross). Irish female soldier who served as a dragoon in Marlborough's army for many years. She became the first female Chelsea Pensioner.

21. A blue-coated trooper of the Prussian 'Lieb' Regiment of Dragoons who served in most of Marlborough's campaigns.

22. Donauwörth town seen from the Schellenberg hill. A bitter battle was fought for these heights July 1704.

Offuz village near to Ramillies. Orkney's British infantry attacked up this slope on 23 May 1706.

The Scheldt River near Oudenarde. Cadogan's advance guard crossed here to engage Vendôme's ench on the morning of 11 July 1708.

25. Marlborough's army moves to cross the pontoon bridges over the Scheldt River, to confront Vendôme's French army on 11 July 1708.

26. The Wynendael tapestry from Blenheim Palace. The battle to hold back the French while the vi supplies made their way to the Allied army besieging Lille in September 1708.
(*His Grace the Duke of Marlborough*)

Detail from the Oudenarde tapestry at Blenheim Palace. (*His Grace the Duke of Marlborough*)

28. The desperate fighting in the woods at Malplaquet on 11 September 1709. The log obstacles chained together by the French defenders can be clearly seen.

29. Marlborough's cavalry move through the Allied gun-line on the afternoon of Malplaquet.

at Albert Camp. 1707.
a Execation of Deserters in Flanders 1707

Discipline could be firmly applied when needed. The execution of deserters in the Allied camp, 1707. A sketch by Marcellus Laroon, a veteran of Marlborough's campaigns.

Off-duty. Soldiers relax in a sutler's tent while in camp. The half-dressed lady indicates that the place was also a brothel. Marcellus Laroon sketch.

32. Siege operations. The methodical battering down of the defences of the formal fortress was a common feature of Marlborough's campaigns.

33. The armorial bearings of John, First Duke of Marlborou[gh]. The double-headed eagle was the crest of the Holy Roman Empire of which he was a prince.

the hard work of the infantry in the early stages of the fighting, setting the duke's French opponents up for the deadly mounted stroke that brought them to ruin. With all their speed and power, cavalry found it difficult to operate effectively on their own, and its influence on the battlefield was gradually declining in western Europe. Infantry weapons and tactics were changing and improving, and tactical formations to counter cavalry, such as the sturdy infantry square, were becoming a notable feature of the battlefield. Rowe's Regiment had tried to form square outside Blindheim village, but the French Gens d'Armes got amongst them before they could do so. Such formations were difficult for cavalry to break other than at great cost. Limitations were increasingly being placed on the free movement and tactical effectiveness of cavalry. Despite this, throughout Marlborough's campaigns cavalry remained in many cases the decisive factor in battle, with Blenheim, Elixheim and Ramillies being the obvious examples. In the fighting at Oudenarde (where cavalry played important roles in both the early and closing stages of the battle) and at Malplaquet, the terrain dictated that the foot soldier took the primary role in the fighting. Even on those two occasions, what fatally undermined the French final position was the inability of their horsemen to hold back the cavalry Marlborough had carefully preserved until the right moment came to strike.

Chapter 5

The Foot Soldier: Lock, Stock and Barrel

All regular armies have the infantry as their backbone, men on whose efforts everything else rests. This has been so ever since the decline of the cavalry as an irresistible fighting force became apparent in the face of rapid and well-directed fire. Nonetheless, Ned Ward, writing in the *London Spy* in 1700, described in clearly disparaging terms how the infantryman was generally regarded in society:

> A foot soldier is commonly a man, who, for the sake of wearing a sword, and the honour of being termed a gentleman, is coaxed from a handicraft trade, whereby he might live comfortably, to bear arms, for his King and country, whereby he has hopes of nothing but to live starvingly. His lodging is as near Heaven as his quarters can raise him, and his soul generally as near Hell as a profligate life can sink him; for to speak without swearing, he thinks it a scandal to his post ... He is generally beloved of two sorts of companions, viz; whores and lice; for both these vermin are great admirers of a scarlet coat.[1]

Despite such sentiments, the common foot soldier, enduring, under-paid and put-upon as he might be, was capable of effective deployment in just about any kind of country. Whether attacking or defending, flexible enough to operate in woods, marshy lowlands, open cornfields, village streets, rocky defiles, on the fire-swept glacis of a fortress or a bombarded covered-way, the foot soldiers could, with their increasing ability to pro-duce powerful and disciplined musketry, dominate a battlefield. The armies engaged in the War of the Spanish Succession comprised about two-thirds infantry, according very well with the estimates given in the previous chapter for the numbers of cavalrymen employed, as the num-bers of those engaged in the other arms, the gunners and the engineers, was quite small in comparison. Like the cavalry and their dragoon comrades, foot soldiers fell into several broad categories – the ordinary 'centinelle' or private soldier, and the grenadiers and fusiliers, who were originally intended for very specific duties. Despite the titles, their role was essentially the same: to occupy the battlefield with 'boots on the ground', wherever and whatever that should be. Mounted troops could, on the right day, roll up an entire opposing army (although in practice they did not manage to do so very often), while gunners could smash holes in fences and walls, disrupt a rank of cavalry or line of infantrymen with round-shot and sweep an attacking force off its feet with canister-shot. Neither the Horse nor the gunners, however, could take and hold ground and deny it to an opponent for critically long periods, and in performing this essential task win or lose a battle – only the humble infantry could do so. The ultimate success of any commanding general rested on the capability to both maintain disciplined formation and deliver effective firepower.

By 1700 there was no longer a need for the employment of massed hedges of long pikes to ward off opposing horsemen and protect vulnerable and slow-firing matchlock-men. The previous vulnerability of infantry to the massed charge of cavalry had diminished with the introduction of the flintlock musket and the bayonet. The infantryman armed in this way could both deliver fire and simultaneously ward off opposing cavalry, defying them to come close and exchange blows, at the risk of having their expensively mounted ranks shredded by blazing musketry in the process. By the time William III had come to the throne in London, the ratio of pikemen to musketeers in his army had dropped to 1 in 5, and over the next few years they faded away almost entirely, the last pikes in English use reportedly going into store in June 1702, although some soldiers continued to regret their passing. By this time, most foot soldiers in western Europe were equipped with the flintlock, but inevitably such a re-equipping of large numbers of soldiers could not proceed quickly or uniformly, or according to any intended programme. In 1704 the Earl of Portmore wrote to the Duke of Somerset that:

> I have the honour of receiving an order from Your Grace directing the storekeeper of this place [Plymouth in Devon] to deliver 450 firelocks in lieu of the like number of pikes which some of the regiments that come from Holland have, as they say, left behind by His Grace the Duke of Marlborough's allowance.[2]

That regiments serving in the Low Countries could, in the same year that saw the victorious campaign for the duke and his troops at Blenheim, still be equipped with the outmoded pike, is surprising. The regiments referred to in the correspondence were on their way to campaign in

Portugal, but that fact offers no real explanation for why they were armed in this fashion before disembarking in England.

To deliver the necessary massed musketry firepower, it was necessary to deploy foot soldiers in extended line when taking up a position. While the French retained the deployment of five-man deep formations for the time being, Marlborough's foot soldiers were arranged in only three ranks. Clearly, the greater number of men who could have a clear field of fire in which to aim a musket and then deliver fire, the greater the effect would be. The steady introduction into common use of the flintlock weapon gave the foot soldier the ability to deliver this effective fire. In the British army it took the form of the 42-inch-barrelled old English musket, eventually to be known by the tender nickname of 'Brown Bess' (taken from the proofing of the barrels against rust). The old drawbacks of the matchlock – the slow rate of loading and giving fire, the heavy weight of the weapon, the unreliability of the match itself – were all done away with. The French, so innovative in other ways, were reluctant to change from matchlock to flintlock and their infantry suffered as a result. At the Battle of Steinkirk in 1692 it had been noticed that Marshal Luxembourg's soldiers were throwing away their own weapons and taking up and using the fallen flintlocks of their opponents whenever the chance arose.

The rate of fire when flintlocks were employed was twice that of matchlock-men, a process made more sure by the introduction of pre-packed cartridges, an elongated paper packet containing the powder, and from 1690 onwards also the ball. The end of the cartridge would be bitten off (requiring foot soldiers to have a good set of front teeth), the action primed and the contents then poured down the musket barrel and rammed home using the paper as a wad to hold the charge securely in place. The flintlock action was then pulled back to the cocked position, before presenting the musket at the shoulder, aimed after a fashion in the right direction, and fired. This ramming-down of the charge was occasionally rather perfunctory, and soldiers keen to maintain a high rate of fire would sometimes just bang the butts of their muskets on the ground to seat the cartridge and ball in a rough manner ready for firing. The subsequent introduction of iron ramrods (despite further complaints about the excessive cost), which were noticeably more robust than their wooden predecessors, added to the speed and reliability of the loading and reloading process. Good training drills and repeated practice would hone this skill, but in the heat and confusion of battle it was not unknown for the ramrod not to be withdrawn and therefore fired like a crude kind of arrow across the battlefield.[3]

Maintaining a good rate of fire demanded set drills to be learned and practised, but it was no simple thing to keep a flintlock in action in the heat, noise, excitement and smoke of a pitched battle. Flints had a tendency to wear out and lose their striking effectiveness after about thirty shots, and would then have to be replaced in the lock, a fumbling process at the best of times. The black powder in use would often burn unevenly, leaving a hard crusty residue in the barrels, impeding swift reloading and ramming a charge home, or producing an exaggerated recoil with resulting bruising to the firer's shoulder to hinder accurate shooting, and occasionally bursting the barrel. Out of the line of battle, soldiers often cleaned their muskets in rudimentary fashion by firing off a charge, sometimes but not always using a blank charge. Camp regulations had to be issued to ensure that this was done safely, and without undue risk to those standing around.

The flintlock musket in British and Dutch use during the War of the Spanish Succession fired a spherical lead ball of 1 ounce weight, a heavier projectile than that in French use, and more likely, because of its greater weight, to travel straighter and more true and to inflict a disabling wound at the receiving end. Some have questioned the actual effectiveness of this weighty ball, but Captain Robert Parker of the Royal Irish Regiment was sure that it was so, commenting on the successful encounter between his own unit and the French-recruited Royal Régiment d'Irelandaise in 1709, that:

> Colonel Kane, who was then at the head of the regiment having drawn us up, and formed our platoons, advanced gently towards [the enemy], with the six platoons of our first fire made ready. When we had advanced within a hundred paces of them they gave us a fire of one of their ranks, whereupon we halted and returned them the fire of our six platoons at once.

This exchange of firing went on for some time, but then the French regiment broke ranks and hurriedly retired into the shelter of the nearby trees. Parker attributed his unit's success to two things:

> The advantage on our side will be easily accounted for, first from the weight of our ball, for the French arms carry bullets of 24 to the pound; whereas out British firelocks carry balls of 16 to the pound, which will make a considerable difference in the execution. Again, the manner of our firing was different from theirs; the French at the time fired by all ranks, which can never do equal execution with our

platoon firing … This is undoubtedly the best method that has yet
been discovered for fighting a battalion.[4]

The disciplined way in which the fire was delivered was, as the gallant
captain said, an essential ingredient in such success, and his reference to
platoon firing is significant. The previous technique was that of having
an entire rank deliver their fire at the same time, as the French did on
this occasion, or sometimes of multiple ranks firing if those soldiers at
the front were kneeling (a posture which made it difficult to reload the
weapon quickly). This method had the advantage of being fairly simple to
control at first, but accuracy would suffer, as soldiers have a natural tendency to fire high, and with entire ranks firing all at once this could not
easily be discouraged. A more complex but undoubtedly effective technique had been developed: dividing a battalion into four grand divisions,
each of which would comprise a group of four platoons. These would be
detailed off as 'firings', each one to discharge their muskets all together at
the given word of command. Although at each discharge there would be
fewer muskets in actual use, and the weight of fire would accordingly
seem to be less than with whole ranks firing, the practical effect was
greater and more accurate with no respite at all from the tormenting
musketry for the opponents. The sergeants and junior officers were also
better able to ensure that the soldiers kept the muzzles of their muskets
lowered, and thus avoided firing too high.

Control of musketry fire was obviously necessary to achieve the desired
effect, but in the press and noise of a battle, shouted orders could often go
unheard or be misinterpreted. Accordingly, the more effective means of
transmitting orders was by that of drumbeat, and, accordingly, the drummers in a battalion had a particularly valuable role to perform. From 1702
onwards all British battalions had a drum major on the strength, and each
soldier would be well versed in the various drumbeats, riffs and flams
given, and would react accordingly, as an automatic drill, learned and
practised well in advance. As important players in the drama of a battlefield, the drummers (few of whom could really be classed as 'boys', despite
numerous heart-rending popular depictions of them as such) would be
bound to attract the unwelcome attention of the enemy, who would seek to
shoot them down as soon as possible. Casualties amongst drummers were,
accordingly, a serious matter, hampering the ability of commanders to
order and reorder their troops quickly when in the thick of an action.

Each regiment of Foot had colours, which were carried by junior
officers. They were used to mark out the position to be adopted when

forming up on parade or ready to go into battle and as useful rallying points when in action. Originally, a regiment would have a Colonel's Colour as well as a colour for each company, but these were reduced by Queen Anne's time to just those of the colonel, the lieutenant colonel and major (or the senior company commander). To this practical purpose of quickly and readily showing soldiers where to stand or rally at times of haste, stress and peril, was added the notional honour of those colours, in that they should never be permitted to be seized by the enemy. An almost religious significance would, in time, be added to these eminently practical signalling devices, with many desperate battles fought, often hand to hand, for the possession of the colours, in a way not at all dissimilar to the fighting for Napoleonic Eagles 100 years later. This was a sensitivity that had yet to develop fully, and in Marlborough's army the colours, while valued, still had an essentially practical purpose.

Although they would not be left unguarded or lightly given up, colours were used as a means to an end, and this can be seen in May 1706 on the ridgeline opposite the marshy Petite Gheete stream near to the village of Ramillies. The British and Danish infantry regiments, under the command of the Earl of Orkney, had forced their way across the marshy valley and driven up the slope towards the hamlet of Offuz in the face of a stout defence by Walloon regiments led by Major General de la Guiche. 'I thought I never had more shot around my ears,' Orkney remembered of that afternoon's fighting, but despite his protests his troops were recalled from pressing home their attack, which could not be supported as the main Allied effort was to be made to the south of the village. To add to the weight of that crucial effort, most of the earl's infantry had to march to join the fray, but their colours and their escorts were left on the ridgeline facing Offuz, to give the clear impression to their French and Walloon opponents on the other side of the valley that the Allied troops were still in place and could attack again at any time.[5] That the foot soldiers who marched south were not in time to have any effect on the outcome of the battle to any great degree does not detract from the point.

The colours had yet to achieve the almost mystical status that would, within a few decades of the Ramillies battle, have made any such leaving behind of these treasured symbols perfectly unthinkable. On the other hand, the colour ensign for Borthwick's Scots-Dutch regiment, James Gardiner, fought fiercely with his small sword to be true to the trust placed in him, and ended up being shot in the mouth and left for dead beside the churchyard wall in Ramillies village as the Régiment de Picardie surged forward in counter-attack, and the loss of the Colonel's Colour of Argyll's

Regiment (the Buffs) at Malplaquet three years later was significant enough to attract comment. Understandably, the colour parties would in the natural course of events attract fierce fire from opponents, who were anxious to shut down these means of communication and command and control, and so casualties amongst those parties were often heavy. 'There had been with me that day fourteen sergeants already killed and wounded while in charge of the Colours, with officers in proportion, while the staff and Colours were almost cut to pieces.'[6]

A battalion on the line of march would be in column, with the companies ranked according to the seniority of the company commander. Once a commanding officer had brought his battalion within effective sight of an opponent, the drumbeat to form from column of march into line would be given, unless the battlelines had already been formed preparatory to the opening of a general action. When required to deploy, tactician Richard Kane wrote that their formation was to be:

> Three deep, their bayonets fixed on their muzzles, the grenadiers divided on the flanks, the officers ranged in front, and the colonel, or in his absence the lieutenant-colonel, on foot, with his sword drawn in his hand, about eight or ten paces in front, opposite the centre, with an expert drummer by him. He should appear with a cheerful countenance, never in a hurry or by any means ruffled and to deliver his orders with great calmness.[7]

The drummers would then beat a preparatory flam to alert the first firing of four platoons to cock their muskets, and look to the priming and flints. The front rank would drop to one knee, with the butts of the muskets to the ground and bayonets foremost to ward off horsemen, and on the next flam the second and third rank would present their weapons and, on the necessary word of command, give fire. As the soldiers in the rear rank would have taken up their position behind and slightly to one side of their comrades to the front, with the left shoulder forward and the left foot locked against the right heel of the front man, they could fire over the shoulder of the forward ranks (at the risk, admittedly, of damaging the hearing of those front men). The kneeling front rank could, if needed, stand and fire while the second and third ranks were reloading their muskets, or reserve their fire until some critical moment presented itself. This drill would be repeated with the second, third and fourth firings in the battalion so that the opposing troops were kept under a constant and galling musketry, and once the first firing had reloaded and regained their correct formation, left leg and shoulder to the front once more, they were ready to repeat the drill as long as the ammunition and necessity lasted – and so it would go on.

In effect, a well-drilled battalion using this platoon-firing technique could keep an opponent under the lash of musketry without respite. The theory was fine, but in the smoke, noise and excitement of a battle, such a neat arrangement was bound to break down after a while, with the natural desire of a soldier to reload and fire off his musket at best speed vying with the discipline necessary for well-measured platoon firing. However, in the opening phases of a clash this advantage could be telling; the Allied armies, who adopted the technique during the latter years of the seventeenth century, benefited to a noticeable degree and generally were able for a time to beat down their opponents in musketry exchanges. The technique was enshrined in a drill manual published in 1708, aptly entitled *The Duke of Marlborough's New Exercise of Firelocks and Bayonets*. The French commanders were, of course, intelligent men and they were soon aware of the disadvantage under which their infantry were labouring. Accordingly, and despite the doubts of Louis XIV about such a novel move, platoon firing was adopted increasingly widely, albeit quite slowly, into the French and Bavarian armies from about 1704 onwards. Not until 1755, however, would the French army formally adopt the new firing method as standard.

It is often said that the smoothbore musket was an inaccurate weapon, but when well handled it was not, even allowing for the looseness in the bore of the barrels to allow a ball to be passed down easily (the windage). In any case, soldiers were not encouraged to take aim at a specific individual target, but to deliver their fire en masse in the right direction. Given that soldiers often reloaded and fired off their pieces in haste and without proper care, a degree of ineffectiveness is not that unexpected, but that is not the same thing as inaccuracy. When necessary, with a cartridge carefully loaded and properly rammed home and a good flint in place, a careful shot at modest range of perhaps 200 yards or so, could be surprisingly accurate. Sharpshooting was not uncommon, particularly during siege operations when a good elbow rest would be had before firing, and this can be seen in the account by Kit Davies of the siege of Ath in 1706, when she went into the trenches and saw a French soldier scavenging for vegetables:

> I took a piece out of one of our people's hand, and called to an officer to see me shoot him; for we had pushed our trenches within thirty-three paces of the palisades. I suppose we were just then perceived;

for the instant I killed the man, a musket-shot from the town, came through the sandbags, split my under lip, beat one of my teeth into my mouth, and knocked me down … General Ingoldsby sent for his surgeon, who sewed up my lip.[8]

Despite such exploits, the build-up of smoke on the battlefield would quickly impair good visibility and easy observation, with an inevitable impact on maintaining the accuracy of fire delivered. A picture of the well-ordered and colourful lines of an army of the eighteenth century drawn up in battle array is easily conjured up in the imagination. Battle scenes of famous engagements such as Blenheim and Ramillies in Marlborough's day are familiar, as are those for Dettingen, Minden, Fontenoy, Borodino, Waterloo – or the Alma, for that matter, almost 150 years later – and all show the neat serried ranks of the armies, usually depicted as mainly comprising infantry, facing up to each other and readied for the deadly contest soon to come. Clearly, to move large bodies of men onto a battlefield and then to arrange them properly to fight at the right time and place in good order required a highly developed system of movements and drills. Orders and instructions transmitted by beat of drum were readily understood and easily heard over the noise of a battlefield, unlike shrill shouted commands, particularly once the artillery had got into place and had begun their deathly work. Such formal arrangements, and well-rehearsed massed movements, were absolutely necessary for the proper arranging of an army getting ready for battle.

As with the effective control of musketry through the use of platoon firing, the good ordering of ranks of foot soldiers when in action would soon start to be a little ragged: as officers and drummers fell, gaps suddenly appeared in the ranks, smoke obscured the field, and the din of guns and musketry grew in volume. Sometimes one side would be beaten down with fire and give way, but combat at close quarters was quite common, and Sergeant John Wilson remembered that the fighting at Malplaquet in 1709 was:

An obstinate engagement for the space of two hours in which there was a great effusion of blood on both sides; the armies firing at each other bayonet to bayonet. And after came to stab each other with their bayonets and several came so close that they knocked each others brains out with the butt end of their firelocks.[9]

To keep formation and order in such circumstances was no simple thing, and Matthew Bishop wrote of the effect of French musketry that day, 'My right and my left hand man were shot dead. I remembered it wounded my captain and took my left hand man, [and] almost swept off those that were on my right.'[10] Strict battle discipline, with each man knowing his correct place in the ranks, the drill to be followed in loading and firing his musket on the word of command, and simultaneously harkening to the beat of drum and shouted commands of officers and non-commissioned officers, helped to ensure that in the heat of a pitched battle some semblance of order was maintained. These things were not simple to achieve, and of necessity were repeatedly practised. John Deane recalled that, while the Allied army was waiting for the French to move out of their entrenchments in 1707:

> His Grace [Marlborough] reviewed the whole army both English and Confederates, Horse and Foot, and on the 29th of May his Grace viewed the English Foot; and the Earl of Orkney, posting himself at the head of our battalion of Guards, saluted the Duke. And, afterwards all the English Foot exercised by signal of Colours and beat of drum, and every brigade fired in platoons before his Grace; in which exercise the English got great applause of the foreigners.[11]

Such disciplined and practised conduct would pay handsome dividends on many occasions, as Captain Robert Parker tells us with his own regiment in the woods at Malplaquet.

The more faint-hearted in such an engagement might find opportunity to take cover or make off to a place of greater safety. Kit Davies wrote that during the fighting on that day in September she went into the shot-torn copses to find her husband and take him some refreshment – a mission that was in vain as he was already lying in one of the piles of the dead. While searching there, she was confronted by a soldier who was 'easing nature', presumably because his bladder was under some pressure, and he had taken the opportunity to turn aside from the firing line to make himself comfortable. On another occasion, during the course of a siege in 1710, she came across a young officer who had fallen out of the line, having been struck by a spent musket ball and fouled his pants in fright, as a consequence of which he never recovered his 'character' (reputation) with his soldiers. On the other hand, instances of outright bravery were not uncommon. When, in August 1704, Brigadier General Archibald Rowe was mortally wounded at the head of his troops during the opening attack on Blindheim village, two of his own officers, Lieutenant Colonel Jonathan Dalyell and Major William Hamilton, ran to his aid, regardless of a heavy French musketry, and were themselves promptly shot down and killed. Such action – going forward regardless of the risk – says much for the sense of duty in the two men, but also for the evident regard and affection in which their brigade commander was held.

'Friendly fire' incidents, as they are euphemistically called when soldiers fire on their own comrades either through carelessness or confusion, are nothing new and a regrettable fact of life on a battlefield. Chaplain Samuel Noyes, serving with Orkney's Regiment at the storming of the Schellenberg in 1704, wrote:

> The English Guards had four officers killed, nine wounded, seventy-four soldiers killed and 127 wounded. Ingoldsby's and Meredith's suffered much, and our two battalions had above 400 killed and wounded. Not that the enemy killed all these; a great many were killed by their own friends. There was such great numbers commanded on the attack that sometimes they were above twenty deep and the hindmost firing sometimes at random (on such occasions there is always some confusion) shot those that were before them.[12]

On many occasions, the main threat to foot soldiers was from opposing cavalry. It is no easy thing to get a horse to charge down a man who is determined to stand his ground, and even more so when that man is wielding a musket tipped with an 18-inch steel bayonet, but it can be done. Infantry in good order, presenting a resolutely unbroken front, shielded by both well-directed musketry and a hedge of glistening bayonets, were relatively secure from a frontal mounted attack, at least until the introduction into western Europe of lancers whose long deadly thrusts could outreach that of the foot soldier, although not of his musketry. Infantry who were taken in the flank, or who had lost their order through confusion and casualties, were at particular risk, as Rowe's Regiment found at Blindheim village, and the manoeuvre that evolved to cater for such an attack by cavalrymen was that of forming the infantry square. This was unavoidably a rather complex procedure, and one that, if mishandled or misjudged under pressure, could make even more vulnerable any infantry battalion under attack. Richard Kane wrote of the intricacies of the manoeuvre to be undertaken when forming a square:

> We will suppose the Colonel has an account that a body of horse are advancing towards us; he orders the drums to cease beating, and the battalion to halt, on which the drums of the first division come out to him, he then gives the word 'Take Care to Form the Square', and immediately after orders the drums to beat a ruffle; upon which the

second division wheel to the right, by the right hand man of the first rank [who will stand still while this wheeling takes place], until their three ranks on the left join the three files on the right of the first division; the third division marches briskly, until they come to the ground of the second [division], and the they begin their wheel to the left by the left hand man [who stands still] of their rear rank; and when they have made their wheel they edge to the right, till their three files on the right take up the three ranks of the left of the first [division].

The commanding officer now had the three faces of the square most likely to be exposed to attack; and then to complete things:

The rear division all this while marches briskly, and takes the ground from which the second [division] wheeled, joining the three ranks on the right to the three files on the right of the second; and the three files on their left take up the three ranks on the left of the third, which closes the square.[13]

This all sounds very complicated, but in practice – and if it was well and often rehearsed, of course – it was a quite simple manoeuvre. Anyone who has watched the Foot Guards troop their colours on Horse Guards Parade in London will recognize the technique of ranks changing front, by forming on the right-hand man, who inclines half right and then stands his ground, and the ranks change front on the pivot thus provided, the second man inclining and taking two paces, the third man three paces, and so on down the length of the line until the wheeling has been completed. Once the square was formed, the officers, the colour party and the drummers would take post in the centre while the grenadiers, in theory the tallest and strongest men in the battalion, would anchor the security of the formation by taking up position on the more exposed corners.

A particularly brilliant example of the employment of this tactic was in July 1705, when Marquis Pierre Caraman, the French infantry commander at the Battle of Elixheim, found that the supporting cavalry had taken themselves off the field. He withdrew his infantry in good order by adopting a large square which defied the determined attacks of Marlborough's horsemen. 'In this form,' Robert Parker wrote, 'they marched, and notwithstanding that our right Wing of Horse and dragoons had surrounded them on all sides, yet they dared not venture within reach of their fire. The square kept marching on, driving the squadrons before them.' The captain added the perceptive note, 'This shows what the Foot are capable of doing against the Horse.'[14] Such admirable attributes had to be supported, of course, with some pretty firm leadership, and things might have gone very differently for the French and Bavarian infantry that day had Caraman not been the robust campaigner that he was, bolstering the strength of the square in the prescribed manner by placing the burly grenadiers at the corners where the formation was at its most vulnerable, 'Moving backwards and forwards to support the parts that were most in danger.'

Soldiers on the march had to carry most of their kit and other belongings with them as they went, since the amount of baggage that could be loaded onto the regimental carts was limited. What could be carried on the carts and taken forward under the overall supervision of the wagon master was liable to be pilfered and plundered on the way, unless a trusted driver or camp follower could be found to keep an eye on things. This problem was particularly acute for the foot soldiers, as they alone of all the arms and services in the army had to rely most on their two legs to carry them along. On going into action, of course, this equipment could not be taken forward any more without impeding the fighting ability of the soldiers. Accordingly, knapsacks, blankets, kettles and other items of comfortable campaign kit had to be dumped at the side of the track as the troops deployed into the battleline. Whether or not they ever saw their belongings again was very much a matter of the fortunes of war, a fickle element at best, but Richard Kane felt that a commanding officer:

> When he finds that there is no avoiding coming to battle, he is to order the soldiers to lay down their knapsacks, tent poles and what is cumbersome, and the Sergeant sends them to some place out of the way, where a sergeant with a few men takes care of them. If we win the day, they will be safe; if not, 'tis no matter what becomes of them.[15]

Kane omits to say that, after any successful encounter, the soldiers could hope to profit from pillaging the abandoned gear of the vanquished. Even so, the simple pace of events in victory might hinder the recovery of possessions, and at Ramillies the pursuit of the beaten French and Bavarians was pushed so rapidly and headlong that few of the Allied soldiers had the chance ever to see again their own knapsacks and kit that they left behind when going into battle, let alone to plunder those of their beaten opponents: 'The Duke pressed so close that he got between their left wing and Louvain which made the disperse ... being so close at their heels, they made off from there, and never looked behind them.'[16] Victory had its rewards, undoubtedly, but there were also practical disadvantages for the common soldier.

Despite the obvious benefits of good order and well-applied discipline, it should not be assumed that infantrymen fighting in the War of the Spanish Succession were always arrayed in neat and solid lines, responding like well-drilled automatons to barked command and riff and flam of drum. Just as the cavalry scouted, foraged and screened as well as charging *en muraille* when called on to do so, the foot soldiers also had their associated duties as sentries, pickets, foragers and labourers, in addition to having to stand their ground in the flame and smoke of the line of battle. There was also probing, screening and skirmishing to be done. This reads a little oddly, for skirmishing and skirmishers, with individual initiative and self-control to the fore, seem to be the preserve of a later generation and to belong to a period when light troops and light infantry tactics employed by more 'educated' troops were developed. However, there was often much to be gained from approaching an opponent by stealth and taking him by surprise, as Sergeant John Wilson recalled:

> The grenadiers of these six regiments were drawn into one body under the command of Colonel Godfery who marched as soon as it was dark in the front of the pontoons in order to cover the lane of the bridges. We arrived at the river a little before daylight without being discovered by the enemy. Notwithstanding they were just on the other side of the river, yet we posted ourselves under cover of a quick set hedge without so much as one shot being fired.[17]

Such an advantage gained with care and discretion and at little cost and fuss was very much to the credit of the commander, and of more value to the unfolding operation than some overt, noisy movement under an officer who might mistake energy and haste for military efficiency. At Blenheim, the wide open plain of Höchstädt was split across by the Nebel stream, which even in the August heat presented a marshy obstacle which had to be crossed before Marlborough could come to grips with Marshal Tallard. To scramble across the brook was both time consuming and not conducive to maintaining a neat military formation, but it was achieved with no great delay, in part because the French commander chose to stand back and allow his opponents to come on before he engaged them.

Soldiers, by and large, do not lack common sense or a sense of self-preservation and what is necessary to perform a task with least cost and effort. Any approach march to battle will in all likelihood be made across ground that is uneven or difficult in some way – marshes, streams, hedges, marshes, fences and walls and so on will impede progress for neat formations. This at the least will slow an advance, and at worst make it impossible to achieve at all. The opening attack at Ramillies was carried out by Colonel Wertmuller's Dutch brigade, coming in hard and fast against the Swiss defenders of Franquenay and Taviers, as John Millner recalled:

> About two in the afternoon, our cannon being planted as most proper, they began cannonading and playing against the enemy, and their's against us, very vigorous and smart on both sides, till a little past three, and then the Duke and Marshal Overkirk ordered the attack to begin on the left with four battalions of Hollands Guards, who courageously attacked a body of French that was posted on foot amongst hedges, who they immediately routed; and then the left Wing advanced, and attacked gradually, as the ground would permit, and the enemies foot, which advanced to the relief was also quickly routed.[18]

So, open and attacking formations were, of necessity, adopted as the particular circumstances required, especially if this was while in close contact with an active opponent. Hampshire-born Tom Kitcher, serving in Meredith's Regiment on that same day, remembered that they had to struggle across the boggy ground of the Petite Gheete stream, clearing French and Walloon outposts and sharpshooters out of the surrounding thickets with the bayonet, and that they:

> Were then commanded to cross the march by means of fascines and many were shot and wounded and maimed, or killed by the French outposts which they carried ... Limbs and bodies, of which it was impossible always to ascertain whether or not they were dead, were used to pass the quagmire ... Some of them I saw turn tail and I spiked one of their officers through the gullet and another through the arse.[19]

Soldiers engaged in siege operations, which was more often the case than action in open field, were obliged to conform to the layout of the siege trenches when taking cover from the fire of the defenders. They were often also employed as labourers in the digging and revetting of the trenches themselves – hazardous enough duty with the defenders doing their level best to pick off the workers with some neat sharpshooting. Such a deadly activity would be partly countered by the besieging troops erecting elevated platforms, known as 'cavaliers', from which their own picked marksmen could try and keep the defenders' heads down while the sapping work went on. Once the sappers had got sufficiently far forward, and the breaching batteries had done their work, an attack might be attempted to seize some important feature: the covered-way, perhaps, or a projecting ravelin. This operation would take the form of a rush forward by a storming party of volunteers, picked men and grenadiers. 'We drove the enemy at once out of the counterscarp,' Robert Parker wrote of the assault on Menin shortly after Ramillies. 'They sprung two mines upon us, and from their works plied us with a most violent fire which we lay exposed to until our workmen had thrown up an entrenchment to cover us.'[20] Volunteers for such hazardous duty were not that hard to find, as bounty money was offered as an inducement to step forward. This money would then be pooled and divided up and paid out to the survivors of the operations, the sums due to the fallen going to swell the pockets and purses of the survivors: 'They took the dead men's wage, and the price of their blood.'[21]

The hand-held bombs, the 'grenades', would be of particular value in the close confines of defensive works. Donald McBane, who served as a grenadier in Orkney's Regiment, recalled on one occasion being engaged in throwing grenades into the French-held covered-way for hours at a time before the defenders could at last be blasted out and dislodged. Such use of grenades was rather limited, though, for they had little effect in the open, and commanders continued to have concerns that the use of such bombs lessened the offensive spirit of the troops, and made them less inclined to get to close grips with their opponents. There were also practical difficulties and hazards, as John Deane of the 1st English Foot Guards explained in 1710:

A sergeant of Preston's Regiment was standing thereby, and he being ambitious to fire [throw] the first grenade against the enemy, not at all considering the bags of powder that lay near him, and he while firing it something burnt his fingers inasmuch that he threw down the grenade and match and blew up about forty of Major General Primrose's men who were standing by. Some were killed, others mortifying most strangely, some were blinded.[22]

Despite such accidents, there was a certain stately formality about siege operations, with various well-known stages to be accomplished before the men could move on to the next – investing a town, establishing lines of circumvallation and contravallation, bringing forward the breaching batteries and placing the guns, summoning the governor of the garrison to surrender, perhaps allowing some of the civilian population to leave and seek a place of greater safety, beginning the bombardment and opening

the trenches, and so on. The actual assault, once the defences were sufficiently degraded by bombardment and mining, was usually a well-
thought-out affair, with a first echelon of stormers establishing themselves
on the edge of the works and, like McBane, bombing out the defenders
with grenades. Then assaulting troops moved forward, reinforced with a
second echelon of fresh men, into the main defences themselves. At this
point, as long as the garrison had not put in some sudden slashing
counter-attack to restore their position, the besieging guns would be
dragged even further forward to continue their work of destruction at
closer range.

These operations were fraught with difficulty and danger, but on occasions the assault might meet with sudden and unexpected success as the
defence, for one reason or another, collapsed in disarray. At the siege of
Venlo, early in on Marlborough's campaigns, Robert Parker remembered
the assault on an important outwork known as Fort St Michael:

> We had carried on our approaches against it, until we came to the
> foot of the glacis ... The Lord Cutts, Brigadier Hamilton, and several
> young noblemen came to see the attack made ... We rushed up to the
> covert-way, the enemy gave us one scattering shot only, and away
> they ran. We jumped onto the covert-way and ran after them. They
> made to a ravelin, which covered the curtain [courtine] of the fort, in
> which were a captain and sixty men.

At this point, with the exertion and excitement of the initial phase of the
attack so far, the stormers might have paused to catch breath and reorder
themselves, but, he goes on:

> We seeing them got into the ravelin, pursued them, got in with them,
> and soon put most of them to the sword. They that escaped us, fled
> over a small wooden bridge, that led over the moat to the fort; and
> here like madmen without fear or wit, we pursued them over that
> tottering bridge, exposed to the fire of the great and small shot from
> the body of the fort.

Parker and his comrades were helped by the laxness of the garrison
commander in inexplicably not keeping the grass on the outer parts of the
defences cut neatly short, as he should have done:

> They that fled before us climbed up by the long grass, that grew out
> of the fort, so we climbed after them. Here we were hard put to it, to
> pull out the palisades which pointed down upon us from the parapet,

and was it not for the great surprise and consternation of those within, we could never have surmounted this very point ... Had not several unforeseen accidents occurred, not a man of us could have escaped. In particular, when we had penetrated as far as the wooden bridge, had the [French] officer drawn the loose plank after him as he ought (for they were laid loose for that very purpose), we must all have fallen into the moat, which was ten feet deep in water ... Had the Governor kept the grass, by the help of which we climbed. close mown, as he ought to have done, what must have been our fate?[23]

The gallant captain could not help but reflecting, as many others have done, that an equal share of danger does not always attract an equal share of glory, and goes on, 'Lord Cutts's orders were crowned with success. In the end his Lordship had the glory of the whole action, though he never stirred out of the trenches till all was over.' The fort was secured in this stirring way, and the governor, Monsieur de Violaine, and nearly 2,000 men were taken captive. As Parker laments, exposure to danger did not always result in a greater share of glory and rewards, but that was the lot of the common soldier and more junior officer, who, lacking connections and influence, sought in this hazardous trade to make his fortune with the sword.

For all the efforts of the cavalry and the gunners, the infantry always had to go forward and secure and then hold the ground, and so complete the defeat of an opponent. Nothing has changed in this over the years, and a cost will always have to be paid by the foot soldier to accomplish this task that no others could or can do. As John Deane recalled of the heavy fighting in the autumn copses at Malplaquet in 1709:

Be sure, abundance of men were lost on our side at these bold attacks, and amongst the rest a great many of our commanding officers ... and abundance of good old experienced soldiers belonging to the several countries concerned in this confederacy died in this engagement. The Hollands army suffering very much, having lost 8,000 men in this action, the second and third battalions of the Blue Guards being bloodily smashed and broke, insomuch that the three battalions all together cannot make above 800 men. And a great many other regiments in the Hollands service being very much broke ... Our battalions of English Guards having lost 240 private centinells, twelve sergeants, and three colonels and two captains, which is a very considerable loss.[24]

The bitter and costly infantry fighting had almost all taken place in close and wooded country, which made formal infantry formations both difficult and tactically irrelevant. Junior commanders, both officers and non-commissioned officers, were to the fore and lost heavily, but Marlborough wrote that the troops 'Behaved themselves extremely well.'[25]

The Scots-Dutch regiments of Murray and Tullibardine, containing many Highland men recruited from the Atholl district, was amongst those units which suffered badly that day. The Marquis of Tullibardine, eldest son of the Earl of Atholl, fell at the head of his regiment, bleeding to death from a musket-shot wound to the thigh.[26] Deane commented that the Dutch Blue Guards, so highly regarded by William III, were mown down in large numbers by the French artillery, and Field Deputy Goslinga remembered, 'The Ditch was so thick with corpses that no inch [of grass] could be seen.'[27] Despite such losses, the Allied army under Marlborough and Eugene was able to shoulder the French aside and, admirably maintaining the pace and tempo of the campaign, press on with the siege of Mons. Villars was wounded, and there was little that Marshal Boufflers could do to interrupt the siege although he attempted to manoeuvre against the Allied lines of supply. Although Deane recalled that they were ordered to make fascines heavily weighted down with stones to bridge the formidable water obstacles encountered, the fortress was given up by the Marquis de Grimaldi on 13 October, scarcely more than a month after the fiercely fought battle at Malplaquet that the young soldier described so vividly.

Chapter 6

The Gunners

They cannonaded us very hard.[1]

The introduction of gunpowder artillery into warfare brought about a major revolution in military thought and practice in the late medieval period, with the application of an awesome destructive power able to dominate parts of the battlefield, bloodily scatter broken men and horses wholesale, and reduce previously stout and otherwise dependable fortresses to piles of rubble. Gunpowder was laborious and expensive to manufacture, and so too were the artillery pieces developed to deliver deadly projectiles. Accordingly, for many years the only armies capable of employing artillery to any real effect were those whose princes had a long enough purse to sustain the expense. In time, of course, no viable army could take the field without artillery, if it was to have any hope of success against a properly equipped opponent. In this way King Charles VIII of France campaigned with great success in northern Italy in the closing years of the fifteenth century, using relatively mobile field artillery pieces on wheeled carriages; his opponents could not yet do so. It was obvious that these new and fascinating weapons, expensive as they were, could not serve on their own: those arms that depended upon mobility and cold steel for effect – the Horse and the Foot – had also to play their part. Accordingly, the intelligent combination of those three key arms – Horse, Foot and guns – together with the essential support of the engineers and the logistics tail, became the set model for all modern armies.[2]

Until relatively modern times, artillery fell into two broad categories – siege guns and field guns. Understandably, the siege train of an army comprised large pieces, cumbersome and heavy, with the power to break open and reduce formal defences of the most complex kind. The heaviest pieces, most generally known in 1700 as 'cannon', ranged in weight of shot from 30 to 50 pounds, although occasionally mighty pieces of up to 64 pounds were used. The demi-cannon fired shot weighing from 20 to 28 pounds, while the lightest effective siege pieces, known as 'quarter cannon' and 'culverin', fired shot from 16 to 19 pounds in weight. These pieces were all regarded as heavy artillery, to be employed from the army's artillery train in formal siege work, and not really capable of effective employment on the field of battle. Such large guns were reckoned to have the capability to penetrate 35 feet of packed earth, when fired at a range of 150 yards. Field artillery, by comparison, was by its very nature of a lighter and more mobile design, with the shot used ranging from the 'demi-culverin' with its 9- and 12-pound shot, through 4- and 5-pounder 'drakes' and 'sakers', to 'falcons' and 'falconets' with 1- and 2-pound shot. These last, very light and nimble pieces, often accompanied the infantry as they deployed for battle and were occasionally known as 'battalion guns'. Such quaint names as these for the various types of guns were gradually falling into disuse by the time of the War of the Spanish Succession (although Kit Davies refers at one point to the shot of a drake coming uncomfortably close), and it became increasingly common to refer to artillery pieces by the weight of the shot they fired – 9-pounder, 24-pounder, and so on.

All artillery, whether the guns were intended for siege or field operations, was heavy, cumbersome and, to a certain degree, tactically quite immobile. The Swedish King Gustavus Adolphus had attempted to improve the mobility of his gunners during the Thirty Years War with light gun barrels bound with leather intended to hold them secure against the bursting pressure on firing. These devices were moderately successful, but the king's greater achievement was to insist on standardization of calibre and weight of shot, with consequent valuable simplification in terms of supply and resupply of ammunition when on campaign. As so often, a really successful general would rely on simple and effective communications and means of supply, and the standardization of artillery would greatly facilitate this process. Bronze was the material of choice when casting artillery pieces, although iron guns were also produced, but these were less robust and had an alarming tendency to burst during sustained firing, to the obvious hazard of the gun crews. However, being cheaper, iron guns could be produced in greater numbers so that, even when due allowance was made for the concerns of the gunners, the employment of iron pieces was often seen as the most cost-effective option.[3]

Types of ammunition similarly fell into three main categories: solid shot, explosive shell and canister shot (charmingly, but incongruously, known as 'partridge shot' to the British). Solid, or round, shot was the commonly recognized cannonball, which achieved its destructive effect by simple physical power, smashing and rending whatever it touched on impact. Round-shot was usually used against formed bodies of troops, opposing batteries, and in siege warfare to breach walls and defences. Ricochet fire, developed by the French engineer Marshal Vauban, was increasingly employed, using reduced charges of powder (with a consequent welcome saving in expenditure of munitions and wear on the gun barrels), with the shot fired at a low trajectory to skip and bound along the ground or over the defensive works. The kinetic effect was surprisingly long lasting, and instances of soldiers seeing round-shot rolling along and playfully trying to stop them with the foot, incurring broken and mangled limbs as a result, were common. Ricochet fire, however, had certain limitations, as modern fortresses of intricate design had few long straight lines along which a round-shot could bound.

Explosive shells were hollowed-out round-shot filled with gunpowder and ignited by an inserted fuse, set to explode either on impact or in the flight as a kind of early airburst munition. These projectiles were commonly used in howitzers, pieces that fired at a higher trajectory than cannon, and also in mortars. The principal use of explosive shell was in siege operations, with the intention that the shell should land and settle at the base of the fortifications before exploding, collapsing the masonry and earth from below. In this way, a practicable breach, easy and wide enough for a soldier to mount with both hands on his musket, could be achieved at least expenditure of powder and shot. To batter away at fortifications with round-shot, by comparison, might simply compact the damaged defences rather than collapse them to create a breach. The calculation of the correct length of fuse for an explosive shell was, of course, a fine one, with an inevitable element of trial and error, although experienced gunners were adept at assessing just what would be most effective in prevailing circumstances. Fuses would occasionally act prematurely, to the peril of the gun crew, or it might go out while in flight or on landing: 'A bomb fell among the officers of Colonel Hale's Regiment without doing any harm, the fuze being stifled, two more fell in the meadow near our Guards, with the same success.'[4]

Canister shot consisted of a bag or tin of musket balls which, when fired from a field piece would spray out like a giant shotgun (hence the sporting reference to partridge shot). This was a close-quarter weapon, effective principally against cavalry and infantry in the open, and could be used with devastating consequences, particularly against close-packed formations of troops. This type of shot could also be employed, with surprisingly good effect, against light obstacles such as sharpened hedges of stakes known as abattis, and defensive palisades and barricades made from doors, carts and furniture in close-quarter battle in villages and farms. During the Battle of Blenheim, near to the village of Oberglau, Colonel Holcroft Blood's efficient handling of a battery firing canister shot defeated a sharp French counter-attack which might have split apart Marlborough and Eugene's armies at a crucial moment. The use of grape-shot in battle is often commented on, but this was really canister, as grapeshot was a naval munition using the same shotgun principle for effect against sails and rigging, and, of course, to clear an opponent's quarter-deck with brutal effectiveness.

Mortars, like howitzers, are high-angle weapons, and were employed in Marlborough's day only in positional and siege warfare. They were simple pieces – 'devilish, murdering, mischief-making engines ... the destruction they make where they fall is prodigeous,' according to John Evelyn – and very effective in searching into dead ground and engaging opposing troops who were sheltering behind fortifications and buildings.[5] Mortars were also useful in bombarding and setting light to buildings in a besieged town, to induce the civilian population to demand an early submission from the governor. This notably occurred at Liège in 1702, Huy the following year and Ostend in 1706, when a fierce bombardment both by Marlborough's gunners and the warships of the Royal Navy lying offshore caused considerable destruction. Explosive shell, or 'bombs', was the munition commonly fired, although heated round-shot was also used to set buildings alight. 'Orders were given for all the cannon to begin to fire this morning at break of day,' the duke wrote during the siege of Ghent in 1708, 'and the mortars and fire-balls at 10 o'clock.'[6] Smaller mortars, known as 'perriers' were also used, projecting showers of fist-sized stones which could inflict appalling casualties on defending troops caught in the open. Although seeming to be a crude technique, the stones fired in this way could be deadly, sometimes penetrating even hard-packed earth to a depth of 6 inches and more, and were said to 'flay' the ground in the target area.

The range at which these artillery pieces operated is often the subject of debate. Trajectories were in general flat, and the most extreme range that could be achieved was at an elevation of the barrel from the horizontal of some 45 degrees. No gunner would blindly fire expensive ammunition away into the hazy distance with no real means of observing the effect at the receiving end. To do so would quickly exhaust the supply of muni-tions, wear out the guns, each one of which was an expensive investment in armaments, and probably produce no good results, to the concern and inevitable wrath of commanders. Gun crews, in effect, had to fire over open sights, and indirect fire was not really practised, other than with the cruelly effective high-angle mortars and stone-throwing perriers. Unless there was some large and unmistakable target, such as a fortress or major building, there was usually no way of observing the fall of shot except at quite close range, and the expensive powder and projectile would otherwise probably have been wasted as a result. 'The effect of a high rate of fire is largely vitiated unless shot and shell are accurately aimed and capable of achieving a good range.'[7] It was also likely that the spent round-shot (being the most commonly used projectile) would be gratefully added to the stock of ammunition of the opponent, who would not neglect to gather up these valuable items once they had come to rest. This simple fact was noted, and taken advantage of, by the Duke of Marlborough, when he adopted a defensive position at Ennetières with his covering army during the siege of Lille in September 1708. The French could not manoeuvre him out of position and were reluctant to make a frontal attack, so in their frustration they began a bombardment. This failed to induce Marlborough to either retire or move out and attack, but the spent round-shot thus secured was promptly sent by the duke to feed his own hungry breaching batteries facing the city.

The ready supply and resupply of ammunition, always bulky and potentially dangerous, was a difficult consideration – any lack in this regard would, of course, render the guns useless. The routine for this necessity, set down by William III in the 1690s, was that once the gun-line had been established at a suitable point of the battlefield, each gun would have a ready-use supply of thirty rounds. The wagons containing the ammunition, vulnerable targets at the best of times, would move with the horse teams to a forward or 'brigade' artillery park sited at a convenient but relatively safe distance to the rear. A detachment of infantry, initially the fusiliers, would be detailed to guard this park. A main artillery park, with the reserve ammunition, would be established in the rear area of the army once deployed, and by dispersal in this way the danger of an accidental explosion, or one caused by enemy fire, was lessened.[8]

The value of well-directed artillery fire in preparing for an assault on an enemy position, whether this was during a formal siege or on the field of battle, cannot be doubted. Colonel Jean-Martin de la Colonie, a French officer in the Bavarian service, remembered Holcroft Blood's bombardment that began the Allied assault on his entrenched position across the Schellenberg hill on 2 July 1704:

> The enemy's battery opened fire upon us, and raked us through and through. They concentrated their fire upon us, and with their first

discharge carried off Count de la Bastide, the lieutenant of my own company with whom at the moment I was speaking, and twelve grenadiers, who fell side by side in the ranks, so that my coat was covered with brains and blood. So accurate was the fire that each discharge stretched some of my men on the ground. I suffered agonies at seeing those brave fellows perish without a chance of defending themselves, but it was absolutely necessary that they should not move from their post.[9]

Steadiness under fire was always a prime military quality, and calmness under such circumstances as de la Colonie describes was, of course, required not only from the soldiers in the ranks. The officers too, high and low, were expected to do their bit, and Johan Wigand van Goor, an officer much valued by Marlborough, had been amongst the first to go down on the shot-torn slopes of the hill. The duke's troops deployed into the open of the plain of Höchstädt a few weeks later were exposed to a French artillery bombardment, while Prince Eugene struggled to get his regiments into position to be ready to make a combined attack. The duke had his men lie down, both to rest under the warm August sunshine and to obtain some measure of cover from the French fire. At one point on that fateful morning, a French round-shot struck the ground under Marlborough's horse, covering both rider and steed with dust. The duke looked around as if in mild surprise, casually wiped some dust from his laced coat, and gave calm orders for the better arranging of his troops ready for the assault. The men would have seen all this, as the duke knew they would, and appreciated with a certain grim humour the sang-froid of their commander who shared the danger.

Two years later, the Dutch Colonel Wertmuller used light and mobile 2-pounder pieces, firing canister-shot, to good effect during his advance on the French-held hamlets of Franquenay and Taviers. Still, the crews working these valuable pieces in such close proximity to their opponents (in this case, veteran Swiss troops) must have been in their turn vulnerable to well-directed musketry, which can have done little to add to their accuracy or rate of fire. Despite this inconvenience, the support Wertmuller received from these light guns was significant, and his determined assault on the two hamlets by his Dutch guards and dismounted dragoons, driving out the Swiss troops at bayonet point, was a key factor in enabling Marlborough to edge his cavalry around the disordered and open right flank of the French army and on to complete victory that day at Ramillies.

We can turn again to the gallant Colonel de la Colonie, who with his Bavarian grenadiers watched the fierce bombardment of the French positions in and around in the woods at Malplaquet in the autumn of 1709. 'The Allies', he wrote:

> Placed batteries of artillery which opened fire on every point, but especially on the Household Cavalry, and as we were exactly in front of these, many shots intended for them constantly carried off someone in our brigade ... At break of day, the battery of thirty cannons opened fire, and by its continuous volleys succeeded in breaching the entrenchments in the woods on our left.

The damage wrought on the carefully prepared French breastworks was severe, and the troops they sheltered were under the merciless lash of the Allied guns, The colonel then got to the crucial point, alluding to the ability, at times, to move guns around a battlefield when necessary, for the Marquis de St Hilaire, the French gunnery commander on the field, was an exponent of aggressive artillery tactics:

> They came on at a slow pace, and by seven o'clock had arrived in line with the battery threatening our centre. As soon as this dense column appeared [French] fourteen guns were promptly brought up in front of our brigade almost in line with the Regiment de Garde Francaises. The fire of this battery was terrific, and hardly a shot missed its mark. I could not help noticing the officer in command, who although he seemed to be elderly was nevertheless so active that in giving his orders there was no cessation of action anywhere, the cannon shot poured forth without a break, plunging into the enemy's infantry and carried off whole ranks at a time.[10]

De la Colonie then repeats the oft-quoted, but erroneous, assertion that the Allied troops had been encouraged with strong liquor: 'a success that owed as much to being drunk with brandy as to martial ardour.' This does his opponents less than justice, especially as the supposedly elite Gardes Français took themselves off the field of battle shortly afterwards to avoid the Allied bombardment – 'Some of our best dressed troops did not think it proper to hold their ground ... They, therefore, made off to a safer quarter' – there was evidently no suggestion that the Gardes had been tippling to any great degree before they left. They might have behaved better for having taken a dram or two, in circumstances where, by virtue of the devastating abilities of the Allied gunners, the bombardment they faced was little short of appalling, smashing and flattening the makeshift French breastworks. This was what artillery could do, and such was the destruction by artillery properly used, that to 'wake the witch with the guns' was often to unleash devastation on a shocking scale. That very same day in September, the concealed French battery sited at Bleiron Farm, under the immediate command of Armand de St Hilaire, achieved much of the destruction wrought in the ranks of the Dutch infantry in their attack on the French right. These guns were firing in enfilade across the front of the French defences, and taking the Dutch infantry in the flank, with each shot able to career on down the line with awful effect, knocking men over like nine-pins.

A French officer wrote, 'A numerous artillery is necessary for forming great enterprises, for attacking a foe with advantage, and for facilitating the defence.'[11] True, perhaps, and the value of artillery was seldom questioned, but the advantages gained had to be weighed against the resources necessary to haul the heavy pieces around the countryside while on campaign, slow moving, and often vulnerable to enemy interference. The pace at which an army could move – theoretically light on its feet where the Horse and Foot were concerned – was reduced markedly by the trains of artillery. Due to their relative immobility, with light gun carriages yet to be fully developed as the century progressed, notwithstanding the Swedish experiment with leather-bound guns, the generally accepted practice for the tactical employment of artillery during the War of the Spanish Succession was for a commander, once his army was committed to fight at a certain place and time, to haul his guns into as good a position as possible and fight them from there throughout the action. If things went well, then fine, although an advance might well mean that the gunners lost their clear field of fire; if the day went wrong, the likelihood was that the artillery pieces would be lost to the victorious opponent. As trophies of war, guns were the most potent prizes to display, almost more significant than regimental colours and subsequently Napoleonic Eagles, demonstrating undeniable victory on the ground, on the one hand, and ignoble defeat on the other. As a consequence, to lose a gun, or guns, was close to the ultimate failure for a devoted gun crew. Such were the fortunes of war, and Marshal Tallard's guns were all lost to Marlborough at Blenheim, as was Marshal Villeroi's artillery at Ramillies. This latter haul of booty was diminished somewhat when the enterprising French governor of nearby Namur sent out teams of men and horses to recover some of the abandoned pieces, left behind as they were by the Allied army as it surged on in pursuit of the beaten French and Bavarians.

The common practice for 'field' guns to be employed in open battle stemmed from their being relatively light and able to be brought to the scene and employed without extraordinary effort.[12] Still, that Whit Sunday in 1706, as Marlborough's army squared up to Marshal Villeroi's troops along the Ramillies–Offuz ridgeline, the duke had thirty 24-pounder guns dragged by oxen teams into position on the highest point of the plateau of Jandrenouille just to the east of the Petite Gheete stream, from which they could batter his opponents around the village before commencing the attack. These were very heavy pieces, really intended for siege work and requiring massive amounts of effort, powder and shot to operate properly; it says a great deal for the efficient organization of the Allied army that they were so well forward on the line of march, and thus could be brought forward in good time across country roads made muddy with recent rain.[13]

Depending upon the energy of a commander, guns could at times be moved around a battlefield once fighting had commenced, despite their bulk and weight; although this was regarded as unusual, it was certainly not unknown. Marlborough had guns hauled over the muddy Nebel stream at Blenheim, and during Prince Eugene's assault on the French entrenchments in the Bois de Sars at Malplaquet, six guns, with their ammunition, were dragged by hand through the tangled undergrowth of those woods, so that he could engage the French cavalry on the open plain to the rear of the battlefield. Later that day, as Marshal Boufflers withdrew his valiant but battered troops from the field to take shelter behind the defensive lines at Valenciennes, Armand de St Hilaire managed to get most of his guns away as the tired Allied army advanced across the shot-torn field. Even so, thirty-five French pieces had to be left behind, mostly those in the earthwork redans in the centre and in the woods to the left where the heavy fighting had left much of their army in some disarray. This loss signifies defeat, but the redoubtable marquis's success in getting the guns on the right off the field under considerable pressure indicates very well once again that artillery could be moved with some rapidity when necessary. Not all the equipment, munitions and stores would be saved, but it was the guns – like the colours, so often seen as symbols of success and failure – that counted, and many of those were got away. Large, cumbersome, valuable and potentially vulnerable, the guns were, with their capability to destroy, dominate and disrupt, nonetheless essential tools of war for an army commander, and had to be cherished as such. Marlborough wrote to William Cadogan from the camp outside Lille on 2 August 1708, with clear concern on hearing that the Marquis de

Caraman's French cavalry squadrons were on the road: 'We have advice here that the enemy has taken post with a considerable detachment upon the Dender ... I doubt not but you are informed of it, and will take all the necessary precautions for the safety of the artillery.'[14]

The movement of large numbers of guns and their associated wagons and equipment, was a monumental task, fraught with risk, as can be discerned from Marlborough's concern expressed to his quartermaster-general. The guns in question were needed to begin the siege of Lille, and their capture or significant damage in a French raid would probably entail the failure of the duke's campaign that year. The great convoy bringing the guns forward from Brussels consisted of 3,000 wagons loaded with munitions and materiel of all sorts, needed to serve the accompanying 154 large guns and mortars of the siege train. No fewer than 16,000 horse, mules, oxen and donkeys were used as the draught animals for this huge enterprise, and once underway the ponderous column covered all of 15 miles of road. The French commanders dithered, each apparently expecting the other to move first, and as a result the convoy came through to Menin on 12 August without suffering the loss of a single gun, cart or animal, and all reached the main Allied camp five days later. The duke wrote to Sidney Godolphin in London, 'You will know by this post that our cannon is arrived safely at Menin, and that I have reinforced Prince Eugene's army with thirty-one battalions and thirty-four squadrons ... This day Lille is invested.'[15] This French failure to even try and interrupt the passage of the siege guns, an obvious target and key component in the campaign, was a major tactical blunder, and openly recognized as such. One of their officers wrote, 'It is an indisputable truth. Never was a daring enterprise so conducted with more skill.'[16]

Chapter 7

The Engineers

Of a sudden, the enemy sprung a mine.[1]

Marlborough's war was, as much as anything, an engineer's war. This may at first glance seem to be strange, given his sparkling successes in the open on the field of battle, successes on which his reputation as a great commander understandably rests. However, all commanders rely upon their engineers to ensure an army's continued mobility, while hindering an opponent's capability in that same regard. In addition, the duke's long campaigns in 1702 and 1703, and those between 1709 and 1711, were unavoidably concentrated on the conduct of siege warfare. After such a succession of defeats at the duke's hands, the French army commanders were understandably anxious to avoid meeting him in open field, if they could possibly do so – failure had made them and their king cautious, and they acted accordingly, placing their faith in fixed defences. In this, they were wise, for by the end of 1708 their armies were exhausted, and in any case an active defence conducted properly is no craven or passive thing; if the balance of probabilities is that more will be achieved by operating in that way, then the conclusion and resulting course of action will be obvious. So, to consider properly the achievements of Marlborough's army in the widest context, it is necessary to look at the activities of his engineers in those two key areas – mobility and siege warfare.

The urgent demands for a commander of maintaining an army's mobility – and its closely associated shadow, counter-mobility – are as old as warfare itself. The relative difficulty in movement for field armies in Marlborough's day, dependent as they were upon poor unmetalled roads that swirled with choking dust in dry weather and were muddy tracks when it rained, limited the capability of large numbers of troops with all their gear to manoeuvre freely and effectively.[2] In addition, rivers, canals and marshes always posed a difficulty, and the ability of an army to cross them without undue delay was an important asset, depending almost entirely upon the skills of the engineers. Bridges were few and far between, and had often been broken down by an opponent. As a consequence, the role of the military engineer was one of particular value and importance, even though it was still regarded as relatively inferior when compared to the more dashing exploits of the Horse, and to a lesser degree, the Foot and the gunners.[3]

There was no formal corps of engineers in Marlborough's army. The Surveyor-General, answering to the Master-General of the Ordnance (who, by happy coincidence, was the duke himself), was responsible for all the affairs of appointing and maintaining engineer officers. The annual stipend for this task in 1702 was the formidable sum of £500. The Surveyor-General also had the services of a principal engineer (annual stipend £300), who had charge of preparing plans and scale models of fortresses that might be attacked, sooner or later, and was expected to be skilled in mathematics (the implication being that most officers at the time were not so skilled). Under the principal engineer were a second engineer (£250 stipend) and third engineer (£150), and in time of war these posts were usually filled by the selection of serving officers, although it was recognized that civilians could be equally expert in military engineering, and their active employment on operations was not unknown. Further down the scale would be junior officers who were interested in, and skilled at, the intricacies of military engineering and siege warfare, and together with clerks and workmen these formed the framework upon which the engineering services developed, in time, to become the Corps of Royal Engineers. More junior officers would serve with the engineer trains which accompanied the army, and in particular had to maintain mobility across water obstacles by the employment of pontoon bridges.

The Flanders Train of 1702 contained a pontoon company intended for the ease of movement for the artillery; the forty 17-foot 'tin boats' were sheathed with tin or copper to prevent rot and damage, and mounted on wagons drawn by horses (or sometimes oxen), which could be brought forward at surprising speed. The bridging company comprised about eighty personnel trained in the particular task, in addition to the civilian drivers for the wagons, together with some 240 horses (assuming a realistic fit of six horses to each wagon). On the march, this impressive and vital assembly would probably take up over half a mile of road, and its protection from enemy interference was of high importance. The loss of the Bavarian pontoon train after the Schellenberg fight in 1704, and that of Marshal Villeroi's pontoons in the dramatic disaster at Ramillies, were seen amongst other misfortunes for France as particularly heavy blows – the resulting loss of mobility could not easily be made good.

In order to get the pontoons into position, some bold soul would always have to swim or wade the stream, marsh or river to start with, and take across an initial line from which all else followed. The boats would be moored across the width of the obstacle, facing into the current and securely anchored in position by means of attachment to a strong cross-cable stretching from one bank to another. Baulks of timber would then be placed across the boats, one to another, to provide a firm platform, and on

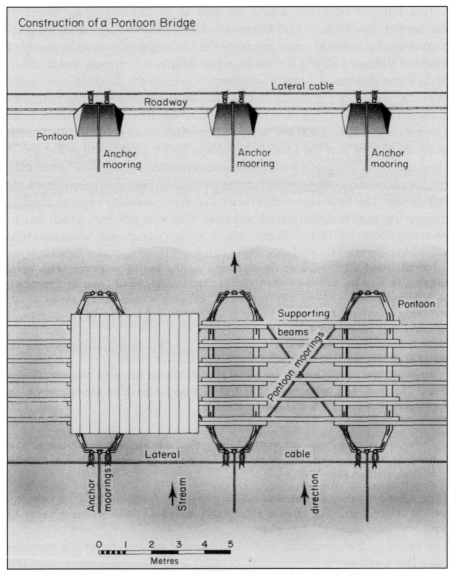

Pontoon bridges: the essential means of providing mobility for an army on campaign.

top of that additional timber sections of pre-prepared plank pathway would be laid. That this was speedily accomplished by both Allied and French armies on numerous occasions, often under pressure and in poor weather, speaks highly for the skills of these specialist troops. The marching soldiers having moved on, the pontoon bridge could be lifted up and carted forward, unless the rear echelons of the army had yet to pass over.

This kind of operation could be seen to particularly good effect at Elixheim in July 1705. Veldt-Marshal Overkirk's Dutch corps used the pontoon train of the Allied army to bridge the Mehaigne stream as he decoyed Marshal Villeroi away to the south, while Marlborough marched north to breach the defensive Lines of Brabant. Three years later, in the hectic opening phases of the Battle of Oudenarde, the pontoon bridges accompanied William Cadogan's advanced guard on their forced march from Lessines on the Dender River to reach the Scheldt and confront the French army. Not only was the Duc de Vendôme sceptical that the Allies could close up to his army so quickly and unexpectedly, but he was apparently (and inexcusably) unconcerned at the efficient bridging capabilities of his opponents. The false sense of security that this gave may explain to some degree the poorly coordinated response that was offered, which led to such a humiliating French defeat. Marlborough's engineers were also sent ahead to construct two temporary wooden bridges in Oudenarde itself, to give better access across the river to the approaching army. One of these bridges laid in the town gave way under the tramp of hundreds of marching feet during the escalating action, delaying the Allied advance; it was inevitable that, despite the best of intentions, things did not always go to plan. Overkirk's delayed arrival that day is at least in part due to the congestion in the narrow streets of the town of large numbers of troops. The mobility given by the judicious use of the pontoons can also be seen later in the 1708 campaign, as the duke moved to reopen the lines of supply which had been disrupted by Vendôme:

> This march was so secret that the French had no notice of the allies directing towards the Scheldt, though they had received advice of their crossing the Lys. The Count of Lottum, on the 17th October, about four in the morning, arrived with the vanguard near to Harlebeck, and instantly laid two bridges, led over his troops, and drew up in order of battle.[4]

The speed of the operation, and the achieving of such complete surprise over the unsuspecting French is evident, and illustrates very well the value that the 'tin boats' conferred on a commander.

The classic skills of the military engineer – to provide mobility for one's own commander by pontoon bridging or building or repairing roads and bridges, and to deny mobility to an opponent by tearing down those same structures – would always be important. A campaigning army that could manoeuvre relatively freely was a living thing, vital and agile, and able through its own strength and resources to strike at an opponent, or conversely to avoid being struck in return. On the other hand, to deny mobility to an enemy by breaking down bridges, obstructing roads and flooding fields, could impose a deadening drag on their ability to operate to good effect. While enduring the toils of French defeat in the summer of 1706, Marshal Vauban would consider breaching the sluices around Nieuport to slow the triumphant Allied advance, and the Duc de Vendôme would do just that two years later in an abortive attempt to halt the Allied siege of Lille.[5] The flooding of the region delayed the siege operations to a limited degree. The supplies were brought through to the Allied army all the same, but at the cost of considerable additional effort, having to come on wagons that had been fitted with oversize wheels to keep their cargoes out of the water. Vendôme even conducted a kind of naval warfare, with heavily armed galleys prowling the flooded fields in an effort, eventually unsuccessful, to interrupt the flow of supplies southwards from Ostend.

For any army commander, the state of most roads meant that the good campaigning months each year really lasted only from late April to early October. At the best of times progress along these highways of the long convoys of hundreds of wagons bringing the mass of supplies, munitions and provisions necessary to maintain a major army in the field was a difficult and time-consuming business, fraught with problems and constant danger of enemy interception. Once the bad weather set in, those roads would become muddy tracks, with the effective movement of large numbers of troops, horses and wagons all but impossible. The waterways of the Low Countries, the numerous canals and navigable rivers, were a major asset in this respect, making the business of supply and resupply faster and simpler, and in consequence command of those waterways – either by holding the fortresses that dominated them, or having control of the sluice gates that regulated the water levels – was of significant military importance. The seizure of Ghent and Bruges after the victory at Ramillies had given the Allies the use of the extensive network of waterways in northern Flanders, greatly simplifying things for Marlborough. Once the duke had recovered the initiative in 1708, he did express his concern that the frozen state of those waterways would impede the resupply of his army as he fought to regain the two towns in the closing days of the year. The essential value of the waterways, and the manner in which they enabled army commanders to operate effectively, was demonstrated in one of the few serious military reverses that the duke suffered. During the siege of Aire in September 1710, French cavalry under the Marquis de Ravignan surprised and seized a convoy of forty boats and barges carrying supplies along the river Lys to the Allied troops in the trenches before the fortress. The 1,200-strong guard, commanded by Frederick Ginkel, Second Earl of Athlone, was routed by the French and the convoy put to the torch. Peter Drake, once more in Allied service, thought that the whole affair was badly mismanaged and could have been avoided:

> The General, having, as it is said, got timely intelligence at dinner, of the French being out to intercept him, might, if his orders would have permitted, have stayed there … perhaps that step might have incurred the Duke's displeasure, and therefore it was thought better to march on.[6]

On receiving the news of the destruction of the precious convoy at St Eloi-Vive and damaging losses inflicted on the escort, Marlborough wrote to London, 'I have sent to our neighbouring garrisons to know what supply of powder and ball they can afford us, and I hope this misfortune, which is the first that has happened to us during the whole course of the war, will not disappoint our sieges.'[7] The massive explosions of the ammunition barges wrecked nearby cottages, and even diverted the course of the Lys for a time, requiring laborious effort to put it right, and reopen the key waterway. Lieutenant Colonel John Blackader remembered that, on getting word of what had taken place:

> We went out in the afternoon, with the few men that could be spared, to try if we could give any help, but when we came within half an hour of the place, we were informed that the convoy was beat, and they were burning and blowing up the ships. This is a very great loss, and great affront. Next day we went out to view the field of battle, and saw a melancholy sight of near 200 men lying drowned on the river side. There seems to have been mismanagement and bad behaviour in this affair.[8]

Despite the setback, the lost supplies were promptly made good and the French governor of Aire, the very capable Marquis de Goesbriand, soon afterwards submitted to avoid a storm once his defences were breached. It had been quite a struggle, however, in filthy weather, and the operation was remembered as one of the toughest sieges that Marlborough's long-suffering army undertook.

The siege train of an army on campaign was formed for that particular purpose under the direction of the commanding general, and was, accordingly, not a permanent body. Suitable officers were selected for the role and appointed on a quite separate basis from the Board of Ordnance. Colonel Holcroft Blood commanded the Blenheim Train in 1704, although he was a gunnery officer. There was no contradiction there, as the 'train' in the wider sense would be required both to provide mobility and to batter into submission any fortress that stood inconveniently in the way; Blood went on to command a regiment of infantry between 1705 and 1707. There grew a feeling, all the same, that special engineer officers, responsible for such important tasks on campaign, should not be 'double-hatted' in this way, but regarded as just that, specialists. This eventually came about, but not while Marlborough was in command of the army. In practice, military engineers operated at two distinct levels when on campaign: the senior officers would be chosen to accompany the army commander, ready at hand to receive broad instructions on what was to be gained and, with their skills and experience, to offer particular advice on ways and means to achieve the aim. Once a formal siege operation had been decided on, a director of trenches would be appointed from amongst these senior officers. His activities would always be subordinate to the instructions of the commander, of course, and were usually at their best when closely supervised in practice. This did not always happen as it should, as could be seen in the early stages of the siege of Lille, which went badly, with the engineers fumbling in their task, until Prince Eugene was wounded and Marlborough took a closer interest in the proceedings. On the other hand, it was the emphatic advice offered to Marlborough in 1711 by his Chief of Engineers, Colonel John Armstrong, that he should press on with the siege of Bouchain, which led to notable success when others urged the duke to abandon the whole enterprise as Marshal Villars' army was so close by.

With sieges such a key element in warfare at the time, it is perhaps the role of the military engineer in these testing operations that most catches and holds the attention. With the use of artillery and subterranean mining as viable means of breaching formal defences, many otherwise strong towns and fortresses had been laid open to attack. The response of military engineers was to develop artillery-proof fortifications, low in profile and sharply sloped backwards to absorb and deflect the impact of artillery fire and negate, to a degree, the effectiveness of mining intended to cause a collapse of high buildings from below. Often these sharply sloped defensive works would be of no grander material than packed earth and grassy turf, although eventually most would be faced with stone and brick.

These fortresses were of the most modern and formidable innovative design, and as a result the ability of an invading army commander to manoeuvre at will was limited. Often an otherwise promising campaign had to concentrate on reducing these places by means of the formal siege. Any such operation was an enormous undertaking, requiring considerable effort and expense, as well as practical and administrative skill, and was not at all considered to be a side-show. Many a good campaign, and many a good military reputation, was built upon the successful prosecution of siege warfare to secure important fortresses such as these, with all the advantages that such a success would bring in terms of prestige, position, security and tax-gathering opportunities in the region – and the concurrent denial of those same advantages to an opponent. That many, if not all, of those same places would be returned to their original owners at the eventual conclusion of peace was not relevant, as they were always valuable bargaining counters with which to wring the best possible result from the negotiations.

The frontier regions of France were studded with fortified places, courtesy of the almost inexhaustible energy of Marshal Vauban, in such notable places of particular interest to the Duke of Marlborough as Landau in Alsace, Lille, Bethune, Douai, Aire sur la Lys and Bouchain in northern France, and Dendermonde, Menin, Ath, Ostend, Tournai and Mons in the Southern Netherlands. The strong defended belt along France's north-eastern border (a border that had yet to take final shape) gave French field commanders the opportunity to manoeuvre in and around the relative safety of those fortresses. The vast expense laid out by Louis XIV's Treasury to construct these defences (he once complained of Vauban's intention to level an entire hill during the reconstruction of Ath) paid handsome dividends in the end, at a time of greatest need for France. This was not how Marlborough wanted to operate, for he had a keen understanding of the demanding requirements and time-consuming nature of siege warfare, but he had to fight the French, not when and where he chose, but when and where he could get them to stand and do so. If that was in defence of some important fortified place, then that was how it had to be. His last great martial success, the capture of Bouchain in the summer of 1711, would feature in no fewer than three of the great tapestries in Blenheim Palace, indicating very well the duke's own appreciation of what had been achieved at that occasion. In addition, a remarkably fine portrait of the duke seen in discussion over the plans of Bouchain with Colonel John Armstrong was regarded by the Duchess Sarah as the best likeness ever made of her husband.

The army commander oversaw the siege operations, of course – his would be the glory of success when the happy moment for capitulation came – but the practical undertaking, subject to his approval, of siege operations fell to the engineers who had to arrange the layout of the siege entrenchments,. The most vulnerable part of the fortress and the angle of attack would have to be assessed and agreed with the army commander, as would the timetable for the operation, and arrangements for the bringing forward from rear areas of the vast quantity of materiel – the gathering of stores, munitions, tools and labourers – necessary for the siege to get underway. How this was to be achieved was a major and demanding task, as enemy interference was to be expected and could only be countered with careful management. The indifferent state of the roads would also always bedevil any commander who wished to move swiftly. Amongst the many tasks that came the way of the engineers, therefore, was to provide mobility yet again, with the repair and maintenance of the route to be used, filling in holes, strengthening the country bridges and draining particularly muddy or marshy stretches. To accomplish this kind of labouring work, mundane but essential, the small company of pioneers who accompanied the train of an army would be augmented with drafts of men taken from their units to wield a spade or mattock, and local peasants would often be impressed – with a mixture of inducements ranging from offers of payment to threats of violence for non-compliance – to take part. The remarkable achievement was that, for all the difficulties and hazards, the movement of large amounts of stores and equipment generally did make good time. In any case, whatever inconveniences were encountered by an army commander were probably just the same as those experienced by his opponent away across the fields somewhere, so the odds were, to a degree, fairly even.

The engineer officers had the specialist duty to prepare the plans for the siege for the army commander's approval, but it was the common soldiers who did most of the labouring work, together with conscripted peasants and civilian labourers who had not been nimble enough to avoid service. They were led in this task by the relatively few specialist sappers; these hard-bitten men knew their hazardous craft and would often wear armour on the head and shoulders to protect against musket shot from the watchful garrison in a fortress. The defenders were on the alert to try and

pick off such specialists, who were always few in number and therefore any casualty would be a sore loss. The army commander would still
have to ensure the continued supply of the siege trenches in good time
over a prolonged period, across roads exposed to enemy raiding, and in
sufficient quantities for the siege work to progress satisfactorily. While
preparing for the siege of Lille late in July 1708, Marlborough had a
convoy of wagons, laden with every kind of munitions and stores and
dragged by 8,000 horses, oxen and mules, brought forward from Brussels
to the camp before the fortress. The duke was unable to take full advantage of the many waterways in the region as the French, even after their
defeat at Oudenarde earlier that month, managed to hold onto the more
important parts of the canals and rivers around Ghent and Bruges to the
north. An even greater convoy followed on 6 August, this time some
15 miles long, and Marlborough wrote to London, 'Our greatest difficulty
of bringing our heavy train of artillery to Brussels is almost over.'[9] For a
variety of reasons, some good and some simply feeble, the French commanders found themselves unable to intercept these huge and invitingly
vulnerable targets while they were on the road and in the process missed
what can only be regarded as a golden opportunity to cripple the duke's
campaign.

Amongst the many activities of Marshal Vauban's long career, he had
set out a model timetable for the conduct of a formal siege of a modern fortress. Assuming that the besieging force was properly trained, equipped
and organized, it was assessed by the masterful French military engineer
that forty-eight days should be sufficient to force a submission from the
garrison, giving a couple of days spare to cater for the unexpected. The aim
was, it should be noted, to force a submission on negotiated terms, not to
carry a place by storm at the first opportunity. Such rash enterprises
almost always involved heavy casualties amongst both the defending
garrison and the besieging troops, and in all likelihood also amongst the
unfortunate civilian population, who would be laid open to sack and
plunder once the fortress was taken. As a result, rash and premature
attacks were discouraged, however much bravery and gallantry might be
displayed by those undertaking them. The measured pace of a formal
siege, for which there were generally well-known and respected rules –
an attempt to introduce a degree of humanity in a fairly inhumane business – was accordingly a common feature of campaigning.

A formal siege had a certain set of procedures to be adopted, if success
was to be had in a timely fashion. Both the opposing commanders would
be well aware of what these procedures were, and approximately when

they would be undertaken, so that a kind of ritual was played out, with the besieging commander getting his troops and stores in place for each successive phase, and his opponent doing what he could to frustrate and delay those preparations. There were also a number of formal niceties to be observed, and at one siege in the late seventeenth century the commander of the Spanish garrison asked to be told where Louis XIV had his quarters, so that his artillerymen should be aware of this, and not disturb the king by firing at the building. The prompt and very neat response was that Louis XIV would be found wherever his soldiers might be, and so the garrison commander did not need to worry himself on that score. Arrangements might also be made to reduce the risk to civilians, and Marshal Boufflers was permitted by Prince Eugene to evacuate a number of the more prominent families from the city of Lille in August 1708, not only reducing the chance of them coming to harm, but conveniently reducing the numbers of hungry mouths in the besieged city that would have to be catered for by the French commander.

Such a measured pace did not indicate, however, that these siege operations were easy, simple or without risk – far from it. The necessity to gain a conclusion to a campaign, in the few short months of fine weather that permitted ease of movement, drove army commanders to demand results, and even Marlborough, who was noted for his concern regarding the welfare of his men, attempted bold and inadequately prepared attacks on occasions. At the same time, any competent garrison commander would be relied on to do his utmost to resist for as long as possible, thereby shackling the campaign of his opponent. The defenders in effect forced battle on ground of their own choosing – always an important military consideration – and imposed delay and inflicted casualties in exchange for whatever was gained. All approaches to a fortress should, ideally, have been kept clear of cover and be able to be swept with fire, and a besieging army would have to inch its way forward using trenches known as saps (from which the term 'sapper' is derived) and under almost constant fire from the garrison. The high water table in the Southern Netherlands meant that it was often not possible to dig down very far, and so the saps would have to be built up on the side exposed to the fortress with gabions, stout and bullet-proof wicker baskets filled with earth that could be hauled into place and then covered with the soil dug up out of the adjacent shallow trench. Casualties amongst those working in the trenches would be frequent, that was the nature of the job, and encouragement for the work to go on at a good pace took various forms, such as bounty money being paid to volunteers for the hazards involved, and ample drink supplied. However, the loss of these skilled men was always regretted, even though 'Sappers often intoxicate themselves at the sap-head, and are then slaughtered like beasts ... There is no safe place in a trench.'[10]

Donald McBane of the Royal Scots wrote of the preparations made to force the pace of a siege and try and bring about a swift conclusion to what might, in other circumstances, have been a rather protracted affair. Early in the war, the commander of the besieged garrison at Liège was thought to be prevaricating too much in the negotiations for a submission to the besieging Allied army:

> About three o'clock in the afternoon the Duke of Marlborough came to the Grand Battery; he commanded twenty grenadiers of each company through the whole army, and ten battalions of the first troops to storm the fort sword in hand, our orders were to give no quarter to none within the fort; we made all ready for the attack, every grenadier had three grenades; our Word was 'God be foremost'; when we came, we came with a loud hurrah, and fired [threw] our grenades amongst them, and small shot without number; we continued this for an hour and a half; then we jumped over the palisades, we then made use of our swords and bayonets, and made a sore slaughter amongst the French, which obliged them to cry for Quarter ... We had mercy upon our fellow creatures and turned them all behind us.[11]

The almost throw-away comment about taking prisoners, contrary to orders, is instructive and indicates a humane understanding between soldiers, and of the strain of campaign life shared by men on both sides over. An opponent who had fought well deserved to not be just butchered.

Sorties by the garrison would be mounted to kill the engineers, sappers and workmen and spoil the trenches; Richard Pope, serving with Schomberg's Horse, remembered that, at Landau late in 1704, the garrison:

> Made a great sally, in which we had twenty-six men killed and wounded. They did no damage to the works, being soon repulsed with much greater loss on their side ... last night the enemy made a great fire from the town, but with very little effect, for we lost but two men.[12]

At Douai, six years later, the French garrison were enterprising enough to come out of their defences and seize some cattle and drive them back into the fortress to supplement their fast-diminishing rations. John Deane recalled that later in the campaign, 'The garrison of Aire sallied out and did beat our men from the trenches for a while at a sore rate, and was very near taking a battery of our guns which they had designed to have nailed up ... A great many men were killed on both sides.'[13] At the siege of Bethune, the Marquis de Puy-Vauban, the great engineer's nephew, wrote of the effects of a sortie: 'A terrible carnage followed. All this was done with audacity and in splendid style, which gave a good example to the rest [of the garrison].'[14]

The ingenious complexity of any fortress constructed to the classic design of the Trace Italienne subtly changed the shape of armies. Firstly, these places had to be adequately garrisoned, otherwise they would be militarily useless piles and liable to be taken with ease. As a result, large numbers of troops were devoted to static defence duties – a necessary and useful, but rather limited, form of military employment. The numbers available for field armies, manoeuvring for position, advantage and eventually outright victory were lessened as a consequence. Given that such a formal defensive barrier was a sound strategic option, to tie troops up in garrison duties was, in fact, unavoidable. However, the Duc de Vendôme found that he had to strip fortresses of their garrisons to rebuild the field army after Ramillies, and Marshal Berwick was aghast to find that most French troops were safely sheltering, almost cowering, in garrisons in the aftermath of the defeat at Oudenarde two years later: 'I went post to Tournai, to have a clearer view of the situation of things. There, I found a great number of straggling parties of the army ... the frontier was entirely destitute of troops.'[15]

The adverse effect of having too many troops in the wrong place can be clearly seen in the case of the bitterly fought siege of Tournai in 1709, when Marlborough used a ruse to trick the French army commander, Marshal Villars, into drawing troops out of that garrison to augment the strength of the field army between Douai and the Lys. Villars then found when it was too late that Tournai was actually the duke's intended target and that Prince Eugene was marching hard to invest the fortress. The French commander had been on the horns of an acute dilemma: if he maintained stout garrisons in all the valuable fortresses that might or might not attract Marlborough's keen attention, then his field army had insufficient strength to operate effectively. By failing to man his fortresses properly he would negate their worth, but if he provided them with enough troops he would risk having to take on a general action in the open with only with a slim chance of success. Villars could not be strong

everywhere, and had he tried to be so, he would have been weak everywhere, and so he had made his choice accordingly, and was intent on
covering the approaches to Ypres. It was the wrong choice, as was soon
clear, and Tournai was invested by Eugene almost immediately the
garrison had been reduced to augment the army, the Allies making good
use of the Lys to move their heavy batteries quickly and open the bombardment of the fortress. To go on campaign was always to take part in a
fast and ever-changing scene, with the balance of probabilities having to be
weighed constantly and choices made to fit; on this occasion the French
army commander badly misjudged things. That the garrison in Tournai
then held out for a very creditable time, inflicting heavy casualties upon
the besiegers says much for the inherent strength of the place, the skill
of the commander, the Marquis de Surville-Hautfois, and the robustness
of the few remaining troops at his disposal. By early September, Tournai
fell to Marlborough and Eugene, after hard and harrowing fighting both
above and below ground, and that was the immediate Allied aim –
another significant erosion of the protection afforded to the French by
their elaborate fortress belt. However, Marshal Villars had not yet been
drawn out into the open to fight to save the place, which was what had
been hoped for, and the chance of a resounding double success – the
seizure of the fortress and the simultaneous defeat of the French field
army – remained elusive.

Such a happy occasion would have to wait, but the loss of such a
fortress as Tournai was not insignificant, and Louis XIV, despite bluster-
ing that the Allied commanders were clearly reduced to a slow grinding
campaign with limited objectives, was quite well aware that, if unchecked,
the Allies would continue to bite their way through the fortress belt, one
place at a time, and eventually Marlborough and Eugene would emerge
into the open fields of northern France. Once there, a battle could not
be avoided, in perhaps the most adverse circumstances. Better to fight
while the fortress belt, to a certain degree, was still intact. Instructions
came to Villars from Versailles that this could not go on, and that Mons,
understood to be the next selected target for Marlborough and Eugene,
was to be saved, no matter the cost. The result was the bloody clash at
Malplaquet, where despite all their valour the French proved unable to
halt the Allied campaign to take Mons, which fell six weeks after the battle.

The very complexity and strength of these modern fortresses demanded
a consequent mighty effort to conduct a formal siege and force a timely
submission from the garrison. The demands on the supply of such an

operation have been mentioned, but the sheer numbers of men required to labour in the siege works, to man the siege batteries and to take part in eventually attacking the outworks, and then move on to assault the main defences when that fateful moment had come, were prodigious. Furthermore, no siege was likely to go unchallenged for long, and any besieging force had two principal and pressing tasks – the first most obviously was to invest and attack the fortress, while the other was to shield those same operations from enemy interference from outside:

> It is best to be stronger, and to have two armies whenever one can: that is to say one which besieges and one which observes. The siege army shuts itself off in its lines, as we shall later show; the army of observation simply covers and occupies the routes by which the enemy may arrive, or takes outlying positions. These two armies must always keep within range of one another, especially in the initial stages, in order to offer mutual support and keep the enemy at a distance.[16]

A bold and active commander, however, would not be closely bound by such caution, as can be seen in 1708 when the Duke of Marlborough manoeuvred freely and aggressively to keep the more numerous, but temporarily demoralized, French army away from the siege works in front of Lille. 'Our troops are in good heart,' he wrote, 'and their Foot are in a bad condition.'[17] That aggressive campaigner, the Duc de Vendôme, then moved to hold the line of the Scheldt River, manning all the main crossing points except at Allied-held Oudenarde in order to disrupt the lines of supply and communication from southern Holland. In response, Marlborough left a scratch force in the trenches to keep an eye on the garrison, while he thrust northwards with almost his whole force to break the French grip on the river line. A simultaneous attempt by the Elector of Bavaria to seize Brussels failed in the face of robust defence by the small Allied garrison there. Marlborough could soon return to Lille to continue the siege, with hardly a beat having been missed in the campaign. At Mons the next year, so confident were the Allied commanders of their superiority over the French, both in numbers and morale, that they did not put their troops to the trouble of constructing the usual lines of circumvallation and contravallation, relying instead on screening and manoeuvre for protection.

Warfare is an inherently uncertain business, and the efforts of Marlborough's engineers in the preparations for the siege of Lille were faulty.

Prince Eugene fired the first shot on 25 August, but although some 120 guns, twenty howitzers, and forty large mortars were in action, it was soon found that the breaching batteries were poorly sited, unable to dominate the guns of the garrison and at too great a distance for proper observation of the fall of shot. Notwithstanding this, the chief engineers with the Allied army, Colonel du Mey and Colonel des Rogues, were confident of early success, with Marlborough writing to London two days later, 'Our engineers promise that we shall have the town in ten days after which we must attack the citadel.'[18] Well, ten days came and went and there was no sign that the town would be taken any time soon, and meanwhile the French field army approached – rather cautiously, it must be said – in an effort to lift the siege. Marlborough had put his own covering army into a strong defensive position between the Deule and Marque rivers and defied Vendôme to attack, which, after a fierce but ineffective bombardment, the French commander eventually decided not to do. This was prudent; with the morale of the French soldiers still fragile after their battering at Oudenarde, the risks were clearly deemed to be too great. Marlborough's nephew, Marshal Berwick, who for the time being still accompanied the army, wrote to the French minister for war that:

> With an infantry already rebuffed and with battalions under strength, we should risk not only a repulse, but even total overthrow thereafter. It is sad to see Lille taken, but it would be even more sad to lose the only army which now remains to us or which can stop the enemy after the fall of Lille.[19]

Such French caution was fortunate for the Allied forces, as the siege operations were, in fact, limping along at an uncertain rate, although a breach was slowly beginning to be made in the north-eastern side of the fortifications. There had clearly been an element of over-confidence in the Allied camp, but all might yet be well, despite an uncertain start, and Marlborough wrote on 30 August:

> This night the Prince of Savoy designs to open the trenches, which I hope he will do with good success. Hitherto the French have not made any motion to disturb us, and cannot do it now with the same advantage they might five or six days ago, since we are at liberty to draw off a considerable strength from the siege to reinforce our army.[20]

On 7 September 1708 an attempt was made to storm the glacis adjacent to the gates of St Andrew and St Magdelane. This was premature, and resulted in an expensive and bloody failure – the artillery in the fortress had not yet been properly suppressed, and *fougasse* defensive mines were blown by the garrison into the faces of the attacking troops. A second attempt met with no more success, and on 20 September Prince Eugene was wounded and concussed while leading a third fruitless assault. The stiffened brim of his hat took the force of the shot, and he soon recovered, but Marlborough was obliged in the meantime to turn his attention from commanding the covering army to the day-to-day siege operations in the trenches. To his dismay, he found that these were poorly laid out and the stores were in many cases faulty, rotten or missing, presumably stolen. The stocks of powder for the breaching batteries, in particular, were lower than he had expected, putting at risk the ability to press forward with the bombardment in any effective way.

Although the chief engineers were undoubtedly at fault, it seemed that they were overworked, overwhelmed by the scale of the siege operations and too distracted to curtail incompetence and theft, rather than being corrupt themselves. The duke wrote to a friend:

> It is impossible for me to express the uneasiness I suffer for the ill-conduct of our engineers at the siege where I think everything goes wrong. It would be a cruel thing, if after all we have obliged the enemy to quit all thoughts of relieving the place by force, which they have done by re-passing the Scheldt, we should fail of taking it by the ignorance of our engineers, and for the want of stores.[21]

The siege of the most important city and fortress in northern France, and a cherished prize of Louis XIV when he was a young man on campaign, proved to be a severe test for Marlborough and his army, and elderly Veldt-Marshal Overkirk died from his exertions during the operations. A valiant defence was put up by the 16,000-strong garrison under the command of the veteran Marshal Boufflers; John Millner of the Royal Irish Regiment recalled: 'It was said that the Marshal said, that if the Allies must needs take Lille before they [the French] had left it, then they must gain it inch by inch; and, indeed, we may safely say that he in a manner was as good as his word.'[22]

All major fortresses had at their heart a strongly built citadel in addition to the formal defences of the town itself. Such prominent structures can be readily identified from the plans and scale models of such places as Lille and Tournai. To breach the defences of the town was an achievement in itself, the result of enormous and well-conducted effort with breaching batteries and mining. This was, however, almost always a rather limited achievement. The garrison commander would be most unlikely to hold out to the last extremity and risk a storm of the defences 'sword in hand'. At an appropriate moment, when the breach in the defences became practicable – wide and easy enough for a soldier to mount unaided with both hands on his musket – the prudent commander would offer to yield up the town, before withdrawing with his surviving troops into the citadel to continue the struggle from there.

Boufflers gave up the town of Lille on 25 October, but the eventual capitulation of the citadel only took place early in December, a submission that the French commander, at the limit of his resources, had no way to avoid, short of risking a bloody storm and sack by the Allies. The king wrote to his old friend with warm words of thanks and praise: 'I cannot sufficiently praise your vigour, and the pertinacity of the troops under your command ... I have every reason to be satisfied.'[23] The simple fact was that while so much had been gained that summer with the daring victory for Marlborough at Oudenarde, the whole promising campaign had then been dragged to a halt by the prolonged siege of the city, an undeniably epic undertaking that took over four precious months to complete. Rarely has the power of a well-directed, and courageous, defence to influence a wider campaign been seen to better effect.

An even sterner test awaited Marlborough and his troops at the siege of Tournai in the summer of 1709 which demonstrated in unmistakable fashion that they lacked the skill and experience of their French opponents in the dark art of subterranean mining and counter-mining. One of Marlborough's commanders, Count von Schulemburg, wrote, 'This is a siege quite different from any hitherto; the most embarrassing thing is that few officers even among the engineers have any exact knowledge of this kind of underground work, and even less of the way of attacking them.'[24] Casualties on both sides were very heavy, as the opposing miners broke into each other's galleries and fought and grappled together in the mud and claustrophobic murk deep beneath the entrenchments. John Wilson wrote of his distaste for this kind of combat:

> Of all the horrid schemes of war, this of bringing of mines and sapping to find out the same was the most doubtful, for it was of great reluctance that even the boldest men in the Army then on this service have turned their backs and given way. Nay, even those who had seen death in all its shapes above ground was shook with horror to stand (as he supposed) on the top of a mine in danger of being

blown up every minute. And those who went underground into the saps had a co-equal reluctance, if not more, they being in danger every minute either of being suffocated or buried.[25]

On 29 July 1709, with the good campaigning weeks of summer speeding remorselessly by, the Duke of Marlborough wrote in some frustration to Queen Anne:

The governor of Tournay having yesterday in the evening hung out a white flag and desired to capitulate for the town, hostages were thereupon exchanged on both sides; but it being very late before those from the town arrived at our quarters we deferred entering upon the treaty for the surrender till this morning. We are now going to assemble in order to settle the articles [of the capitulation]; in the mean time I thought it my duty to lose no time in acquainting Y.M. with this good news by express, and hope it may not be long before it is followed by that of the surrender of the citadel.[26]

The duke's optimism was misplaced, and the French garrison commander, the Marquis de de Surville-Hautfois, maintained a stout and valiant defence of the citadel, inflicting heavy losses on Marlborough's troops. Marlborough wrote from the siege lines on 12 August 1709:

We are obliged to carry on our attack on the citadel with great caution, to preserve our men from the enemy's mines of which they have already sprung several with little effect. Our miners have discovered one of their galleries at each attack, but dare not advance to make the proper use of this discovery because of the enemy's continual fire of small shot under ground. We are preparing to roll bombs into these galleries in order to dislodge them.

The effect of counter-mining in slowing the progress of a siege was evident, as the duke wrote three days later: 'We find that by reason of the enemy's mines they go on with much more caution than were to be wished, so that I am apprehensive we shall not be masters of the place as soon as was expected.' Again, on 22 August he wrote:

Yesterday a new battery of fifteen mortars began to fire at [from] M. Schuylembourg's attack. Our miners had the good fortune to discover a mine under this battery, out of which they took eighteen barrels of powder, the enemy deferring to spring it till we should begin to fire.[27]

The work had been arduous, grim and bloodily expensive, and John Blackader of the Cameronians, when writing to his wife, remembered that:

> The progress of the besiegers was much retarded by being obliged to adopt the slow and laborious method of sapping; the enemy having wrought all the ground into mines, which rendered it unsafe to approach from the hazard of explosion. Every step they took was under the apprehension of being blown into the air. Hostilities were carried out chiefly under ground, and in total darkness.[28]

The garrison had done their level best, and the conduct of the French troops in defence was commendable, reaching out towards the besieger's entrenchments to slow and harass the progress of their work with explosive mining, or in hand-to-hand combat, by breaking into the underground chambers where the miners worked, and where pistol, dagger and a smartly wielded sharpened spade were most effective. Their ingenuity was such that a mine might be discovered, and made safe, only for the Allied soldiers to find that another, deeper, device had been laid beneath, ready to be detonated once enough curious soldiers had gathered on the spot to see what was going on.

> In the night, between the 16th and 17th [August], there happened a long and fierce combat in the mines, which ended at last in favour of the besiegers. On the 20th M. De Surville caused a wall to be blown up which hung over a sap, and thereby smothered a captain, a lieutenant, thirty soldiers and five miners.[29]

Such ambuscades were made easier by the common practice, at least in fortresses of Vauban's innovative design and construction, of building subterranean chambers into the defences. The locations of these secret voids would, of course, be unknown to the attackers, and so adequate measures to counter them would be difficult, and the apprehension amongst the soldiers labouring in the saps would be that much the greater. The defending garrison, with time aplenty to pack the chambers with explosives and wait for the most propitious moment for detonation, could watch with gleeful anticipation as the besiegers crept with such enormous effort towards the fateful devices. The redoubtable Kit Davies recalled that, at Tournai, 'Our engagements were more terrible than in the field, being sometimes near suffocated with the smoke of straw which the French fired to drive us out; and the fighting with pickaxes and spades, in my opinion, was more dangerous than with swords.'[30] Grim work indeed, with little opportunity in the darkness for dash, gallantry and chances of recognition, and it was here and in such circumstances that the grit and mettle of an army would be tested to the full. Aware of the nervousness amongst their soldiers at this kind of warfare, both Marlborough and Eugene made frequent visits to the trenches to inspect the progress and, by example, to try and hearten the men.

The defence, stout as it proved to be, was overcome and the Tournai citadel was given up by de Surville-Hautfois in early September, although Marshal Villars would have preferred that he resisted longer. To secure such a place was undoubtedly a major military achievement, commensurate with the enormous expense and effort required in the undertaking. Still, the main purpose of any fortress was to hold up an opponent's progress and impose as much of a drag on his freedom of action as possible. The garrison commander, no passive participant in such an affair, would be fighting on ground of his own choosing, prepared long in advance with every conceivable advantage bestowed on the defenders, ready for just such a day. It is only fair to say, of course, that even with all such advantages, it was known that any fortress would fall if enough time, resources, effort and energy were devoted to the task by the besiegers. The effort necessary was prodigious, and the achievement of the Duke of Marlborough and his commanders in capturing so many of Vauban's elaborately designed fortresses between 1706 and 1711 must attract the attention and admiration that such repeated success demands. These things took time to accomplish, however, and – unlike his opponents – that was the one thing that the duke did not have in abundance.

Made cautious by defeat in open battle, the French commanders had for some time adopted a very careful strategy of shielding their army behind extensive lines of defence. These works comprised earthen redans, fortified farmhouses and hamlets, and flooded meadows where rivers and canals did not already provide such an obstacle. Marlborough had overcome such defences in July 1705, when he broke through the Lines of Brabant, and after the grim campaign of siege warfare in 1710 he did so once again the following year. He once again tricked Marshal Villars, decoying him away to the west before deftly getting his own advanced guard across the defences at Arleux, with a bare hour to spare, and going on to seize the fortress of Bouchain in 'a virtuoso exhibition of his mature genius'.[31] The engineering effort that the French put into the preparation of these defended lines, however, had paid handsome dividends, for on numerous occasions Marlborough found his plans frustrated by not being able to come to close grips with his opponents. That was just what was intended, and such a strategy was no indication of a lack of French resolve, for Louis XIV and his generals understood very well the advantages of playing a waiting game, while the time available for Marlborough to force a battle and win a decisive victory crushing enough to win the war for the Grand Alliance was limited. This became more so as the duke's political support in London faded away, something of which the French king was, as we have seen, very well informed.

Chapter 8

Logistics

No-one ever heard of a quartermaster in history.[1]

The fighting troops in any army on campaign were always only the sharp point of a large and complex operation that kept it in the field, for behind the teeming field of battle or the trenches of a siege there stood many hundreds of wagons and carts laden with supplies to sustain whatever was being attempted. It remains an odd fact, though, that while most readers of military history will avidly want to know who stuck a bayonet in someone, or at whom the slash of a cavalry sabre or thrust of a lance was directed, relatively few will be as interested in just how those men got to that part of the field at the right time and in good order with all their kit, or how they were provided with a hearty and sustaining breakfast and an encouraging tot of rum or gin that morning. This is perhaps not that surprising, as the cut and thrust of combat on the field of battle naturally excites attention and admiration. However, good logistics – reliable and coordinated provision of supplies – has always been essential for the effective maintenance of an army on campaign, and where this is lacking so too in equal measure is diminished the effectiveness of that army. Valiant soldiers whose exploits catch and hold the attention so well would have been nothing without the diligent efforts of those who ensured that food was provided, sore feet had good shoes and ball cartridges were in the pouch ready for use. Furthermore, soldiers who are not regularly paid seldom maintain good discipline for long, and become an unreliable mob. In 1704 the French army under Marshal Tallard struggled through the Black Forest, and the logistical arrangements for this operation were far from perfect, the troops having to scavenge their food on the march. The result was that they were not in the best or freshest condition when they reached their destination in southern Germany. The march of the Duke of Marlborough's army that same summer, though, was a model of good planning and sound logistics, and the difference in the way in which these operations should and should not be undertaken could not have been more stark.

To send an army to war it is plainly necessary that the resources to fight and succeed are put at the disposal of the commander, as a prerequisite to entering upon a campaign. Any significant lack in this respect would be viewed as scandalous, and wasteful of the energy and lives of good soldiers. In early 1702, however, when England declared war on France and the French claimant to the Spanish throne, Parliament in London authorized the raising of troops for the purpose, but it did not at the same moment take the trouble to set in place the measures by which those men should be supplied and maintained. For all armies involved, supply would in varying degrees be a lasting problem, and David Chandler wrote, 'The powers failed to rise to the challenge they set for themselves; they never proved capable of solving the basic problem of supplying the armies effectively while in the field.'[2] National wealth, and the vigour of rulers, could recruit and impress large numbers of troops to take the field, but the arrangements to sustain those superficially impressive forces was ill-formed, intermittent and sometimes lacking altogether, and, when they were in place, not that effective. The threadbare state of Prince Eugene's Imperial Austrian troops in Italy early on in the war has already been mentioned, and some of Marshal Villars' officers would sell their coats to provide food for their men in the calamitous summer for France of 1709. In part, such problems were caused by a lack of foresight and planning, not least because money was often not available (or was withheld) to purchase the necessary quantities of materiel and supplies. Funds to pay for war were voted on an annual basis, both in England and Holland, a system that provided a check on what might otherwise have become overly powerful and ambitious commanders, as well as restating the over-riding power of the politicians who held the purse strings.

The supply of any army out on campaign has always been an enormous and never-ending undertaking, and in 1708 at the height of the campaign to seize Lille, Marlborough wrote to the Earl of Stair, whose troops were on a foraging expedition, that 'All our happiness depends upon your getting a good quantity of corn.'[3] The sheer scale of the stores, provisions, munitions, fodder and materiel involved in sustaining an active campaign was staggering. A glimpse into this can be seen in the duke's almost casual reference in a letter written later in that year when, after forcing a passage over the line of the French-held Scheldt River, and in so doing lifting the blockade of his own army in the siege trenches, he commented that he had ordered a fresh supply of gunpowder to be sent forward, as soon as possible, to replenish the breaching batteries before the citadel:

> I have this minute received a letter from Prince Eugene, writ last night, that he hopes by Thursday to have all his batteries ready, and

then he will summon the Marshal and at the same time let him know that he [Boufflers] may send an officer to see our cannon and ammunition ... The 1,000 barrels of powder I send to Lille are this morning come out of Ath and will be with the Prince on Wednesday night.[4]

The duke was clearly taking care to make proper arrangements for his army's continued siege operations, an approach that appears to be simple common sense and application to the task at hand. All was not so straightforward, however, as this was still an age when armies were to a large degree expected to live off the land across which they operated, and to share the resources of the much-put-upon populace, who would routinely, and repeatedly, see their crops, herds and horses seized by whatever needy soldiers came their way.

That armies on campaign were unpopular and rarely welcomed was inevitable. Even Marlborough, who took pains to warn his soldiers against looting and pillaging, and whose commissaries had the money necessary to pay for supplies (unlike their French opponents), was for many years burned in effigy in some Flemish villages in retribution for the past depredations of his troops. 'You never saw so wretched a country,' Francis Hare wrote in 1705, 'there is not a soul to be seen in the villages, the peasants flying as we came, either into places of defence or to the woods.'[5] Foraging by small groups of soldiers – 'partizans' as they were known – was common, with these activities sometimes resembling private enterprises, and the booty gathered being sold by those taking part to quartermasters and sutlers. Donald McBane wrote, 'I got thirty men that was willing to be at my command, so we went to the Duke of Marlborough's Secretary and got a warrant to go partizanning; that night we went out very quietly to try what we could make.'[6] The rascally grenadier and his band accosted a party of French who were acting as escort to a baggage train and brought in their booty, together with sixteen prisoners and their horses. Their opponents would as a matter of course attempt the same kind of enterprise, as John Millner recalled that, during the march to the Danube, 'We that day took a party of forty French, which had been lurking by the roadside in a scrub, from the garrison of Trarbach, in order to catch some of our stragglers.'[7] To live off the land in this way was precarious, as illustrated by Marshal Tallard's struggle to feed his troops on his march to the Danube, while soldiers on both sides had to take care not to stray too far and alone from their encampments. As John Deane so graphically described in 1710, locals would sometimes act with great barbarity against those who brought such distress and want for the

•

common people, who, as often as not, had no real stake or interest in whatever desirable but distant cause was being fought for.

Assuming that rulers and politicians would acknowledge that their armies had to be properly provided for, the first great obstacle to overcome was that of adequate transport. Such matters were far from simple, as movement along the poor roads of the early eighteenth century, or on the waterways of the region campaigned over, were always subject to interception and interference by an opponent's cavalry raiders. Marlborough's correspondence during the protracted siege of Lille reflects this concern again and again. Movement over the high seas – for the duke the important link across the Channel to southern England – was dependent upon wind and wave and could be slow and hazardous, and prey to enemy commerce raiding. The aggressive French privateers, operating out of such places as Dunkirk and heirs to the tradition and practices of Jean Bart, were a particular problem. Such was the difficulty that the demolition of the defences and installations of that particular port were made a part of the eventual peace agreement that brought the war to an end.

Long experience of fighting wars with the French had taught the Dutch the necessity of good logistics, and in this respect the commissaries employed by the States-General were more adept and better organized than their English allies. The victories in battle were Marlborough's, but the essential logistics of his army lay in the experienced hands of his Dutch allies for much of the war:

> The army of the United Provinces [of Holland] became one of the best supplied in 17th Century Europe, and the system of relying on contractors worked so well that it was retained, with some modifications and additions into the early 18th Century. It was Dutch contractors who supplied the Allied British army throughout the Nine Years War and the War of the Spanish Succession, and provided the logistical basis for Marlborough's victories.[8]

A prime factor in all this was finance and the ability to purchase those supplies without having to seize or confiscate them by force. The financial capability of the British and Dutch in this respect must be regarded as one more essential tools of the war, although when operating in enemy territory, as in Bavaria in 1704 and in northern France after Oudenarde, less scrupulous attention had to be given to this aspect, and the duke's cavalry raided and pillaged the outskirts of Arras as early as the autumn of 1708.

In Queen Anne's army, the administration fell into two categories: the Army General Headquarters in Whitehall, under the control of the commander-in-chief (the Captain-General), which attended to the Horse and the Foot, and the Board of Ordnance under the Master-General of the Ordnance, controlling the activities of the artillery, the engineers and munitions. By good fortune, and courtesy of his close friendship with the queen, Marlborough was both Captain-General and Master-General of the Ordnance between 1702 and 1711, and this ensured that the two organizations worked well together during the crucial years of the war. Boards of commissioners for both the supply and transport functions tended to the provisioning and movement of stores on campaign, and again, the duke's influence was enough to ensure that they worked well. It would only be fair to say, however, that Marlborough's attention was fixed firmly on his own campaign in the Low Countries and, briefly, in southern Germany, and operations in other theatres of war such as Spain and Portugal did not receive the same close care and attention, to the detriment both of the Allied cause and the welfare of the troops campaigning there. The Duke of Argyll's problems, when appointed the commander in Spain, have already been recounted.

All armies would be accompanied by a field train, an essential component in pursuing an effective campaign. The train comprised specialists: a curious mix of professional soldiers, civilian experts and hired civilian workers. There was plenty of room in such arrangements for friction, professional jealousy and bickering; rank, standing and privileges were counted and disputes, both petty and significant, were commonplace. Officers were frequently 'double-hatted' and employed in more than one role at a time (for which there was a welcome increase in pay, naturally). Richard King, a Scottish officer, served at the siege of Menin in 1706 as a controller of the train, then as supervisor of rations and munitions, as an engineer in the trenches and as a gunner in command of one of the breaching batteries. This remarkable tally was all accomplished in the space of less than five short weeks and demonstrates not only the good captain's energy and range of talents, but the flexibility that was plainly expected. It was a common arrangement in Marlborough's army when in action: the demands of the service clearly had to be met. It may be assumed that King acquitted himself well in these roles, as his career prospered, but whether every officer thus employed was so adept and flexible might be questioned.[9]

To this mix of personalities and talents could be added the civilian contractors in the train, the suppliers of stores and the drivers of the hundreds of wagons and carts that accompanied an army; the boatmen who plied the waterways were no less valuable. Armies did not have wagon parks with their necessary draught animals waiting ready to transport the supplies out on the campaign trail. To move the huge quantity of stores involved, many hundreds of these equipages and teams would have to be hired locally. These civilians were recruited for the duration of a particular campaign, and in many cases they were veterans of such operations, known and trusted by commanders, experts in their chosen field, and largely able to be relied on. They were not subject to military law, the Articles of War were not read to them, and, effectively working on contract, they took full advantage of the fact. The drivers would often be the owners of the vehicles and animals concerned, and anxious to see that they did not come to harm. Whether they would be stout-hearted and reliable when things were not going well would have to be seen and occasionally, of course, pressure would be applied to keep them at their posts, possibly at bayonet point, but they were aware of their rights and of their value to the army, so it was inadvisable to trifle with civilian contractors, or use them brusquely, too much or too frequently. In the event, the simple but invaluable ability of a commander to pay regularly and well for these services would be inducement enough, and by and large the seemingly rather haphazard system appeared to work well.

For all the apparent imperfections of the system, armies composed of many thousands of troops did subsist themselves, one way or another, and campaign for months at time. The troops led by Marlborough and his commanders could cover considerable distances, at a good pace and in timely order. The most prominent and well-known example of this must surely be the renowned march to the Danube in the summer of 1704: 19,000 men set off from the Low Countries to cover almost 300 miles across country that varied from water-meadows to rocky mountain passes, and in weather that was often unseasonably bad. Food, fodder and replacement clothing and footwear was stockpiled along the route, all paid for in advance and ready for use. The marching pace was easy – exhausted soldiers would be of no use – but the distances covered were impressive, and the administration of the army on the road was of a highly regulated and efficient order. Captain Robert Parker wrote:

> As we marched through the countries of our Allies, commissaries were appointed to furnish us with all manner of necessaries for man and horse; these were brought to the ground before we arrived and the soldiers had nothing to do, but to pitch their tents, boil their

kettles, and lie down to rest. Surely never was such a march carried on with more order and regularity, and with less fatigue.[10]

The army arrived at its destination on time and in good fighting trim, attacking the Franco-Bavarians on the Schellenberg on 2 July 1704, without pausing for even a day's rest. The strategic shift accomplished by the march, and the resounding, but bloody, tactical success on the hill is often commented on, but the logistical success was of an equal, if not greater, proportion – little like it had been seen before, so it is useful to look at how it was accomplished.

First among the great assets that the duke enjoyed was his capacity for good management, careful planning and attention to detail. He also chose his servants carefully, and those officers detailed for a particular task rarely let him down. All this rested, however, on his ability to pay for supplies – the financial strength of Great Britain, and the widely held understanding that London's credit was sound, stood him in very good stead. Crucially, his financial agent, Henry Davenant, was able to ensure that funds were readily available. Gold in sufficient quantity was carried in the duke's military chest, to ensure prompt payment as necessary, and in consequence stores were put into stockpiles at regular intervals ready for the quartermasters of the marching army to draw. The troops that Marlborough set out to take up the river Rhine were accompanied by 1,700 supply carts, each capable of carrying 1,200lb of stores and altogether drawn by some 5,000 draught animals, horses and mules.[11] Additional supplies were purchased from farmers on the route and by the sutlers who accompanied the troops to sell their wares on an informal basis. Marlborough's soldiers were not reduced, as his French opponents and Imperial allies often were, to excessive foraging, forcible confiscation and downright theft and pillage in order to be fed and shod. The electors of the various regions through which Marlborough's army made its way were united in their opposition to Louis XIV and his schemes, and were assured in advance that Marlborough's troops were well disciplined and would pay for the provisions that were required. At Heidelberg, for example, the troops received new shoes, indicative of considerable forward planning – the marching had been by relatively easy stages, with frequent rests, but the distances covered were impressive and shoe leather soon wore out.

There was also the necessity to pay the troops, and once again Marlborough's access to ready funds ensured that this was never a serious problem, although the Imperial commanders Prince Eugene and the

Margrave of Baden were unable to be so sure at times, and much of the pillaging and looting that was reported to occur when their armies were on the march resulted as much as anything from the lack of cash in the pockets of the soldiers with which to obtain a few necessities or occasional comforts. Even with the generally excellent arrangements in Marlborough's army for pay for the troops, problems did occur, and his soldiers were not particularly saintly; a degree of private enterprise and pilfering was almost inevitable, although the penalties the duke pre-scribed for such offences were severe. The redoubtable female soldier, Kit Davies, also recalled an occasion when 'The Corporal having received the company's money, instead of paying it to them, lost it at play, and then desperately shot himself through the head.'[12]

The careful timetable for the march up the Rhine had been so arranged that the troops should not over-exert themselves, and supplies were avail-able at convenient points on the road, in the right quantities and at the right time. These arrangements were all admirable and attracted wide approbation, particularly from the inhabitants of the regions through which the army passed. An early start was made before dawn, with a march through the cool of the morning to the next designated bivouac site. Robert Parker's approving comments were echoed by John Millner:

> I must say that he performed that march with very good conduct, by beginning every day's march by break of day or sun-rise; so that every day, before it was extreme hot or Noon, we were fully en-camped in our new camp; so that the remaining part of the day's rest, was nigh as good as a day's halt.[13]

It is as well not to dwell too much on these fine arrangements, as, almost inevitably, things did not always go smoothly or pleasantly. John Deane of the 1st English Foot Guards wrote rather ruefully that:

> It hath rained 37 days together more or less and miserable marches. We have had for deep and dirty roads and through tedious woods and wildernesses and over vast high rocks and mountains, that it may be easily judged what our little army endured and what unusual hardship they went through.[14]

Still, some rather more cheerful soldiers were sprightly enough to notice that the German girls in the villages that they marched through were considerably prettier than had been expected.

The Margrave of Baden had given assurances that supplies would be available to Marlborough on his arrival on the Danube, but this proved not to be so, no doubt the subject of a pointed, but diplomatically polite, conversation with the normally urbane duke on the matter of 100 missing bread wagons. Also, human nature and venality being what it is, the simple knowledge that the Allied army would pay for its supplies in hard cash induced local producers to increase their prices to take best advantage of the commercial opportunity presented. John Deane recalled that 'Everything grew to be at an excessive dear rate that there was scarce living for a soldier and the nearer came every day to the Grand [Imperial] Army, the dearer everything was.' It was also to be expected that these fine arrangements would be intercepted by the French and their Bavarian allies whenever the opportunity arose, for to delay and disrupt the supplies of an opponent could bring significant advantages at every level. Deane added, 'A partizan [patrol] of the enemy fell upon some of our sutlers and plundered them, and so made off.'[15]

However proficient the logistical arrangements in the duke's army, the soldiers themselves could not be expected to behave like angels; that is not in the nature of troops when on campaign, particularly when operating in the territory of their opponents. On occasions, official policy demanded a grim and brutal form of campaigning, rather along the lines of the French habit of having their armies 'eat up a country' so that nothing could then subsist there in the following months, neither civilians nor opposing forces. It was calculated that a region capable of supporting a peacetime population of thirty-five souls per kilometre was necessary to adequately provision an army 60,000-strong operating without the benefit of fixed magazines.[16] The wants and needs of the civilians would suffer, of course, if an army was subsisting itself in an area, whether they were paying for their supplies or simply taking them by force. Relatively few regions at the time were so well populated that they could sustain, willingly or otherwise, those kinds of numbers for long. To march, manoeuvre and campaign over rough country, with few ready supplies and extended lines of communication was dangerous, if not impractical. That Marlborough did so in his march to Trier and Trarbach on the Moselle late in 1704, while attempting to drive home his success at Blenheim that summer, indicates very well his capacity for innovation and risk-taking, when the potential prize made it worth doing so.

A forced lack of provisions, destruction of shelter and imposition of want could be ruthless tools of war. After the success at the Schellenberg, in an effort to induce the Elector of Bavaria to abandon his alliance with the French, Marlborough sent his cavalry and dragoons deep into the surrounding countryside to burn, harry and destroy, an activity that was embraced with some enthusiasm by many of those who took part. Kit Davies remembered that the duke sent out 'Parties on every hand to ravage the country, who pillaged above fifty villages, burnt the houses of peasants and gentlemen, and forced the inhabitants, with what few cattle had escaped to seek refuge in the woods.'[17] On 16 July 1704 Marlborough wrote to a friend in London, 'We are now advancing into the heart of Bavaria to destroy this country, and oblige the Elector one way or the other to a compliance.'[18] Learning of criticism being voiced at the opening of such a brutal campaign, he wrote again with assurances that British troops were not being used in this way, but this was not true. For Tallard and Marsin and the Elector of Bavaria, the belief that the duke could not winter his army in a region so picked clean of supplies led them to assume that he would withdraw northwards to take advantage of stock-piles of supplies gathered in central Germany. In this they made a terrible mistake, and were in their over-confidence surprised on the plain of Höchstädt as a result.

The logistical tail of an army on campaign would be enlarged by the numbers of coaches, wagons and other equipages of the senior officers and their entourages. These commanders were men of standing and posi-tion, expected to put on some show even when out on in the field, and were well aware of what was due to them in consequence. The occasion of Marshal Tallard sitting as a captive in Marlborough's own coach after the Battle of Blenheim is well known and demonstrates very well that such vehicles would be close up behind the firing line, and could provide a very useful practical function as a kind of mobile office. This was seen when the duke issued his orders to his generals from his coach as the army began to move through the Schwenningen defile that momentous morning. On other occasions they were less useful, and the Dutch General Slangenberg – 'brave and bloody and obstinate' – insisted that his per-sonal baggage wagons should have precedence over the artillery on the road during the march to the river Yssche in August 1705. The delay that this caused was not the reason for the failure of Marlborough's plans to attack the French, but was indicative both of how such clumsy arrange-ments could be an impediment, and also how obstructive some officers could be when they chose. Marshal Villeroi neglected to have the baggage of his army cleared away from just behind his line of battle at Ramillies, and this added to the awful confusion of his troops as Marlborough's great flank attack came in late that Sunday afternoon. The humble foot soldier, trudging the roads of Flanders and Germany and casting envious eyes at officers' elegant equipages, could at times take their revenge.

During the march to Lessines in 1708, on the way to join battle at Oudenarde, the troops detailed to guard these vehicles instead tipped them into the roadside ditches, regardless of their elegant contents, to clear the way, and hurried on through the heat of the July day towards the sound of battle.

It is as well not to impose modern notions of what is acceptable onto the practices of the early eighteenth century, and at first glance it seems that the medical, surgical and dental care, both on the battlefield and in camp, was of a highly rudimentary nature in Marlborough's day. However, there was a well-developed system for medical care, even if the arrangements seem to modern eyes to have been basic. Each regiment had a surgeon and a surgeon's mate on the strength, and the skills that they deployed were often considerable, and were in any case not less than commonly enjoyed by most people at the time. The risks attendant in a soldier's life, of course, were of a higher order than for most, but few common people would have access to anything like a surgeon or physician for treatment of everyday ills and woes. The treatment provided may appear to have been coarse and to a degree brutal, and survival for the wounded on the battlefield would often depend, not just on the chance and arbitrary direction of a musket ball or sword slash, but on the wounded soldier being found by friends or well-disposed locals (and even merciful enemies, on occasion) and taken to receive assistance. James Gardiner was left for dead at Ramillies churchyard, suffering with a dreadful wound that threatened to suffocate him as his mouth and throat were congested with blood. Two French soldiers ran over, apparently hoping to gain a little loot from pillaging the fallen man, but on hearing him mutter something in Latin, they assumed Gardiner to be a Catholic, and on that score probably an ally of theirs, and so carried him to where he could receive some medical aid. The more common alternative would often be a sharp knock on the head to induce compliance while the pockets were rifled.

By and large, soldiers were and are a tough lot, and their ability to survive quite extensive wounds was remarkable. Surgeons usually did their best in adverse circumstances, but occasionally performed their duties carelessly, and James Cathcart recalled that a brother officer died through the negligence of a surgeon who was aggrieved at the poor rate of his pay.[19] Sergeant George Depp was amongst the wounded at Ramillies, with a French musket shot to the abdomen, but remarkably he lived on for another fourteen years, despite having a severely prolapsed double-barrelled colostomy.[20] Kit Davies suffered a fractured skull from a shot on the same day, and was too stunned to conceal her sex from the surgeon, and so her secret was out and she had to leave her regiment after many years masquerading as a man. The roguish Irishman 'Captain' Peter Drake, while serving with the French cavalry at Malplaquet, also had his skill fractured and the brain ('the dura matter') exposed, and the Duke of Marlborough gave instructions that he should be attended to (his main complaint, in actual fact, was that his shirt was caked with dried blood – his own and others – and having it removed from his back was like being flayed alive). With regard to Drake's injured skull, he wrote that it was difficult for him to wear a hat for some weeks afterwards, but appeared to suffer little other inconvenience. It seems that the medical and surgical attention that soldiers in the duke's day received was quite often of a surprisingly good standard, but there is a certain grim self-selection in such matters. The more severe the wound, the less likely the fallen soldier was ever to come before a surgeon or his mate for attention, and it may often have seemed to be more kind to end the suffering of a stricken man on the spot with the blow of a musket butt, or simply to shrug the shoulder and move on from an apparently hopeless case. Donald McBane received one of several wounds during a hard-fought siege when taking up a grenade that proved to be both ready primed and faulty. The exploding munition:

> Killed several about me, and blew me over the palisades, burnt my clothes about me. Carried into a house, that the surgeon might dress our wounds, when he saw me he said 'It was needless to apply any things to me, for before morning I would be dead.'[21]

The grenadier was tougher than the surgeon thought; he lived for many years despite his wounds being treated with salted onion juice, and survived long enough to see his scurrilous and highly entertaining memoirs published twenty-six years later.

Despite such heartening instances of surprising longevity, the care and attention provided to the wounded and sick in the duke's army, and the other armies of the period, can only be described as basic, mixed with a fair degree of well-meaning but off-hand improvisation. After the severe fighting for the Schellenberg hill in July 1704, when the advanced guard of the Allied army suffered more than 5,000 casualties in one short brutal evening, the sheer scale of the numbers of wounded lying all over the slopes and requiring attention (not including the hundreds of vanquished Bavarian and French soldiers, who were apparently left to their fate) overwhelmed the local arrangements. Certainly the regimental surgeons and their mates could achieve little in the heavy rain that followed the battle, and so transport was arranged to take the stricken men over 20 miles northwards to the walled town of Nordlingen, where makeshift arrangements had been set up by John Hudson, Marlborough's Commissioner for Hospitals. The duke, anticipating the heavy fighting to come on the hill, had written on 1 July to Hudson that he should 'Hasten away to Nordlingen and to march day and night till he had settled with it [the supplies of the hospital] there.'[22]

The 'widows' of the army – a euphemism for the female camp followers, whether properly married or enjoying a rather more informal relationship with the soldiers – who had gone with their menfolk on campaign to southern Germany, were now ordered to go to Nordlingen and provide what nursing care they could. That there were so many women who could be classed as 'widows' indicates the scale of the loss on the hill that day. Samuel Noyes noted also that not only had just one-third of his fellow chaplains been present with their regiments at the Schellenberg, but none at all had thought it necessary to accompany the wounded to Nordlingen. He went on to recall the suffering of Lieutenant Colonel William Palmer, who was shot through the body while commanding Lumley's Horse during the attack:

> Whether mortal or not I cannot say, I found him up with his clothes on, to my great surprise. I asked him how he did. He told me he was full of pain, for the ball was still in ... He was very uneasy 'til his bed was made, that he might lay down ... The bullet was not found, when the surgeon was last with him.[23]

Two weeks later, Noyes could write, 'There was a report in the camp that Colonel Palmer was dead, but ... they have found the ball and taken it out, and he was recovering very fast and past all manner of danger.' Despite this good news, less than a week later Noyes noted, 'That very day, about four in the afternoon, the Colonel died. He swooned away as his wounds were dressing and never came to himself again.'

Perhaps not relishing the rigours of the bone-jarring journey to Nordlingen, several wounded officers had insisted on staying in lodgings in Donauwörth to receive treatment. Those wounded men who survived their ordeal, if they had become incapable of rejoining their regiments and soldiering on, had to be transported back to their home country; stricken soldiers could not just be abandoned, that was not the duke's way, and in any case sentiment in the army would not permit this – morale in the ranks would suffer, and questions would undoubtedly be asked in London. Donald McBane remembered that after the victory at Blenheim:

> The wounded men at Hochstadt, lay up and down the fields, with a guard to look over us, until they got wagons to carry us to a town called Marelykin in Swapperland [Swabia] ... a grand hospital was there but very scarce of Surgeons; there was four thousand men. I had some money wherewith I employed a Surgeon for myself.[24]

In this respect, at least, Marlborough's troops were better served than those in the Imperial armies, where such humane arrangements were noticeably lacking. Early in 1705 John Hudson, as Commissioner for Hospitals, was allowed the seemingly lavish sum of £9,360 for the medicines, necessaries and transport of sick and convalescent men by way of the rivers Rhine and Meuse, as part of the clearing-up of the previous year's campaign in Germany.

The fate of the wounded men of a beaten army was inevitably less happy, as they were likely to receive little or no attention or care from the victors. Looters and plunderers, whether in uniform or not, would scour any battlefield as soon as possible once the action was over, although, as James Gardiner had found in Ramillies churchyard, these scavengers often did not wait for the firing to cease before coming forward to see what could be had. A soldier's comrades were not always sympathetic or helpful. 'The Dutch of our Army', Donald McBane remembered as he lay waiting to be helped after Blenheim, 'came a plundering, and stripped me of all except my shirt.'[25] However, five years later, after the murderous battle at Malplaquet, the Duke set guards on the strewn battlefield to prevent plundering, and sent William Cadogan under flag of truce to find Marshal Boufflers and ask that he send wagons back to collect and take away the hundreds of French wounded that were lying everywhere in the woods and could not be tended to.

Whatever care was available to wounded and injured soldiers, warfare is an inescapably risky business, and a man whose wound might at first glance seem to be slight, could see it fester and worsen rapidly, at a time when infection control and the practice of good hygiene was imperfectly understood. The smashing effect of a musket ball or – no less deadly – a canister shot would also carry into the wound cavity dirty clothing from the soldier's torn coat and shirt, taking infection deep into the body. There was little that could be done in such cases: probing for a ball by a surgeon was time consuming (and therefore often not undertaken), agonizing and often unsuccessful. The wound, accordingly, would simply be closed up and perhaps stitched up, and the best hoped for.

Once her sex had been discovered, the resolute Irish-woman Kit Davies continued with the army until the end of the war, marrying more than once and running one of the small sutler's tents that provided welcome comforts for the soldiers. She proved herself to be just as determined and enterprising in this role as when she had stood or ridden in the ranks, and at Malplaquet in 1709 she remembered:

> I entered the wood with small beer for my husband; though the shot and bark of trees flew thicker than my reader, if he has not seen action, can well imagine; not a few pieces of the latter fell upon my neck, and gave me no small uneasiness by getting down my stays. My dog at the entrance to the wood, howled in a pitiful manner, which surprised me as it was unusual. A man near me, who was easing nature, said 'Poor creature, he would fain tell you his master is dead' ... I ran among the dead ... before I found my husband's body.[26]

However, her trials continued, as she had to recount that her next man, Richard Wells, was wounded in the thigh by a French musket ball during the siege of the small fortress of St Venant in 1710. 'His comrades carried him to the trench, where Mr White, the surgeon, who searched and dressed the wound, said it was but slight, but the next day finding the bone broken judged it to be mortal.' Wells was taken to a hospital in Lille, but, 'My husband grew daily worse, had his wound laid open [presumably lanced to drain away the pus], but at length it turned to mortification and in ten weeks after he received it, carried him off.'[27]

At a time when even a simple fracture of a limb could cause infection and gangrene, amputation was often the necessary recourse for surgeons when dealing with soldiers coming off the battlefield with shattered arms and legs. Some surprisingly serious wounds were survived, and amputation was commonly the way to avoid infection, gangrene and a certain slow death, although at the risk of the patient succumbing to shock and loss of blood. The development of effective anaesthetics was far in the future, but a degree of welcome delirium might be induced with a good tot of rum or gin, then as the patient was held down by assistants and friends, it was down to the surgeon with his knife and saw, all too often blunted with much use, to get the job done as quickly and as well as could be. Speed was thought to be important to avoid gangrene – 'mortification' – of the limb. Dr J. White wrote, 'Where amputations are required they succeed ten to one better if the operation is performed immediately after the misfortune, than four or five days after. This all our surgeons in the army know very well.'[28] The procedure for amputation was simple and gruesome: 'Bind the part two inches above the place which is to be cut off ... with a sharp razor or dismembering knife made for that purpose being somewhat crooked, cut the flesh round to the very bone ... then with your saw take away the bone.'[29] Such apparently rudimentary methods would remain commonplace as part of a soldier's lot for another 150 years or so, and the merciful introduction of anaesthetic would come even more slowly. Stoicism amongst the patients on such an occasion was a necessary quality, and was often displayed. Although the limb did not have to go when Marshal Villars was shot in the knee at Malplaquet, the French surgeons' efforts to find and remove the musket ball proved unsuccessful, despite the most agonizing probing. Villars lived on for many years, semi-crippled, with his mangled leg held fast in an iron brace (depictions of the marshal leading a charge on foot over the Allied defences at Denain in 1712 can only be regarded as fanciful).

Wounds suffered on the field of battle were not the only concern, for sickness and everyday accidents also took their toll, and the men suffering these required attention if they were to hope to take up their place in the ranks once more. Marlborough wrote to his general of infantry, his younger brother, Charles Churchill, on 22 June 1704 during the long march to the Danube, requiring him to leave behind sufficient wagons to transport the 1,200 sick and injured men (sprained ankles being very common) who had to be brought on over the rocky passes of the Swabian Jura after the main body of the army had marched through. An army on campaign is a living thing, not just a collection of armed men, and it is as well to remember the valuable service provided by the camp followers – in many cases the women who, very often with their children, accompanied their men to war, and who were able to provide day-to-day nursing of great value to the care for common ailments.

Those men rendered unfit for further soldiering, whether by wound, injury or illness, were in most cases discharged to what might be beggary and poverty, especially as they would be less than able in a society that had little allowance for such things. Receiving centres for Queen Anne's veterans were established in the Kentish towns of Deal, Rochester, Gravesend and Folkestone for those returning from campaigning in Flanders or Germany. A lucky few could hope for a gratuity on account of their wounds and disablement; some might seek service or charity with a retired officer who remembered them from their time in the field, while others might be able to enter the Royal Hospitals at either Chelsea, then just outside London, or Kilmainham in Dublin. Many hoped for such assistance in vain, as pensions were usually not made available to time-served or discharged soldiers, other than to a few senior officers who might expect to receive special payments from their grateful sovereign or prince, or be appointed to some lucrative post with generous emoluments but little in the way of onerous duties. In this way, George Hamilton, 1st Earl of Orkney, one of Marlborough's best commanders, was appointed to be governor of Virginia, rather to the dismay of Colonel Daniel Parke (who had ridden, it will be remembered, to London with the Blenheim dispatch in his pocket in 1704), who hoped to secure the post for himself. Junior ranks could petition for special grants to alleviate hardship, as Ensign Gordon of Primrose's Regiment did successfully in 1710, after losing a leg at the siege of Douai.[30] The lack of proper provision for discharged soldiers and their naval counterparts – and their dependants – was acknowledged, as was the need of the widows and orphans of those who fell in battle. It became the practice to enlist non-existent 'widow's men' into the ranks, and for the pay allowed for those phantoms to be put towards the relief of old and infirm veteran soldiers and their bereaved or destitute families. This financial sleight of hand was officially sanctioned, and Queen Anne took a keen interest in the effectiveness of the measure: 'The Queen has directed that a man per troop should be mustered under a ficticous name, whereby the fund for the Flanders widows would be enlarged.'[31]

Admission to the Royal Hospitals at Chelsea or Kilmainham, as either an in-pensioner or out-pensioner, was available to a few. Places were greatly sought after, with personal intervention by some person of rank often the key, although even this could be qualified by prevailing circumstances. Adam Cardonnel wrote on 27 July 1703:

> Lord Orkney having recommended the bearer, Thomas Mackay, a soldier who has served long in the Royal Regiment of Foot, and is disabled by his wounds received therein, from further service, as a fit object of Her Majesty's bounty, my Lord Duke of Marlborough is pleased to command me to signify his directions that he be taken into the Royal Hospital at Chelsea, if there be room, or as soon as there is a vacancy.[32]

These fortunate few in-pensioners occasionally included women soldiers, as was seen with Kit Davies, who was admitted as an in-pensioner on

19 November 1717, and described as 'A jolly fat-breasted woman, received several wounds in the service, in the guise of a man.'[33] Out-pensioners might be old soldiers who were either waiting, as Tom Mackay was, for a place in the hospital, or perhaps were sufficiently young and hearty enough to be enrolled in one of the invalid companies formed for garrison duties or home defence. Such service would certainly be more congenial to the veteran, when past his best, than to have to live in penury and beggary and dependent upon the occasional casual charity of others. John Blackader, writing to his wife in her lodgings in Ghent after the bloody fighting at Malplaquet, gave advice to pass on to her friend, the widow of Lieutenant Colonel James Cranstoun who had been killed that awful day. She had been offered a commission as ensign for her young son as a mark of recompense for her loss, but was also being urged by others to seek a pension from Queen Anne rather than accept a widow's gratuity:

> I humbly differ from them. The gratuity is a certain thing; she comes to it, of course, without any trouble. The other is uncertain and depends upon interest and friends. Let her once enter herself into the first and afterwards if she can procure a better pension, it is well, but a bird in the hand is worth two in the bush.[34]

The colonel had too much delicacy to add that a pension from the queen, if it could be obtained, would die with her, at some perhaps not too distant point.

The victory achieved at Blenheim had been so startling that a special bounty was paid to those British troops who took part in the campaign in Bavaria. In March 1705 the bounty was declared, at an overall figure of £65,000 – a staggering amount for the day. A double amount was paid out to those who were wounded, and who had served as staff officers if their own regiment had been engaged in the battle, while payments were also made to the widows of those who had been killed or had died from their wounds while the list was in preparation. The Duke of Marlborough, as the army commander, quite naturally received the largest sum, £600, although he remitted this so that the overall fund for more junior ranks could be increased; given various anecdotes of his meanness and caution with money, this is a telling indication of the true care he had for his men. Private soldiers, at the other end of the scale, received £1, as did drummers, but the disparity in the two sums is not surprising, for the duke was the guiding hand behind the whole campaign; without him nothing would have been achieved, and in any case he did not claim the sum due. There were many and varied levels of payment under this bounty, with Marlborough's brother Charles Churchill receiving £300, Lord John Cutts had £240 and William Cadogan £60, although the quartermaster-general also got £123 for being colonel of his own regiment of Horse in the battle. In the dragoons, Lord John Hay got £105 plus £80 for being on the staff, while his adjutant, James Scott, received £15. In the same regiment, Captain Thomas Young was killed, and his widow and children were awarded £93. In the line regiments, the exiled Huguenot Captain Jean Ligonier of North and Grey's Regiment got £30, while Lieutenant Colonel John Dalyell of Rowe's Regiment, having been killed while going to the aid of Archibald Rowe outside Blindheim village, his widow and children received a bounty of £102 (the deceased brigadier general's own orphaned children received £90). Lieutenant Robert Falconer of the same regiment was awarded £14 for his efforts, while Rowe's surgeon, Alexander Renton, got £12.[35]

All campaigning armies had, as a necessary part of their 'tail', a substantial group of camp followers, composed partly of the families of the soldiers, who went with their man rather than stay at home to eke out their lives in penury, and partly of those following a trade or profession in the service of keeping the troops in good form and better spirits than might otherwise be the case. Often, these arrangements were informal and not officially recognized, but the well-being of solders was usually understood to be tied in to the provision of a few comforts when off-duty, of a nature that the army itself could hardly provide. Discipline had not to suffer, of course, and instances of drunkenness could lead to impromptu ale tents being shut down, while comfort of a more intimate variety might lead to incapacitating venereal disease, and the brothels that routinely accompanied an army would in turn be closed and the women and girls employed there driven away. Overly strict measures could, however, be self-defeating, for fighting soldiers depended on the provision of the essential, mundane but comforting services provided by the shadow army of these camp followers. Donald McBane combined his own military duties with running one of the brothels that accompanied the duke's army, while sutlers like Kit Davies provided a variety of entertainments for those with a few pence to spare in the wet canteens and market tents that would spring up as soon as an army went into its encampment.

The sutlers, official and unofficial, in practice performed a key function in Marlborough's army, for commissaries provided only bread as a staple ration to the soldiers. All other food and drink had to be purchased, each regiment having one established 'grand' sutler and each company a 'petty' sutler. The range of produce offered, the correct weight and quantity given, and the prices to be charged, were closely regulated, other than for strictly recreational services such as strong drink and other forms of off-duty entertainment. It was also stipulated that produce should be fresh and wholesome, and assuming that this was so, this was certainly an advance on what much of civil society could enjoy at the time. Some sutlers certainly ran a good shop and prospered by their trade, and a soldier who married the widow of one of his fallen comrades wrote contentedly that 'She was a pretty little Scotchwoman and got a great deal of money by keeping a suttling tent.'[36] Whether the man was attracted by her feminine charms or by the size of her purse is not clear, but perhaps it was the former.

In some of the armies that fought against Marlborough, the arrangements were of a more elaborate nature, and amongst the huge pile of booty that fell into Allied hands after the victory at Blenheim was a number of coaches containing the officers' ladies, clad in a variety of exotic and revealing dress. The women on campaign were not all offering their services for cash, however, as can be seen with Kit Davies, who was permitted to accompany the army after her deception was discovered. Nor did all soldiers by any means relish having their loved ones with them in the field, and at times it was certainly inappropriate. The Comte de Merode-Westerloo had interrupted his participation in the fighting at Eckeren in 1703 to pay his compliments to Countess Tilly, whose coach had been apprehended by French dragoons as she attempted to escape the fighting in the village. He recalled with some regret that his gallant efforts at making small-talk were unavailing, due to the heavy musketry all around at the time. 'She returned me only a short salutation.'[37] The Duchess of Marlborough stayed in England, where she could exercise her influence over the queen, an advantage that was, however, dwindling at increasing speed, while John Blackader, who in many ways demonstrated a rather bleak character, would write in affectionate tones to his wife in May 1705 while he was away with the army in the briefly promising, but ultimately doomed, Moselle campaign:

> My inclination would lead me to have you always with me, and if both of us had our wills and wishes, we would never be parted at all … I am persuaded it is your duty to remain in Rotterdam, considering that you have good gospel there, good company, edifying

conversation, time and opportunity to serve God, advantage of living by faith, and trusting Him with a husband who is far from you.[38]

Despite such solicitous comments, the lady clearly found some cause to complain of her husband's apparent neglect of her and her wishes, for he wrote two weeks later:

> You have no reason to quarrel, for I have taken all occasions upon the march to write: and sometimes after fatiguing marches, when others lay down to sleep, I sat up and wrote to you ... I think I could part with all other comforts pretty easily, without much regret, except thyself.[39]

Whether or not the colonel's wife was mollified by such soothing words we cannot know, but the concern Blackader clearly felt for her lends a perhaps softer hue to the otherwise rather austere picture we might have of him.

Chapter 9

Marlborough's Legacy

When the War of the Spanish Succession began in the spring of 1702, England was a military power of moderate, even negligible, quality and reputation. The shifting fortunes of the Stuart reign in the previous century had seen varying degrees of internal division, religious differences, brutal civil war, despotic yet ineffective royal rule and equally unsatisfactory parliamentary government and even military dictatorship. With such distractions, England counted for little in the wider context of European affairs. After the Restoration in the 1660s, the impecunious but astute King Charles II allied himself to Louis XIV of France, covertly at times and then openly, in return for large cash payments from the French Treasury. His brother, James II, a good soldier but a bad king as it was said, was obliged to flee to France by the arrival of his Dutch son-in-law at the Glorious Revolution of 1688. Once William III was established on the throne his earnest efforts to link the power of Holland and England in a war to curb Louis XIV and his overbearing ambitions led to only limited military success. England was inevitably involved in a lengthy war, with a series of grinding and expensive battles being fought in the 1690s – Walcourt, Leuze, Steenkirk and Landen, and the sieges of Maastricht and Liège – with little evidence amongst the English troops and their Scottish, Irish and Welsh compatriots of martial skill and prowess other than dogged and bloody-minded bravery.

This all changed with the Duke of Marlborough, whose appointment in 1702 as Queen Anne's Captain-General and to the command of the Anglo-Dutch armies had the appearance of being almost a happy accident. He had, after all, been often out of royal favour for much of the last decade of the previous century, even spending some time incarcerated in the Tower of London, before emerging once more as a person of influence. The duke, as he became after his early successes in the Low Countries, brought together the talents and energy of the army of Queen Anne and that of the States-General of Holland in a remarkably successful way, and went on to lead the combined forces of the two countries to great, arguably unprecedented and hardly ever equalled, victories – 'Amid all the chances and baffling accidents of war, he produced victory with almost mechanical certainty ... nothing like this can be seen in military annals.'[1] All this is true, and but for casually negligent and unforgiveable fumbling by politicians who had never so much as smelled a battlefield, those successes would have secured for the Grand Alliance everything that it had sought in the War of the Spanish Succession. Such a welcome result would, of course, have had its own inherent perils for it does not do to grind your opponent, especially one as proud and resourceful as Louis XIV and his people, too finely. Sober judgement was called for before, during and after the war, and that was plainly lacking – on both sides, it should be said. However, during the long course of that war, British generals and commanders such as Cadogan, Argyll, Orkney, Sabine, Webb and Lumley, working in close harmony with their Dutch allies, proved themselves in unmistakable fashion. Furthermore, Marlborough's reputation as a great military leader soared and has endured, and he showed clearly that coalition warfare, with all the stresses and strains that were inevitably entailed, could succeed against an opponent whose absolute rule, while paradoxically having certain limits, could command resources that were very deep indeed. Given the inevitable strain of coalitions in wartime, the success that was achieved, although less than it should have been, was still far greater than what might have been hoped for at the outset.

The numerous tactical successes achieved by Marlborough and his armies between the summer of 1702 and the end of 1711 marked the duke out as one of the greatest captains in history. The duke's close partnership and friendship with Prince Eugene of Savoy, another of the great captains, must also be acknowledged, for the war was, of course, a joint effort and little could have been achieved but for the skill, valour and sheer sustained effort of the officers and men of many nationalities that Marlborough led, and who repaid his care and concern for them with widespread respect and affection. Not for nothing was the duke known to his men as 'Corporal John' – no mean compliment as any soldier will confirm. To appreciate Marlbrough's achievement, and what may be claimed to be his legacy, we should look briefly once more at the man as he was when he was removed from the scene as a military commander by an ailing and disappointed monarch. Corporal Matthew Bishop wrote in dismay on hearing the news of his commander's dismissal, 'I concluded that the Neck of War was broke, and that I should be disappointed of the pleasure of seeing Paris that Year; though we were in hopes of arriving to the honour.'[2] Field Deputy Sicco van Goslinga, staunch and obstinate as he was in pursuit of what he saw as his duty, and at the same time both an admirer and sharp critic of Marlborough, could still write of him:

> His mind was keen and subtle, his judgement both clear and sound, his insight quick and deep, with an all-embracing knowledge of men which no false show of merit can deceive. He expresses himself well, and even his very bad French is agreeable; he has a harmonious voice, and as a speaker of his own language he is considered one of the best ... He has courage as he has shown on more than one occasion; he is an experienced soldier, and plans a campaign to admiration.

Not for nothing did van Goslinga also have something of a reputation for being argumentative; he went on:

> Now for the weak points which I consider I have discovered in him. He is a profound dissembler, all the more dangerous that his manner and his words give the impression of frankness itself. His ambition knows no bounds ... Moreover, he lacks the precise knowledge of military detail which a Commander-in-Chief should possess. But these defects are light when balanced against *the rare gifts of this truly great man.*[3]

While he was undeniably gifted, perhaps few would really argue that Marlborough was perfect; far from it, he was certainly ambitious both for himself – that was how advancement was gained in uncertain times – but also ambitious for the common cause against France and certainly no worse for that. His ability to flatter and cajole, learned in part when he was a young courtier, was turned to excellent effect over ten strenuous years while keeping together the various strands of a confederate army engaged in outright warfare with a resolute and skilful opponent. The duke clearly understood that good generalship entailed the judicious use of available resources, rather than a simple augmentation of numbers. Much depended upon his calculation of what should be done, by whom and where, and he rarely misjudged the matter.[4]

If Marlborough lacked, as the field deputy suggests, the required knowledge of military detail, then his victories flowed with 'almost mechanical certainty' all the same, and he had received, after all, no lengthy formal training in the art of warfare and had few opportunities before 1702 to command large bodies of men in the uncertainties of active campaigning. That he remains one of the most notable captains of history, 'a truly great man' as Goslinga said, is nonetheless beyond dispute. Where

Marlborough was at his weakest was on the political scene, which, despite his close friendship with such adept operators as Lord Treasurer Sidney Godolphin, he could not control with all its twists and turns; his power base in London faltered and then slipped away. This was perhaps inevitable and no great surprise: different and differing forces were in play, some well meaning but others less admirable. His ill-judged requests to be made Captain-General for life were refused by Queen Anne, as they must always have been, for Stuart memories of Cromwell and the Interregnum would not ever fade, and Marlborough was the weaker for ever having asked the question. Men were suspicious of his true motives: 'I believe there is no instance that ever a man who had tasted of absolute power could ever retire to a private life and become a good subject.'[5] Unable to procure the complete victory for the Grand Alliance that had seemed possible at one fleeting point, with his influence with the queen fading and his political opponents gaining ground, the duke's dismissal became inevitable. Although out of favour in London and at some risk of malicious prosecution, his reputation in the courts and council chambers across Europe, even in Versailles, remained high. Whether the outcome of the war would have been significantly different had he retained the command is hard to judge. The terms of the treaties of Utrecht, Baden, Rastadt and Madrid, agreed between 1713 and 1715, at last bringing the tired war to an untidy close, appeared to leave France with its hands on much of the spoils, but in actual fact the principal aims of the Grand Alliance, as originally set out in 1702, had largely been achieved. A great deal of this success was due to the efforts and abilities of the Duke of Marlborough, for he had carried forward the effort against Louis XIV and France to a degree that was unmatched by any other individual.

For much of the war, Great Britain (as it was from 1707 onwards) had been the paymaster of the Grand Alliance. The large numbers of men mustered to fight the French and their allies were mostly paid for by gold from the Treasury of Queen Anne, made available by the simple expedient of trustworthy credit and the establishment of the national debt. This was a novel idea, whereby a government could borrow money it never intended to return but would pay the interest accruing on the sums instead, and be relied upon to do so. Against all expectations, this system worked very well, despite heartfelt protests from many Britons outside the City of London at taking on such a burden for the nation. The queen and her ministers, as a result, were able to raise and maintain the large sums necessary to prosecute the war for so long; only towards the end of the conflict did this ability begin to flag, but burdensome taxation was sapping the will of all the protagonists, not just those in London. In the end, Great Britain turned its back on solemn undertakings given to the Alliance, and tiring of a pointless war, made a separate peace with France in 1712. In effect, Queen Anne took her troops off the field, but Marlborough had been dismissed by then. The two events were not unrelated, for it is inconceivable that the duke, despite all his political acumen and vaulting ambition, would have connived, as his successor did, in attempting to mislead friends and allies in the way that was done. He had become, therefore, an inconvenience who had powerful and clever enemies and so could be set to one side and blamed for all that had not gone right. However, the war had by now run its course, if only people could see that this was so. Stubbornness born of frustration was in the air – so much having been gained and then allowed to slip away – and there was no easy or elegant way to bring matters to a close.[6]

As was only to be expected, blame was heaped on Great Britain for having secured a peace to its own advantage, but this criticism was largely manufactured, as the only alternative was to go on with a ruinously expensive war that could not be won. The French prince was secure and popular in Madrid and that, when all was said and done, was that. In any event, the main aim of the Grand Alliance had been achieved, and what had not been secured were the ill-judged additional ambitions of members of the Alliance that grew with the repeated successes won by the army under Marlborough's command. In fact, the British pragmatically arranged advantageous terms with Versailles, well knowing that Holland would have to follow suit before long and Austria would not have the will or capability to fight on alone, particularly as the Austrian claimant to the Spanish throne was now Emperor Charles and comfortably installed in Vienna; he would never visit Spain again.

The wider consequences of the war, away from lofty considerations of what had been political and dynastic gain or loss for France, Spain and Austria, were profound. The martial power and prestige of France, so apparently absolute at the close of the seventeenth century, was reduced, while Austria happily took its gains in northern Italy and the Southern Netherlands, and otherwise turned its back on the west to become distracted again by the Ottoman threat in eastern Europe. Vienna remained oblivious to the growing power of German states, most noticeably that of Prussia, a strategic error it would come to regret. Holland, so valiant and staunch in its opposition to France, had regained its barrier towns in the

Southern Netherlands, albeit reduced in extent. Not having been able to secure the full fruits of the peace – unlike Great Britain, which made sure of doing so – the Dutch were broken financially by the long war and slipped from view as a world power, In consequence, the maritime commerce on which the States-General had built their trading empire lost much ground to growing British power and the effectiveness of the Royal Navy. Spain had its French king, Philip V, who abdicated and then came back to the throne, and by and large the people were very satisfied with the arrangement. Internal divisions and a lack of strategic direction, and an inability to reform the cumbersome control of its still wide empire, meant that the decline in effectiveness and influence of Spain as a power continued with a certain remorseless inevitability.

The exciting days when the Duke of Marlborough led Queen Anne's army and that of her allies to victories cast a glow over subsequent events. Never again would Great Britain be militarily of little account, for the duke had by his repeated successes shown what could and should be done. 'By stopping France, and by showing that Britain possessed a land capability, the army ensured that Britain played a major role.'[7] King George I, the Protestant heir, came to the throne in 1714 once Queen Anne died, and the wasteful distraction of whimsical Jacobite rebellions, 'risings', in 1715, 1719 and 1745–6 were a military irrelevance, while British influence and empire-building gained pace. French efforts to establish a wider empire would falter; the war for Spain, Marlborough's war, for all its untidy endings, had weakened France to a perceptible degree. Throughout the eighteenth century French ambitions and French concerns in Europe and overseas would bring conflict back again and again, with France and Great Britain engaged in warlike activities for a staggering forty-three years in all. These ambitions and worries were not irrelevant or frivolous, for France was striving to make an empire for itself as others, notably Great Britain, were so busily doing. However, only the extraordinary days of revolution in Paris and the rise of Emperor Napoleon, with all his brilliant and baleful talents, would enable France to throw Europe back into quite as much turmoil as had been seen in the heyday of Louis XIV and his ambitions.

In the meantime, Great Britain would have to relinquish the bulk of its first empire, that of North America, but this stemmed as much from financial considerations, and greater opportunities for wealth elsewhere in the world, as interference from perennial antagonists such as France and Spain. British military fortunes varied, inevitably, and for every success at places such as Minden, Havana, Montreal or at the conclusion to the long siege of Gibraltar in 1783, there was a grim day such as Fontenoy in 1745, Saratoga in 1779 and Yorktown in 1782. On the credit side, though, could also be counted somewhat forgotten successes at such fields as Emsdorf, Warburg and Brandywine. In the closing years of the century, British troops commanded by the much-maligned Duke of York carried the day at Beaumont, Lincelles and Willems, pretty well a century after Williams III's laboured efforts over much the same ground, although for this duke the enemy was the Republican French rather than the Sun King. What was clear was that the belief in success and the regard in which the British army was held, and held itself, was firmly established, both at home and abroad; after the Duke of Marlborough nothing was ever quite the same. Mothers might declare that they would prefer their sons dead than to see them in a red coat, but no one treated the sight of British soldiers arrayed for action on the field of battle with anything less than marked and grudging respect. 'It would be very important to have particular attention to that part of the line which will endure the first shock of the English troops.'[8] The French king's admonition to Marshal Villeroi as he began his march to defeat at Ramillies in 1706 was sincerely meant and would find echoes on many other battlefields.

For all that, good fortune would not return on a scale seen by Marlborough's soldiers until the campaigns in Spain under Arthur Wellesley, Duke of Wellington, some 100 years after the triumph at Oudenarde and the grim day of trial at Malplaquet. Hard-fought actions on such fields as Bussaco, Talavera, Albuera, Salamanca, Vittoria and Orthez would cement afresh a military reputation for British soldiers and British generalship. The crowning achievement for Wellington came in 1815 at Waterloo (a potential field of battle with which Marlborough was well acquainted). Unlike 'Corporal John', Wellington was able to bring to a neat and glorious end the war against the French, and the memory of Waterloo and the reputation of the men who fought and won there has been enhanced to a greater degree as a result. This is not surprising, but while Waterloo may come to the public mind far more readily than Blenheim or (more notably perhaps) the unequalled triumph at Ramillies, the battles are closely linked, for on each occasion there was a driving force, a dominating and guiding hand that could control the battle as a true master of the field. Marlborough and Wellington may be said to be linked in this way, and it is not stretching the point too far to suggest that either duke would have recognized, and been at home on, the battlefieldsfought by the other

– the doughty lines of the 'long red wall', the waving colours, thrilling flams of the drummers and the obscuring smoke of cannon and rattling musketry would surely have been familiar to both commanders. So, too, would have been the polyglot nature of their armies, for both Marlborough and Wellington could only operate by working in close conjunction with their allies – Marlborough with Overkirk and Eugene, Wellington with Blücher. It is invidious to quibble, as it might be tempting to do, regarding the relative merits and conduct of Marshal Tallard or Marshal Villars, on the one hand, and Marshal Soult or Emperor Napoleon a century or so later, on the other. For those tempted to ascribe the Allied success at Waterloo to the Prussians under Blücher (a good if not entirely convincing case can be made for it), then Prince Eugene can claim the credit for tying down, at enormous effort and expense, the Bavarians while Marlborough achieved his success over the French on the open plain of Höchstädt. Such comparison is pointless, for great men will rise above such trivia, and Marlborough declared after Oudenarde, when Eugene was admired for his handling of the fighting along the Ghent road while Overkirk belatedly got his corps into place on the Boser Couter hill, that there could never be any difference (argument) between himself and the prince over where the credit lay. In just the same way, Wellington and Blücher had each a like feeling for the pressing needs of the other on that fateful day in June 1815 on the field of Waterloo.

The upshot of all this was that the reputation of the British and their army, first established by the Duke of Marlborough, was confirmed and enhanced – with occasional setbacks – over succeeding decades as the British Empire grew and prospered. That the empire depended upon the Royal Navy having command of the seas does not diminish the role of the army in imperial matters. Almost without knowing it, Great Britain became a nation with a proud martial reputation, and British soldiers became known for a certain rough-and-ready self-confidence. 'This is a terrible war,' one lady well-wisher would say to a wounded Irish soldier. 'Yes ma'am,' came the murmured reply, 'but tis better than no war at all.'[9] There were, of course, setbacks on the way, such as the gross mismanagement of the campaign in Afghanistan in 1839–40, in the Crimean winter of 1854 and 1855, or repeatedly in two wars against rough-hewn Boer farmers in South Africa. German Chancellor Otto von Bismark might comment, rather wittily, that if he had trouble with England he would send a policeman to arrest the British army, but the dogged fighting abilities of the British Expeditionary Force in late 1914 and the rapid raising of a huge citizen army by Field Marshal Lord Kitchener may be said to have laid that thought to rest for the shades of the bluff old gentle-man. The essential point remained the same: despite a by no means un-blemished record, the belief in eventual success which Marlborough's soldiers undoubtedly carried with them as they tramped the roads of Germany and Flanders became deep-rooted in the army. A casual self-confidence was set in the minds of future British soldiers, officers and men alike, and the claim that 'We'll do it, what is it?' was no mere puff or boast.[10]

Timeline for the War of the Spanish Succession

Unless otherwise stated, all dates are given in the New Style, which was eleven days later than the Old Style (OS).

1700

1 November	Death of King Carlos II of Spain in Madrid.
16 November	King Louis XIV proclaims his grandson, the Duc d'Anjou, as King Philip V of Spain.

1701

February	French troops occupy Barrier Towns in the Southern Netherlands
18 February	King Philip V enters Madrid.
8 August	Marlborough appointed Captain-General.
7 September	The Grand Alliance formed between England, Holland and Austria.
17 September	Louis XIV acknowledges the 'Old Pretender' as King of England.

1702

19 March	Death of King William III, accession of Queen Anne of England.
15 May	The Grand Alliance declares war on France and Spain.
1 July	Marlborough takes command of the Anglo-Dutch army.
23 August	Missed chance to attack the French at the Heaths of Peer.
September	The Elector of Bavaria and the bishopric of Liège ally themselves with France.
25 September	The Allies capture Venlo.
7 October	The Allies take Ruremonde.
26 October	The Allies capture Liège.

1703

15 May	Marlborough captures Bonn.
30 June	The Battle of Eckeren, near to Antwerp.
26 August	The Allies take Huy on the Meuse.
13 September	Archduke Charles declared King Charles III of Spain.
27 September	The Allies capture Limburg.

| November | The Duchy of Savoy joins the Grand Alliance. |
| December | Portugal joins the Grand Alliance. |

1704

May	Failed Allied advance from Portugal into Spain.
19 May	Marlborough begins the march up the Rhine.
30 May	The Allies fail to capture Barcelona.
2 July	Marlborough beats d'Arco at the Schellenberg.
6 August	Anglo-Dutch forces capture Gibraltar.
11 August	The Margrave of Baden begins siege of Ingolstadt.
13 August	The Battle of Blenheim.
29 October	Marlborough captures Treves (Trier).
28 November	The Allies capture Landau.
20 December	The Allies capture Trarbach.

1705

5 May	Death of Emperor Leopold I, succeeded by his son, Joseph.
10 June	The French capture Huy.
11 July	Marlborough retakes Huy.
18 July	The Battle of Elixheim and the passage of the Lines of Brabant.
18 August	The 'Unfought battle of Waterloo' on the river Yssche.
6 September	The Allies capture Leau.
14 October	Barcelona taken by the Allies.
December	The Allies occupy almost all of Valencia.

1706

19 May	Marshal Villeroi advances to challenge Marlborough.
22 May	Barcelona relieved by Royal Navy during French siege.
23 May	The Battle of Ramillies.
28 May	The French abandon Brussels.
17 June	The Allies occupy Antwerp.
23 June	The Allies take Cartagena.
27 June	The Allies enter Madrid.
9 July	The capture of Ostend by the Allies.
4 August	Madrid evacuated by the Allies.
22 August	Marlborough captures Menin.
7 September	Prince Eugene wins victory at the relief of Turin.
9 September	Dendermonde submits to the Allies.
13 September	Majorca and Ibiza occupied by the Allies.
1 October	The Allies capture Ath.
11 November	Marshal Berwick retakes Cartagena.

1707

13 February	France and Austria agree to cease operations in northern Italy.
25 April	The Allies defeated at Almanza.
22 May	Marshal Villars storms the Allied Lines of Stolhoffen.

22 August	Failure of Prince Eugene's operations against Toulon.
14 November	Berwick captures Lerida from the Allies.

1708

30 April	An Imperial army arrives in Catalonia.
5 July	The French capture Bruges.
7 July	The French capture Ghent.
11 July	The Duc de Vendôme defeated at Oudenarde.
August	Sardinia occupied by the Allies.
	The siege of Lille begins.
29 August	Minorca captured by the Allies.
19 September	The Battle of Wynendael.
10 December	Surrender of the Lille citadel by Marshal Boufflers.

1709

2 January	The Allies retake Ghent, and the French abandon Bruges.
7 May	Defeat of the Allies at Val Gudina in Portugal.
June	Louis XIV rejects the Allies' treaty terms.
3 September	Marlborough captures Tournai.
11 September	The Battle of Malplaquet.
20 October	Mons captured by the Allies.
29 October	First Anglo-Dutch Barrier Treaty agreed.

1710

25 June	The Allies capture Douai.
27 July	Allied victory at the Battle of Almenara.
20 August	Allied victory at Saragossa.
28 August	The capture of Bethune by the Allies.
August	King Charles III enters Madrid.
29 September	The Allies take St Venant.
8 November	Aire captured by the Allies.
9 December	Stanhope defeated at the Battle of Brihuega.
10 December	Bloody French victory at Villaviciosa.

1711

25 January	Berwick takes Gerona.
17 April	The death of Emperor Joseph; accession of his brother, Charles.
7 August	The passage of the Lines of Non Plus Ultra.
14 September	The capture of Bouchain by Marlborough.
22 September	Emperor Charles leaves Spain.
31 December (OS)	Marlborough dismissed from all his offices.

1712

4 July	The Allies capture Le Quesnoy.
16 July	British troops withdraw from active operations.
19 July	Dunkirk handed to the British by France.
24 July	Marshal Villars' victory at Denain.

30 July	The French capture Marchiennes.
2 August	Failure by Dutch and Imperial troops to capture Landrecies.
8 September	Douai retaken by the French.
2 October	Hostilities suspended in Spain.
3 October	The French recapture Le Quesnoy.
19 October	Bouchain recaptured by Villars.
3 November	Hostilities suspended in Portugal.

1713

30 January	Second Anglo-Dutch Barrier Treaty agreed.
11 April	The Treaty of Utrecht agreed between Britain, Holland and France.
9 July	Barcelona declares continued allegiance to King Charles III.
13 July	Anglo-Spanish Treaty agreed.

1714

6 March	Treaty of Rastadt agreed between France and Austria.
26 June	Treaty agreed between Holland and Spain.
31 July	Death of Queen Anne; accession of King George I.
17 August	Marlborough reappointed as the Captain-General.
7 September	Treaty of Baden agreed between France and Austria.

1715

6 February	Treaty between Spain and Portugal agreed.
15 September	Death of Louis XIV; accession of his great-grandson, Louis XV.
15 November	Barrier Treaty signed between Holland, Austria and France.

Marlborough's Regiments

Note: 1881 and 1914 titles are added in brackets. Those given in italics only served under Marlborough during the years indicated.

Cavalry and Dragoons

Lumley's Horse — (Queen's Regiment) (1st King's Dragoon Guards)
Harvey's Horse — (2nd Dragoon Guards, the Queen's Bays)
Wood's Horse — (3rd Dragoon Guards, Prince of Wales's)
Cadogan's Horse — (5th Dragoon Guards, Princess Charlotte's)
Wyndham's Horse — (6th Dragoon Guards, the Carabiniers)
Schomberg's Horse — (7th Dragoon Guards, Princess Royal's)
Raby's (Royal) Dragoons, 1702–3 — (1st, The Royal Dragoons)
Hay's/Stair's Dragoons — (2nd Dragoons, the Royal Scots Greys)
Ross's Royal Irish Dragoons — (5th Royal Irish Lancers)
Kerr's Dragoons, 1711 — (7th Queen's Own Hussars)

Foot Guards

1st English Foot Guards — (Grenadier Guards)
Coldstream Guards, 1708–11 — (Coldstream Guards)
3rd (Dutch Blue) Guards, 1702 — (transferred to the Dutch Establishment)

Infantry

Orkney's (the Royal Regiment) — (1st/Royal Scots, the Royal Regiment)
Bellasis's (Queen Dowager's), 1703 — (2nd/Queen's Royal West Surrey)
Churchill's, 1704–11 — (3rd/Buffs, Royal East Kent)
Webb's (Queen's) — (8th/King's, Liverpool)
North and Grey's — (10th/Royal Lincolnshire)
Hill's, 1702–3, 1709–11 — (11th/Devonshire)
Livesay's, 1708 — (12th/Suffolk)
Barrymore's, 1702 — (13th/Somerset Light Infantry, Prince Albert's)
Howe's — (15th/East Yorkshire, Duke of York's Own)
Derby's — (16th/Bedfordshire & Hertfordshire)
Bridge's, 1702 — (17th/Royal Leicestershire)
Hamilton's, Royal Irish, 1703–11 — (18th/Royal Irish)
Row's, Scots Fusiliers — (21st/Royal Scots Fusiliers)
Ingoldsby's — (23rd/Royal Welch Fusiliers)
Seymour's — (24th/South Wales Borderers)
Fergusons, Cameronians, 1703–11 — (26th/Cameronians)
De Lalo's, 1704–6 — (28th/Gloucestershire)
Farrington's, 1704–8 — (29th/Worcestershire)
Huntingdon's, 1702–3 — (33rd/Duke of Wellington's)

Lucas's, 1708–11	(34th/Border)
Meredith's	(37th/Hampshire)
Stringer's, 1704–11	(Disbanded 1713)
Temple's, 1704–11	"
Evan's, 1704–11	"
Macartney's, 1704–11	"
Prendergast's, 1708–10	"
Wynne's, 1708–11	"
Townshend's, 1708–11	"
Johnson's, 1708	"
Moore's, 1708	"
Dormer's, 1708–9	"
Creighton's, 1708	"

The augmentation in strength from 1704 onwards is evident. The total British regiments deployed by the Duke of Marlborough during his victorious year of 1706 was seven regiments of Horse and dragoons, one Foot Guards regiment and eighteen regiments of Foot. All those units that had gone with him to the Danube were present in the Order of Battle for that year, in addition to Farrington's Regiment which had not been on the famous march to the south. By comparison, the British troops serving in Spain and Portugal in that year comprised eight regiments of Horse and dragoons, one Foot Guards regiment (the Coldstream) and twenty-seven regiments of Foot. See also, Leslie, N., *The Succession of Colonels of the British Army from 1660 to the Present Day*, 1974, and also Barthorp, M., *Marlborough's Army 1702–1711*, 1980, pp. 20–7, for additional interesting comments on these totals.

Notes

The following abbreviations are used in the notes and bibliography:

BCMH: Journal of the British Commission for Military History.
DNB: Dictionary of National Biography.
JSAHR: Journal of the Society for Army Historical Research.
RUSI: Royal United Services Institute.

Introduction

1. This doggerel verse, in various forms, enjoyed wide and lasting popularity amongst soldiers, being often sung by the Duke of Wellington's soldiers a hundred years or so after Marlborough's campaigns: 'Now courage boys 'tis one to ten, that we all return as gentlemen, when conquering colours we display, over the hills and far away.' See Weinstock, L., *The Songs and Music of the Redcoats*, 1970, for interesting comments on this.

2. Lediard, T., *The Life of John, Duke of Marlborough*, 1736, Volume I, p. xxiii. Where quotations are taken from accounts written in the eighteenth century I have amended – I hope sympathetically – the occasionally idiosyncratic grammar, spelling and syntax, where it seems appropriate, to modern usage for greater uniformity and convenience. Additional comments inserted for clarification are enclosed in square brackets.

3. As a young man Marlborough served at the French siege of Dutch-held Maastricht, alongside King Charles II's illegitimate son, James, Duke of Monmouth. On one notable occasion they were involved in the storm of an outwork, in which the young Claude-Louis-Hector de Villars (one day to be a Marshal of France) also took part, as did Captain d'Artagnan, hero of Alexandre Dumas' novels. The captain was killed in the failed attempt.

4. Churchill, W., *Marlborough, His Life and Times*, 1947, Book I, p. 556.

5. Chandler, D. (ed.), *A Journal of Marlborough's Campaigns during the War of the Spanish Succession, 1702–1711*, (JSAHR) 1984, p. 43.

6. St John, B. (tr. and ed.), *Memoirs of the Duc de St Simon*, 1879, Volume I, pp. 290–1. Not in living memory had a main French field army been defeated so thoroughly, and numerous officers of high ranks were captives in Allied hands. To add to the general air of astonishment and mortification, the abject surrender of thousands of French infantrymen trapped and impotent in Blindheim village, was an unwelcome and inexplicable sensation. See also Miller, H., *Colonel Parke of Virginia, the Greatest Hector in the Town*, 1989, p. 137 for a fuller text version.

7. In the House of Lords, the adulatory address to Marlborough on his resounding success in Bavaria ran in part:

   The happy success that has attended Her Majesty's Arms, under your Grace's conduct in Germany the last campaign, is so truly great, so truly glorious in all its circumstances, that few instances in former ages can equal, much less excel the lustre of it. Your Grace has not overthrown young and unskilful generals, raw and undisciplined troops; but your Grace has conquered the French and Bavarian armies, that were fully instructed in the arts of war; select veteran troops, flushed with former successes and victories, commanded by generals of great experience and bravery. The glorious victories your Grace has obtained at Schellenberg and Höchstädt are very great, very illustrious in themselves; but they are greater still in their consequences to Her Majesty and Her Allies ... My Lord, this most honourable House is highly sensible of the great and signal honour your Grace has shown Her Majesty this campaign, and of the immortal honour you have done the English Nation.

See Chandler, D. (ed.), *Military Memoirs, Robert Parker and Comte de Merode-Westerloo*, 1968, pp. 49–50.

8. Petrie, C., *The Marshal Duke of Berwick*, 1953, pp. 235–7. Louis XIV could not have been oblivious to the trials and hardship of the French people after so many years of ruinously expensive and unproductive war. The harsh winter of 1708/9 was particularly severe: ink was seen to freeze on the pen before reaching paper, sentries froze to death at their posts, and starvation haunted some French districts.

9. Brereton, J., *History of the 4/7th Dragoon Guards*, 1982, p. 79.

10. Churchill, Volume II, p. 913.

11. Anon., *The Compleat History of the Treaty of Utrecht*, 1715, p. 109.

12. At the start of the eighteenth century the old Julian calendar (OS) was still in use in the British Isles, whereas the Gregorian calendar (NS) – which from 1700 onwards was eleven days ahead – was used on the Continent. As almost all the events described took place outside the British Isles, the dates given, unless stated otherwise, are in the New System. Therefore, the battle of Blenheim was fought on Wednesday 13 August 1704 (NS) although in some old accounts this is given as being on 2 August (OS). In addition, the New Year was held to start on Lady Day, 25 March, so that in older accounts, for example, what we understand as February 1709 is given as still being in 1708, but the modern understanding of the commencement of the New Year being on 1 January is used throughout

Chapter 1: The War for Spain

1. St John, B. (ed.), *Memoirs of the Duc de St Simon*, 1879, Volume I, p. 183. Louis XIV had little doubt of the trouble the acceptance of the Spanish throne by a French prince would cause, commenting rather prophetically, 'Whatever course I adopt many people will condemn me.'

2. The terms of the Treaty of Grand Alliance, signed in September 1701, were sufficiently vague that they would be acceptable to all parties. From the Earl of Marlborough's point of view that mostly meant the Parliament in London, which was wary of foreign entanglements. The terms set out were that the Allies (England, Holland and Austria) would seek to obtain:

   (a) Binding guarantees that the thrones of France and Spain would always remain separate. Note: It was not stipulated that the Duc d'Anjou would have to give up the throne in Spain – that requirement, fatal in outcome, would come later.

   (b) Austria to receive the Milanese, Naples and Sicily, the Balearic Islands, the Spanish Netherlands and the Duchy of Luxembourg.

(c) Holland would regain the Barrier fortresses seized by French troops.

(d) The Elector of Brandenburg would become King of Prussia in return for his active support for the Alliance.

(e) Financial subsidies would be paid to German Princes and Electors, guaranteed in return for providing troops for the Alliance.

(f) England and Holland would have a free hand to conduct trade in the West Indies.

(g) No separate peace to be made without consultation.

There is some contradiction between clauses (b) and (c) which would cause difficulties between Holland and Austria once the Southern Netherlands were secured for the Grand Alliance in 1706.

3. Brown, B., *The Letters and Diplomatic Instructions of Queen Anne*, 1935, pp. 82–3.

4. George, Elector of Hanover, had a close personal interest in how things would turn out in the war, as once his mother died, he was the Protestant next in line to the throne in London.

5. Falkner J., *Marlborough's Wars, Eye-Witness Accounts*, 2005, p. 4.

6. Trevelyan, G., *Blenheim*, 1948, p. 238.

7. Brown, pp. 145 and 208. Financing the war was not least amongst the concerns of Queen Anne when dealing with England's partners in the Grand Alliance. Still, a lack of energy and perhaps good faith were suspected, and she wrote to her ambassador in Portugal in December 1706 'You shall use your best endeavour to penetrate into the private interests and management of the Ministers and discover who have the most credit with the present King, and by all proper means to engage them to at zealously and vigorously for the good of the Common Cause.'

8. Miller, H., *Colonel Parke of Virginia, the Greatest Hector in the Town*, 1989, p. 117.

9. Coxe, W., *Memoirs of the Duke of Marlborough*, 1847, Volume I, p. 127.

10. McBane, D., *The Expert Swordsman's Companion*, 1729, p. 120. McBane was wounded four times with spent musket balls during the fighting for Blindheim village, and repeatedly stabbed with bayonets, before being stripped and plundered by marauders.

11. Dalton, C., *The Blenheim Roll, 1704*, 1904.

12. Chandler, D. (ed.), *Military Memoirs, Robert Parker and Comte de Merode-Westerloo*, 1968, pp. 51–2.

13. McBane, p. 122. See also Chandler, D. (ed.), *A Journal of Marlborough's Campaigns during the War of the Spanish Succession, 1702–1711* (JSAHR), 1984, p. 26.

14. The individual Dutch states appointed their own field deputies whose task it was to accompany the field army, and ensure that their soldiers operated to the agreed terms, and were not put at undue risk by the Duke of Marlborough and his schemes to defeat the French. At times these men, who were all civilians with limited military experience, could be obstructive, but they were stout enough, with hearts in the right place, and most of them respected the duke and his abilities, and their presence with the army, although occasionally causing friction, was necessary and gave Marlborough a useful degree of cover from criticism from The Hague.

15. Taylor, F., *The Wars of Marlborough*, 1921, Volume I, p. 370.

16. Although the Hanoverian contingent of troops was not at Ramillies, disputes with the elector over the terms of their service not yet having been settled, two of their

officers, Colonel Brunck and Colonel St Pol, were killed that day. Presumably they were serving on the staff of the duke.

17. Chandler, *A Journal of Marlborough's Campaigns*, p. 33.
18. Tindal, N., *The Continuation of Mr Rapin's History of England*, 1738, p. 505.
19. Taylor, Volume II, pp. 264–5. Louis XIV regretted that his commander in northern Flanders, the Comte de la Motte, had submitted when he did, feeling that such a move was premature. However, despite the valiant defence of Lille by Marshal Boufflers, the French had been thoroughly demoralized by their unexpected defeat in July 1708 and subsequent failure to prevent the loss of that great fortress. The comte was an accomplished soldier and had done his best, but he risked being isolated if he tried to hold the line of the Ghent–Bruges canal to the last extremity, with no hope of relief or reinforcement from the main French field army, which had already gone off to its own winter quarters.
20. Brown, p. 275.
21. Chandler, D., *Marlborough as Military Commander*, 1974, p. 251. Given the boisterous temperament of Marshal Villars, such an instruction from the king to save Mons was effectively carte blanche to offer battle in the open, despite the threadbare state of his troops and the repeated reverses of the previous campaign.
22. Taylor, Volume II, p. 379. Not until Borodino in western Russia 109 years later would another battle be fought with such large casualties on both sides. The loss at Malplaquet to Marlborough and Eugene's 120,000-strong army, although variously given, seems to have been about 20,000 killed and wounded. Marshal Villars' casualties were some 13,000 of the 85,000 men he had in action that day, but of these only about 500 were left behind as unwounded prisoners, a good measure of the order in which he and Boufflers got their battered troops off the field. However, Villars had to abandon thirty-five guns in the woods on his left flank, and despite the valiant defence by his army, he failed entirely in his given task, Louis XIV's instruction being to save Mons no matter what the cost. See Corvisier, A., *La Bataille de Malplaquet, 1709*, 1997, for interesting comments on the respective casualties suffered in the battle.
23. Coxe, Volume III, p. 149. The siege of Aire was particularly trying for the Allied army, as foul weather had set in and the trenches were half flooded, with the soldiers having to stand knee-deep in cold water. John Deane's comments given in Chapter 7 below are of particular interest in this regard. In addition to the inevitable casualties resulting from the very stout French defence, large numbers of men also had to go sick.
24. The principal terms of the treaties of Utrecht, Rastadt, Baden and Madrid (1713–15), which brought an end to the War of the Spanish Succession, were that:

    (a) The French claimant, Philip V, was recognized as King of Spain and the Indies. The crowns of France and Spain were always to be kept separate, with Philip irrevocably renouncing any potential claim to the French crown.

    (b) Naples, the Milanese in northern Italy, Sardinia and the Southern Netherlands to go to Austria. The Southern Netherlands was to be under Austrian rule, with Barrier Towns guaranteed to Holland – Furnes, Ghent, Mons, Charleroi, Namur and Tournai. Fortresses beyond the Barrier, most significantly that of Lille, were to be restored to France.

(c) France was to retain Alsace and Strasbourg, but to relinquish the fortresses of Kehl, Breisach and Freiburg on the eastern bank of the Rhine.

(d) The electors of Cologne and Bavaria were to be restored to their domains.

(e) The Hanoverian succession to the throne of Great Britain to be confirmed once Queen Anne died. French support for the Jacobite cause was to be withdrawn.

(f) Great Britain was to retain Minorca, Gibraltar, Newfoundland, Hudson's Bay, Arcadia and St Kitts. Both Great Britain and Holland to have access to trade in designated Spanish ports.

(g) The French defences of Dunkirk to be demolished.

(h) The Duke of Savoy to receive Sicily and a part of the Milanese.

(j) Portugal to regain trading rights in the Amazon region from Spain.

Under the provisions of (d), the Duke of Marlborough lost his principality of Mindelheim, which had been bestowed on him by the emperor after the victory at Blenheim. He retained the title, however. Austria would continue, half-heartedly, to maintain a campaign in Catalonia, but nothing came of that endeavour, apart from additional distress for the Catalans, who were eventually forced to submit to Philip V on harsh terms. Such were the complexities of the war and the political, dynastic and diplomatic maneouvring over the disputed succession, that Victor Amadeus II, Duke of Savoy, did not abandon his own rather spurious claim to the throne in Madrid until 1720.

25. Chandler, D. (ed.), *Military Miscellany, The Journal of Sergeant John Wilson, 1694–1727*, 2005, p. 90. Wilson calculated that in eleven years of war, 1702–13, Marlborough's Anglo-Dutch army lost 71,723 men killed in action, with a further 17,606 dying of their wounds subsequently. Deaths from natural causes over the same period came to 9,204, giving a grand total of mortalities of 98,533, to which could be added the 18,876 men discharged as no longer fit for service, due to wounds and other injuries (notably hernias) sustained while on campaign. Not surprisingly, the heaviest losses were recorded for 1704 (Blenheim), 1708 (Oudenarde and Lille) and 1709 (Malplaquet), although the grim sieges warfare of 1710 made that a testing year also. The years 1702, 1703 and 1705 saw relatively light losses, no doubt due to the lack of general engagements in the Low Countries, and also 1706, despite the resounding victory at Ramillies. These figures are, of course, very precise and should be treated with some caution as a result, but the late Dr David Chandler accepted their worth. Wilson had enlisted into Leslie's Regiment in March 1695, at the age of 14 years.

Chapter 2: Finding an Army

1. With the increased speed in the pace of modern warfare, and the vastly greater means of ready communications, the vital role of signals as a fighting arm of service is not forgotten. In the early eighteenth century, however, signalling was a relatively basic process, usually carried out by handwritten note, face-to-face verbal order, or by beat of drum and flourish on trumpet. Logistics, for Marlborough – meaning providing the food for his army, horses and other draught animals so that those supplies could be gathered and transported, and fodder so that the animals themselves were in turn be fed – was always of fundamental importance, and will be discussed in detail in Chapter 8.

2. Churchill, W., *Marlborough, His Life and Times*, 1947, Book Two, p. 318.

3. Brown, B., *The Letters and Diplomatic Instructions of Queen Anne*, 1935, p. 145.

4. Crichton, A. (ed.), *The Life and Diary of Lieutenant-Colonel J. Blackader*, 1824, p. 171.

5. Nec Pluribus Impar Website, *Dutch Army Order of Battle in 1702*, 2011. Amongst the Huguenot Frenchmen who left to take up the service of others could be found Lieutenant John (Jean) Ligonier, who joined the British army and distinguished himself as a junior officer under Marlborough, and rose to become a field marshal, and one of the most influential British officers of the eighteenth century. He was taken prisoner on a later occasion by the French, and was introduced by Marshal Saxe to Louis XV; the king declared that the laws that prevented such a gallant soldier as Ligonier from fighting for the country of his birth were plainly mis-conceived. See also Whitworth, R., *Field Marshal Lord Ligonier, the British Army 1702–1770*, 1958.

6. Ibid.

7. Notable amongst the Walloons who changed their allegiance from Philip V to Charles III was the Comte de Merode-Westerloo, and he took his locally recruited regiment of excellent dragoons with him when he did so. However, to his credit, he had announced the change a year before the calamity to French arms suffered so dramatically at Ramillies. However, a perceived lack of appreciation of his services, and lack of advancement, rather than anything finer seems to have been behind the move: 'Nothing was further from my thoughts than to dictate to monarchs how they should comport themselves; they were the masters and might promote whomsoever they pleased.' Still, the comte goes on 'I was also born a free man, and I would not serve a moment longer if such an injustice was done me, after my giving so much service.' Chandler, D. (ed.), *Military Memoirs, Robert Parker and Comte de Merode-Westerloo*, 1968, p. 188.

8. Dalton, C., *English Army Commission Lists and Registers*, 1904, Volume III. p. xvi.

9. Portmore's, Stewart's, Stanhope's, Barrimore's and Bridges's regiments of Foot were sent to Portugal in 1702, joined later by Raby's (the Royal) Dragoons. See Willcox, W., *The Historical Record of the 5th (Royal Irish) Lancers*, 1908, p. 79.

10. Chandler, D., *The Art of Warfare in the Age of Marlborough*, 1976, p. 66. The gradual augmentation of Queen Anne's troops can be seen from the votes in Parliament for 31,524 'British' troops in 1702, 50,000 in 1706 and 75,000 five years later. A feeling for the enormous financial contribution made by Queen Anne's Treasury to the Allied war effort, a contribution which no others could attempt, can be seen in the vote of supplies (money) by the Parliament in London in December 1707, which included such considerable sums as:

£894,272	40,000 troops on the Flanders Establishment
£177,511	10,000 additional troops for Flanders
£ 34,251	for Palatine troops
£ 43,251	for Saxon troops
£ 22,957	for Hessian troops
£404,680	subsidies to the Allies
£500,000	subsidy to the Duke of Savoy
£100,000	additional subsidy to the Duke of Savoy (presumably for his expenses in the abortive 1707 campaign against Toulon).

See Tindal, N., *The Continuation of M Rapin's History of England*, 1743, p. 506, for additional details on this vote of money for the 1708 campaign. Many of the British regiments raised for service in the war were subsequently disbanded, only to be hastily re-raised with the eruption of the 1715 Jacobite rising, and survived from then onwards. See also Black, J., *Britain as a Military Power, 1688–1815*, 1999, for interesting additional comments on this aspect of the war.

11. Brown, p. 184.
12. Scouller, R., *Queen Anne's Army* (JSAHR), 1956, p. 221.
13. Scouller, R., *Purchase of Commissions and Promotions* (JSAHR), 1984, p. 131.
14. Scouller, *Queen Anne's Army*, p. 219.
15. Rennoldson, N. (ed.), *Renaissance Military Texts, Warfare in the Age of Louis XIV*, 2005, p. 84.
16. Brereton, J., *History of the 4/7th Dragoon Guards*, 1982, p. 49.
17. George MacArtney was described by Henry St John as a brave and experienced officer but a notorious rake. Although not present at the Schellenberg and Blenheim during the Danube campaign in 1704, he ably commanded his regiment at Ramillies and the siege of Ostend two years later, but was taken prisoner in 1707 at the defeat at Alamanza in Spain. Deprived of his regiment for misconduct, he served on as a volunteer and subsequently regained his command in recognition of his good conduct at Malplaquet, much to the resentment of those such as Argyll and Lord North and Grey, who heartily disapproved of him, his firm allegiance to Marlborough, and his raffish ways. MacArtney certainly seemed to attract trouble, and his opponents managed to see that he was cashiered once more, in 1710, for allegedly showing a lack of respect to the government and reportedly drinking a toast to the confusion of ministers. Two years later MacArtney had to flee England for taking part in a notorious duel where, as a second, he was said to have intervened to finish off one of the participants as he lay wounded on the ground. Much of the allegation had, once again, to do with the malicious political manoeuvring at a torrid time as Queen Anne's reign came to a close and, following the Hanoverian succession, the colonel was acquitted of this charge. MacArtney's Regiment was one of those 'hostilities only' units that were disbanded in the reductions of 1713 at the close of the war.
18. Neave-Hill, W., *Brevet Rank* (JSAHR), 1970, p. 86.
19. Kemp, A., *Weapons and Equipment of the Marlborough Wars*, 1980, p. 14.
20. Whitworth, p. 17.
21. Crichton, p. 236.
22. Davies, G., *Recruiting in the Reign of Queen Anne* (JSAHR), 1950, p. 155.
23. Robinson, J., *The Princely Chandos, A Memoir of James Brydges*, 1893, p. 41.
24. Scouller, *Queen Anne's Army*, p. 55. The Coldstream Guards establishment was 1,143 men in fourteen companies. A fully recruited French battalion in 1702 was smaller than its Allied counterpart, with just some 650–700 officers and men. See also Atkinson, C., *Queen Anne's Army* (JSAHR), 1958, p. 53.
25. The uniform for an officer of the British artillery train in 1708 was described as being a scarlet coat faced with blue and with brass buttons, and blue waistcoat and breeches. See Carman, W., *Notes* (JSAHR), 1939, p. 48.
26. *London Gazette*, 1711
27. The lengthy old English (William III pattern) musket was found to be unsuitable and unwieldy for service in the West Indies, partly as the inferior quality of manufacture caused the locks to quickly rust in the moist climate, unlike their more

robust French counterparts. In October 1702, English commanders had to ask that the shorter and lighter fusee be supplied instead. See Atkinson, C., *Queen Anne's War in the West Indies* (JSAHR), 1946, p. 86, for more details on this difficulty.

28. Tylden, G., *The British Infantryman* (JSAHR), 1969, p. 60. See also the Nec Pluribus Impar website for interesting details on the dress of the Swiss regiments in Dutch service.

29. Parker, G., *The Military Revolution*, 1998, p. 72.

30. Scouller, R., *The Clothing of Queen Anne's Army* (JSAHR), 1969, p. 211. See also Barthorp, M., *British Infantry Uniforms since 1660*, 1982, p. 21. The dress of a junior officer in Marlborough's army was described as:

> Black felt hat, turned up, edged with silver lace.
> Plain white neckcloth with collarless shirt.
> Red coat, lined with buff and turned back sleeves to show the lining. Silver buttons, buttonholes edged with silver lace.
> Buff leather gauntlet type gloves.
> Crimson sash and gilt gorget.
> Red waistcoat as the coat.
> Red breeches, Grey woollen stockings fastened with garters below the knee.
> Black leather shoes with silver buckles.

See also, Kemp, A., *Weapons and Equipment of the Marlborough Wars*, 1980, p. 142 for further details.

31. Depictions in portraits of officers wearing full or half-length armour are almost always fanciful, denoting simply the wearer's status as a distinguished (usually) soldier. The practice had largely died out by 1702, other than for cuirassiers, although Prince Eugene was seen to be wearing a breastplate under his coat at Blenheim two years later. See also Kemp, p. 140.

32. McBane, D., *The Expert Swordsman's Companion*, 1729, p. 98.

33. McBane, p. 98.

34. Holmes, R., *Marlborough, England's Fragile Genius*, 2006, p. 367.

35. Atkinson, C. (ed.), *Gleanings from the Cathcart Mss* (JSAHR), 1951 p. 25.

36. Ibid., p. 48.

37. Johnson, S. (ed.), *The Letters of Samuel Noyes, 1703–1704* (JSAHR), 1959, p. 69.

38. Chandler, D. (ed.), *Military Memoirs, Robert Parker and Comte de Merode-Westerloo*, 1968, p. 212.

39. Phelan, I., *Marlborough as Logistician* (JSAHR), 1989–90, p. 109. The veterans of Marlborough's army provided some examples of surprising longevity with Alexander Kilpatrick dying in 1783 (seventy-nine years after he fought at Blenheim); John Jackson, a gunner, having fought in nineteen actions under the duke, lasted until 1799, while MacLeod of Inverness walked to London from his Highland home in nineteen days in 1782 to petition King George III for a pension on account of his services under the duke. He died eight years later. See Grant, J., *British Battles by Land and Sea*, 1880, for further details.

40. Fortescue, J. (ed.), *The Life and Adventures of Mrs Christian Davies (Mother Ross)*, 1928, pp. 149–50.

41. Atkinson, *Gleanings from the Cathcart Mss* (JSAHR), 1951, pp. 24–5.

42. Atkinson, C., *Wynendael* (JSAHR), 1956, p. 77.

43. Phelan, p. 39.
44. Chandler, D. (ed.), *A Journal of Marlborough's Campaigns during the War of the Spanish Succession, 1702–1711* (JSAHR), 1984, p. 86.
45. Crichton, p. 52.
46. Ibid., p. 247.
47. Chandler, *A Journal of Marlborough's Campaigns*, pp. 48–9.
48. Ibid., p. 65.
49. Coxe, W., *Memoirs of the Duke of Marlborough*, Volume II, 1847, pp. 343–4.
50. Fortescue, p. 115.
51. Ibid., p. 106.

Chapter 3: The Commanders
1. Rowse, A., *The Early Churchills*, 1956, p. 320.
2. The warlike King Charles XII of Sweden was courted by Louis XIV in an attempt to involve him in the war for Spain, and by so doing to draw off to the north some of the many excellent German troops hired for service in the Grand Alliance. Amongst the Duke of Marlborough's most significant diplomatic coups was a visit he paid to Charles in 1707, to persuade him to stay out of the conflict. In this he was successful, and the king turned instead against Russia, and met defeat at Poltava two years later.
3. George, Elector of Hanover, was a man to be reckoned with, adroitly expanding his own territory and influence, and with the formidable assistance of his elderly mother, Electress Sophia Dorothea, was becoming one of the most prominent of the electors in their dealings with the emperor in Vienna. George also had an eye to the likely succession to the throne of Great Britain, as, after the early death of the Duke of Gloucester, Queen Anne would almost undoubtedly remain childless, and he was alert to any diplomatic manoeuvrings that might have a bearing on that process. He was also a capable field commander, providing large numbers of very good troops for service with the Grand Alliance, and might have had a greater influence on the military course of the war, particularly along the Rhine and France's eastern borders, had Marlborough and Eugene been more inclined to take him into their confidence. As it was, the elector was largely kept out of things, and remained in the dark over the plans for the march from the Moselle valley of Eugene's troops during the 1708 campaign. George was snubbed, in effect, and never forgot the fact. It is also true that not all the minor princes and electors who provided the Grand Alliance with troops shared the aims of the Alliance itself, or felt any particular animosity towards the French king. Their prime motive in many cases was the money provided in return for sending their soldiers to war.
4. Alison, A., *The Military Life of the Duke of Marlborough*, 1848, p. 112.
5. Ibid., p133.
6. Goslinga, S., *Memoires Relatifs a la Guerre de Succession de Espagne, 1706–1709 et 1711*, 1857, p. 5.
7. The low ridgeline between Ramillies and Offuz was generally thought to be a bad place to fight, whether it be on the attack or the defence. The marshy ground of the Petite Gheete stream was held to be a major obstacle to easy movement in an advance, particularly for cavalry. On the other hand, the extended nature of the field, with strongpoint villages situated out on each flank which would have to be

held, risked overstretching any army defending the ridge. Simultaneously, any attacking force was in endanger of being encircled by an enterprising commander who had to reach forward in that manner. Despite such concerns, Marshal Villeroi was not so enterprising, Marlborough took the risk, the battle was fought and still ranks as one of the most extraordinary and crushingly successful general actions of all time.

8. Coxe, A., *Memoirs of the Duke of Marlborough*, 1847, Volume I, p. 127.
9. Ibid., Volume II, pp. 371–3.
10. Murray, G. (ed.), *The Letters and Despatches of the Duke of Marlborough*, 1845, Volume IV. pp. 482–3. These valuable but forgotten documents were discovered unexpectedly in a records room on the Blenheim estate in 1842, and fortunately were recognized for what they were. Murray, Master-General of the Ordnance at the time, undertook to edit the mass of papers, and they were published three years later. 'No one', Winston Churchill wrote in the 1930s, 'can read the whole mass of the letters which Marlborough either wrote, dictated, or signed personally without being astonished at the mental and physical energy which it attests … disposed of day after day by a general manoeuvring equal or smaller forces in closest contact with a redoubtable enemy who often might engage in a decisive battle at no more than one hour's notice' (Churchill, W., *Marlborough, His Life and Times*, 1947, Book Two, p. 488).
11. Ibid.
12. Ibid., pp. 912–13.
13. Ibid., p. 964.
14. Ibid.
15. Henderson, N., *Prince Eugen of Savoy*, 1964, p. 13.
16. Ibid., pp. 9–10.
17. Atkinson, C., *Marlborough and the Rise of the British Army*, 1921, p. 333.
18. Chandler, D. (ed.), *Military Memoirs, Robert Parker and Comte de Merode-Westerloo*, 1968, p. 31. See also Watson, J., *Marlborough's Shadow*, 2003, p. 34.
19. Wykes, A., *The Royal Hampshire Regiment*, 1968, p. 29. Tom Kitcher was a Hampshire-born farm boy who served in Meredith's Regiment throughout Marlborough's campaigns and related his exploits to the rector in his home village when he left the service. See also Falkner, J., *Great and Glorious Days, Marlborough's Battles, 1704–1709*, 2002, p. 113.
20. Dalton, C., *English Army Commission Lists and Registers, 1660–1714*, Volume I, 1904, p. 38.
21. Dickson, A., *Red John of the Battles, the 2nd Duke of Argyll*, 1973, p. 97. See also, Dalton, C., *George the First's Army, 1714–1727*, 1910, p. 9. Although Marlborough clearly preferred to have his close friend William Cadogan in charge of suppressing the Jacobite rebellion in 1715, the Duke of Argyll had already requested to return to London to attend to some private affairs before the order of recall was made. He remained a controversial figure, and was subsequently dismissed from all his official posts by George I in 1717, but reinstated the following year. George II then removed Argyll in 1740, only to reinstate him, once again, the next year.
22. Ibid., p. 116.
23. Fortescue, J. (ed.), *The Life and Adventures of Mrs Christian Davies (Mother Ross)*, 1929, p. 138.

24. Dalton, C., *George the First's Army*, p. 5. Letter to Lord Raby.
25. Rowse, p. 316.
26. Fortescue, p. 156.
27. Belfield, E., *Oudenarde, 1708*, 1972, p. 24.
28. Johnson, S. (ed.), *The Letters of Samuel Noyes, 1703–1704* (JSAHR), 1959, p. 131. See also Atkinson, C. (ed.), *Gleanings from the Cathcart Mss* (JSAHR), 1951.
29. Miller, H., *Colonel Parke of Virginia, the Greatest Hector in the Town*, 1989, p. 204. Daniel Parke caused a scandal, the first of several, when he left his wife and children behind in Virginia and travelled to London with his mistress to lobby for a lucrative government appointment. He attempted to get into Parliament, but was censured for the overt and brazen attempts made to bribe voters (these must have been extreme indeed, given that such practices were commonplace). His attachment to Marlborough's army in the Danube campaign seems to have been a part of this attempt to secure a permanent office, as he had no formal appointment in the army, his commission as 'colonel' being that he held with the Virginia Militia.
30. Chandler, *Military Memoirs*, p. 161.
31. Ibid., pp. 165–6.
32. Ibid., p. 201.
33. Ibid., p. 206.
34. Churchill, Book One, p. 893.
35. Ibid., Book Two, p. 168. Vendôme blamed the defeat at Oudenarde on the Duc de Bourgogne, the eldest grandson of King Louis XIV, and eventually the heir to the throne of France. This was a dangerous game to play, as Vendôme's own hot-headed and ill-judged behaviour was in large part responsible for the loss, and in any case the French king could hardly, in public at least, acknowledge that his grandson had been at fault. Although partisan in-fighting between the competing factions in Versailles, with most of those involved prudently supporting Burgundy, saw that Vendôme was dismissed, Louis XIV could not do without his undoubted abilities for long, and he was soon reinstated.
36. Petrie, C., *The Marshal Duke of Berwick*, 1953, p. 334. Marshal Villars was on his own deathbed when the news of Berwick's death was brought to him.
37. Dalton, C., *The Blenheim Roll, 1704*, 1904, p. 3. The Earl of Stair also received a purse of 1,000 guineas when he brought news of the victory at Oudenarde to London in 1708. The bringer of the news of the Allied victory at Saragossa in 1710, however, was rewarded with just 500 guineas, which may be an indication of general increased weariness with the war, or a certain renewed caution in Queen Anne's Treasury.
38. Coxe, Volume II, pp. 40–1.
39. Murray, p. 183.
40. Muller, J., *A System of Camp Discipline*, 1757, pp. 200–1.
41. Burn, W. (ed.), *A Scots Fusilier and Dragoon under Marlborough* (JSAHR), 1936, p. 85.
42. Ibid.
43. Chandler, *Military Memoirs*, p. 60.
44. Crichton, A. (ed.), *The Life and Diary of Lieutenant-Colonel J. Blackader*, 1824, pp. 351–2.
45. Ibid., p. 219.

Chapter 4: The Horse

1. Chandler, D., *The Art of Warfare in the Age of Marlborough*, 1976, p. 53.
2. Dr David Chandler gave the proportions of cavalry in the armies engaged in Marlborough's most notable victories; as Blenheim (1704) 32.4%, Ramillies (1706) 27%, Oudenarde (1708 on unsuitable ground for cavalry) 24.1%, and Malplaquet (1709) 27.3%. General Max Weygand estimated that, at the close of the War of the Spanish Succession, the French army comprised just 25% cavalry and dragoons, out of a total strength of approximately 300,000 men. See also Chandler, *Art of Warfare*, pp. 30–1.
3. Kemp, A., *Weapons and Equipment of Marlborough's Wars*, 1980, pp. 55–6. During the Blenheim campaign, 356 horses ridden by the rank and file were lost by the British Horse and dragoons, to enemy action and disease. The cost to Queen Anne's Treasury of providing remounts was £6,725, in addition to the officers having to obtain and pay for their own replacements. Richard Pope lamented that he had lost six mounts, and commented on the prevalence of sickness amongst the horses at the time. The effect on the French cavalry of the sickness 'glanders' is well documented, but it affected the Allied armies as well, although to a lesser degree, The comparable losses at the end of the following year, a campaign that, despite Marlborough's best efforts, saw no major general action, were 882 horses. See Cormack, A., *Equine Losses in the Campaign of 1704* (JSAHR), 2013, pp. 60–5, and Rennoldson, N. (ed.), *Renaissance Military Texts, Warfare in the Age of Louis XIV*, 2005, p. 90.
4. Scouller, R., *The Armies of Queen Anne*, 1966, p. 252.
5. Murray, G., *The Letters and Despatches of the Duke of Marlborough*, 1845, Volume III, p. 126.
6. Chandler, D. (ed.), *Military Memoirs, Robert Parker and Comte de Merode-Westerloo*, 1968, p. 202
7. Brereton, J., *History of the 4/7th Dragoons Guards*, 1982, p. 79.
8. Sir Arthur Hazelrigg's cuirassiers in the English Civil War were nicknamed 'Lobsters' for the amount of armour they wore, at a time when it was gradually fading from use. However, Hazelrigg himself, in flight after the Parliamentarian defeat at Roundway Down in Wiltshire in 1643, was set upon and struck repeatedly with a sword about the head by a Royalist horseman, and suffered only minor injuries in the affray.
9. Brereton, p. 53.
10. Ibid.
11. Murray, Volume I, p. 331.
12. Ibid., Volume I, p. 336.
13. Ibid., Volume I, p. 338.
14. Taylor, F., *The Wars of Marlborough*, Volume I, 1921, p. 385. Lieutenant General Wood's energy flagged at last with increasing age, and Charles Colville, serving with the Cameronians, remembered him in 1710 as a 'very old infirm man who did not stir out of his house and not often out of bed for the whole winter'. Sumner, P., *Military Memoirs of Lieutenant-General Charles Colville* (JSAHR), 1947, pp. 56–7. Wood died in 1712.
15. Cannon, R., *History of the 2nd (Royal North British) Dragoons*, 1836, p. 48. 'Both corps were distinguished from other regiments by being permitted to wear grenadier caps.'

16. Kemp, p. 56
17. Chandler, *Art of Warfare*, p. 53.
18. Chandler, *Military Memoirs*, pp. 156–7. The good order in which Marlborough's troops arrived in southern Germany, after their long march from the Low Countries, attracted wide approving comment. Prince Eugene's comments, of course, were highly complimentary and diplomatically aimed at pleasing Marlborough, whose assistance, at some considerable professional risk, was essential to the Imperial war effort in southern Germany. 'The Prince who was surprised to see them in such good order after so long a tedious and quick march, praised the goodly appearance of their clothes, accoutrements and horse. See Millner, J., *A Compendious Journal*, 1712, p. 88. Eugene, fine field commander that he was, often led troops who were shabby if not actually ragged, as the Imperial finances could not support their armies on campaign. There is, however, no reason to really doubt the good condition of Marlborough's troops after their long march up the Rhine, and the comments of Millner, Parker and Kane, men who all took part in the famous exploit, support this.
19. Rennoldson, N. (ed.), *Renaissance Military Texts, Warfare in the Age of Louis XIV*, 2005, pp. 88–9.
20. Chandler, *Art of Warfare*, p. 54.
21. Ibid.
22. Horsley, W. (ed.), *Chronicles of an Old Campaigner*, 1904, pp. 311–13. Despite all this wisdom, old habits clearly died hard, even when they were thoroughly bad habits. The British 15th Light Dragoons overthrew a squadron of the French 13th Hussars who had remained stationary to receive them at Tarsac in southern France during the closing stages of the Duke of Wellington's 1814 campaign.
23. Turnbull, S., *The Art of Renaissance Warfare*, 2008, pp. 77–178. The *en muraille* technique for delivering a massed cavalry advance was a simple development of the wedge-like formation (*en host*, as it had been known), adopted by the German reiters in the sixteenth century. 'Reiters' was the term that had come from the word *schwartzreiter* (black rider), mounted cavalrymen who, clad in blackened armour to prevent rust, made use of wheel-lock pistols while mounted as their particular speciality in breaking up massed formations of foot soldiers armed with the pike. The caracole movement allowed the riders to fire and then turn about and retire to a sheltered rear position, to reload their pistols well away from the return fire of their opponent's arquebusiers, before riding forward to the attack once more. Such a movement had to be well drilled and practised to maintain any semblance of order, and to avoid firing into one's own ranks in error. It was also common for the pistol to be discharged in such a way that the lock mechanism was uppermost, to avoid a loss of priming powder while riding forward, but this hampered correct aiming and meant a degree of inaccuracy to what was being attempted. There was also the danger of shooting the ears off one's own horse. A further development of this tactic was to use the same method against opposing horsemen, but this was dismissed by some as 'a pretext for doing nothing while seeming to do much'. An alternative and rather more dynamic option was to go in to the charge when the opposing cavalrymen retired in the caracole movement. The rearward movement of the caracole, superficially so logical and prudent in gaining time and space in which to prepare for the next attack, could rapidly be

turned into confusion, rout, panic and flight by an opponent thrusting home with the sword.

24. Chandler, *Military Memoirs*, p. 276.
25. Burrell, S. (ed.), *Amiable Renegade, The Memoirs of Captain Peter Drake*, 1960, p. 167.
26. Kemp, p. 70. See also Chandler, *Art of Warfare*, p. 47.
27. Burn, W. (ed.), *A Scots Fusilier and Dragoon under Marlborough* (JSAHR), 1936, p. 40.
28. The quality of swords, particularly those issued to the common trooper, varied widely and the difficulty in getting and maintaining a keen cutting edge to the blade was often commented on. This problem lasted for many years, although the 1796 British light cavalry sword was generally recognized to be a superb and murderously effective weapon, unlike its more clumsy hatchet-pointed heavy cavalry counterpart, such that it raised protests from French commanders for the dreadful wounds that were inflicted by its use. The swords in the hands of the British troopers in the Crimea were generally reported to be of poor quality, and more like a cudgel with which to batter and bruise an opponent than able to inflict any serious cutting or stabbing wound. By contrast, the tulwars wielded by rebel Indian horsemen in the 1857–9 Mutiny were noted for their sharp edge, and on one occasion one such downward stroke was seen to sever not only a saddle crupper, an achievement in itself, but the spine of the unfortunate horse too. See Holmes, R., *Redcoat, the British soldier in the Age of Horse and Musket*, 2004, p. 233. As late as August 1914, a British cavalry officer in the 12th Lancers would notice that that his shiny new Wilkinson sword bent like a bow, instead of fully piercing the breast of a German soldier from Queen Victoria's Dragoons of the Prussian Guard, in a gently sloping field just to the south of St Quentin. The Troop sergeant's older-pattern cutting sword 'well sharpened', however, was said to have gone in and out like to a pat of butter. See: Stewart, P., *The History of the XII Royal Lancers*, 1950, p. 254.
29. Atkinson, C., *Marlborough and the Rise of the British Army*, 1921, p. 295.

Chapter 5: The Foot
1. Neuburg, V., *Gone for a Soldier*, 1989, p. 18.
2. Holmes, R., *Marlborough, England's Fragile Genius*, 2006, p. 205.
3. Leopold, Prince of Anhalt-Dessau, introduced iron ramrods into use in his own regiment in 1698 at his own expense, despite concerns that their use would cause sparks to be struck in the barrel, with the possibility of premature discharges. Twenty years later they were coming into general use. See Scurfield, R., *Smoothbore Firearms* (JSAHR), 1957, pp. 86–9.
4. Chandler, D. (ed.), *Military Memoirs, Robert Parker and Comte de Merode-Westerloo*, 1968, p. 89. Robert Parker was not at Malplaquet, as he was rather reluctantly in Ireland on recruiting duties in September 1709, but the engagement at the edge of the woods was described to him by his brother officers in the Royal Irish Regiment soon afterwards.
5. Falkner, J., *Ramillies 1706, Year of Miracles*, 2006, p. 69.
6. Haythornthwaite, D., *The Armies of Wellington*, 1996, p. 80. It was not only the colours of Allied regiments that had yet to achieve the status or diligent care that they would, in time, be accorded. The thirty-four French standards and eighty-three colours taken at Blenheim were paraded through the streets of London on

3 January 1705 and taken to Westminster Hall to be displayed in triumph. Through neglect they then rotted away in St Paul's Cathedral, so that 131 years later there was no longer any trace to be found. See Dalton, C., *The Blenheim Roll, 1704,* 1904, p. xv.

7. Kane, R., *The Campaigns of King William and Queen Anne,* 1747, pp. 111–42.
8. Fortescue, J. (ed.), *The Life and Adventures of Mrs Christian Davies (Mother Ross),* 1928, pp. 85–6. Rifled weapons were occasionally in use, although they were usually expensive sporting weapons, and a Parliamentary officer was killed by shot from one of these pieces at the siege of Litchfield in Staffordshire in 1644.
9. Chandler, D. (ed.), *The Journal of John Wilson, 1694–1727* (Army Records Society), 2005, p. 78.
10. Falkner, J., *Guide to Marlborough's Battlefields,* 2008, p. 199.
11. Chandler, D. (ed.), *A Journal of Marlborough's Campaigns during the War of the Spanish Succession, 1702–1711* (JSAHR), 1984, p. 48.
12. Johnson, S. (ed.), *The Letters of Samuel Noyes, 1702–1703* (JSAHR), 1959, pp. 131–2.
13. Kane, pp. 136–7. HM 44th Foot misjudged this movement badly at Quatres Bras in June 1815 and were mauled by Marshal Ney's cavalry as a result.
14. Chandler, *Military Memoirs,* p. 55.
15. Kane, p. 113.
16. Ibid., p. 68.
17. Chandler, *Journal of John Wilson,* p. 59.
18. Millner, J., *A Compendious Journal, 1701–1712,* 1733, pp. 171–2.
19. Wykes, A., *The Royal Hampshire Regiment,* 1968, pp. 29–30.
20. Chandler, *Military Memoirs,* p. 64.
21. Burn, W., *A Scots Fusilier and Dragoon under Marlborough* (JSAHR), 1936, p. 89.
22. Chandler, D. (ed.), *A Journal of Marlborough's Campaigns,* pp. 107–8. Concerns at a loss of offensive spirit, with bombing out with grenades taking the place of closing with the bayonet, were felt by both Allied and German senior officers in the trench-fighting tactics of the First World War.
23. Parker, pp. 22–3. David Chandler, in his admirable work, *Marlborough as Military Commander,* 1974, p. 105, states that this exploit was at Liège, but it was, as Parker makes quite clear, actually at the siege of Venlo.
24. Chandler, *A Journal of Marlborough's Campaigns,* pp. 94–5.
25. Snyder, J., *The Marlborough–Godolphin Correspondence,* 1975, Volume III, p. 1363.
26. Alison, A., *The Military Life of John, Duke of Marlborough,* 1848, p. 275.
27. Falkner, J., *Marlborough's Battlefields,* 2008, p. 197.

Chapter 6: The Gunners

1. McBane, D., *The Expert Swordsman's Companion,* 1729, p. 101.
2. When the Duke of Marlborough took command of the Anglo-Dutch army in 1702, the 'Flanders Train', the artillery provided by Queen Anne's Treasury, comprised a headquarters staff, two artillery companies with fifty-nine all ranks each, a twenty-two-strong pioneer company, a pontoon bridging company with twenty-three men, with thirty-four guns and howitzers. See Chandler, D., *The Art of Warfare in the Age of Marlborough,* 1976, p. 161.
3. Bronze guns had a tendency to warp with the heat of sustained firing, and to droop at the muzzle as a consequence. Marshal Vauban planned the formal

defence of Paris in the 1680s, and he advocated equipping those defences with the cheaper iron guns to ease the strain on the Treasury of King Louis XIV. This project came to nothing, not because of any doubts over the iron guns, but because the king was not convinced of the value of having Parisians sitting secure behind their defences and quite possibly defying him. When Baron Haxho, an engineer officer who had served with distinction under Napoleon, completed the long-delayed defences of the French capital city in the nineteenth century, the ordnance that was provided was indeed that of iron guns.

4. Chandler, *The Art of Warfare*, p. 185.
5. Anon., *The Diary of John Evelyn* (edited), 1818, p. 88.
6. Murray, G. (ed.), *The Letters and Despatches of the Duke of Marlborough*, 1845, Volume IV, pp. 381–2. See also the *Journal of the Society of Army Historical Research*, 1923, p. 147 for interesting additional comments.
7. Chandler, *The Art of Warfare*, pp. 141–2 and 192. The maximum range for artillery pieces when fired at an angle of 45 degrees was held to be 4,600 yards for a 24-pounder gun, 3,600 yards for a 12-pounder, 3,360 yards for an 8- or 9-pounder, and 2,920 yards for a 4-pounder. However, wasting shot at unrealistic distances was discouraged and battle ranges of about 1,000 yards were more practical. Chandler felt that to engage at ranges over 600 yards were unusual, with canister employed at no more than 300 yards, p. 211. The effective range for breaching batteries engaged in siege work was often much shorter, and the gun emplacements and their crews had to be heavily protected from the fire of the defenders.
8. Chandler, *The Art of Warfare*, pp. 209–11. See also, Hughes, B., *Open Fire, Artillery Tactics from Marlborough to Wellington*, 1983, for useful additional useful information.
9. Horsley, W. (ed.), *Chronicles of an Old Campaigner*, 1904, pp. 182–3. Holcroft Blood's father had infamously attempted to steal the crown jewels from the Tower of London during the reign of King Charles II. Colonel Blood, a skilled artillerist much valued by Marlborough, died in 1708.
10. Horsley, pp. 338–9.
11. Chandler, *The Art of Warfare*, p. 146.
12. Ibid., p. 211.
13. Chandler, D., *Marlborough as Military Commander*, 1974, p. 173.
14. Murray, Volume IV, p. 144.
15. Churchill, W., *Marlborough, His Life and Times*, 1947, Book Two, p. 425.
16. Coxe, W., *Memoirs of the Duke of Marlborough*, 1847, Volume II, p. 301. The complete inability of French commanders to seriously interfere with the preparation for the siege of Lille indicates very well the state of disarray, and low morale, in their army after the shock of the defeat at Oudenarde.

Chapter 7: The Engineers
1. Churchill, W., *Marlborough, His Life and Times*, 1947, Book Two, p. 579.
2. To their credit, it should be said that armies could move with remarkable nimbleness at times – Prince Eugene's forced march northwards from the Moselle and Marshal Berwick's shadowing march, with Marlborough then driving his troops forward to overtake the Duc de Vendôme on the river Scheldt in July 1708, being excellent examples. The French commander's well-known comment, 'If they are

there, the devil must have carried them, such marching impossible,' indicates a lively scepticism that the Allied troops could make such good time on the road from the Dender River. Vendôme was perhaps thinking that the troops concerned were actually from the garrison in Oudenarde. The famous march by Marlborough's army through the August night in 1711, to breach the vaunted Lines of Non Plus Ultra, is yet another when speed was a strict necessity. See also Churchill, Book Two, p. 360.

3. The reputation established by skilled military engineers such as Sebastien le Prestre de Vauban and his Dutch counterpart, Meinheer van Coehorn, was slow to deliver the full recognition that was so obviously deserved by their essential activities. The French engineer was eventually made a Marshal of France in January 1703, but it was widely seen as late in coming, and even at that time surprise was expressed that Vauban, as simply an engineer, was so honoured by the French king.

4. Fortescue, J. (ed.), *The Life and Adventures of Mrs Christian Davies (Mother Ross)*, 1929, p. 107.

5. In the late summer of 1914, the Belgian army breached the same sluices around Nieuport that had attracted Vendôme's attention in 1708, intending to slow the thrusting German advance after the evacuation of Antwerp which threatened both to expel King Albert's army entirely from its homeland and to lay hands on the important ports on the Channel coast. The staunchly patriotic Belgian civilian lock-keepers, knowing the mechanics of how this could be accomplished and who, had they been apprehended, would almost certainly have been shot by the Germans as saboteurs, easily outshone their military counterparts. See Pul, van P., *In Flanders Flooded Fields*, 2006, for additional interesting details on this campaign of sabotage.

6. Burrell, S. (ed.), *Amiable Renegade, the Memoirs of Captain Peter Drake, 1671–1753*, 1960, pp. 198–9.

7. Murray, G. (ed.), *Letters and Despatches of the Duke of Marlborough*, 1845, Volume V, p. 127.

8. Crichton, A. (ed.), *The Life and Diary of Lieutenant-Colonel J Blackader*, 1824, pp. 339–40.

9. Murray, Volume V, p. 126

10. Chandler, D., *The Art of Warfare in the Age of Marlborough*, 1976, p. 255.

11. McBane, D., *The Expert Swordsman's Companion*, 1729, pp. 107–8.

12. Rennoldson, N. (ed.), *Renaissance Military Texts, Warfare in the Age of Louis XIV*, 2005, p. 88.

13. Chandler, D. (ed.), *A Journal of the Marlborough's Campaigns, 1702–1711* (JSAHR), 1984, p. 117. John Deane also wrote that during the siege of Aire, 'The trenches being so very dirty and miserable for the men who could neither sit nor lie to rest themselves, but was obliged to stand always come life or death', p. 120. To hammer a nail into the vent-hole of a cannon would render it unusable until it could be drilled clear again, a laborious and slow process.

14. Reeve, J., *The Siege of Bethune, 1710* (JSAHR), 1985, p. 203. The garrison commander, Major General Michael Roth, was an émigré Catholic Irishman serving in the French army on account of his religion – yet one more example of the oddities of military life in the eighteenth century.

15. Petrie, C., *The Marshal Duke of Berwick*, 1953, p. 229.
16. Parker, G., *The Military Revolution*, 1998, p. 70.
17. Coxe, W., *Memoirs of the Duke of Marlborough*, Volume II, 1847, p. 305.
18. Ibid.
19. Churchill, Book Two, p. 436.
20. Murray, Volume IV, p. 177.
21. Coxe, p. 310.
22. Millner, J., *A Compendious Journal, 1701–1712*, 1733, p. 250.
23. Petrie, p. 232.
24. Murray, Volume IV, p. 577.
25. Chandler, D. (ed.), *The Journal of John Wilson, 1694–1727* (Army Records Society), 2005, p. 75.
26. Murray, Volume IV, p. 556.
27. Ibid., Volume IV, pp. 572–7.
28. Crichton, p. 346.
29. Coxe, p. 426.
30. Chandler, *Art of Warfare*, p. 258.
31. Kenyon, *Stuart England*, 1978, p. 328.

Chapter 8: Logistics

1. Phelan, I., *Marlborough as Logistician* (JSAHR), 1989–90, p. 254.
2. Chandler, D., *The Art of Warfare in the Age of Marlborough*, 1976, p. 13.
3. Murray, G. (ed.), *The Letters and Despatches of the Duke of Marlborough*, Volume IV, 1845, p. 299. The Duke of Marlborough's campaign in the Moselle valley early in 1705 came to grief, at least in part, as the commissary officer left in Trier, a Mr Centery, had failed to gather enough flour, forage and grain, but then sold the stores he had acquired and pocketed the money, before deserting to the French to avoid the retribution he so richly deserved. 'The commissary employed there in chief to do it has either been in correspondence with France and treacherously neglected it, or else has spent the money and could not do it, so the magazines fall mightily short of what is necessary.' See: Falkner, J., *Marlborough's Wars*, 2005, p. 80, also Chandler D., *Marlborough as Military Commander*, 1974, p. 155.
4. Coxe, W., *Memoirs of the Duke of Marlborough*, 1848, Volume II, p. 339.
5. Falkner, J., *Marlborough's Wars*, p. 181.
6. McBane, D., *The Expert Swordsman's Companion*, 1729, p. 129.
7. Millner, J., *A Compendious Journal, 1701–1712*, 1733, p. 83.
8. Trim, D., *Mars & Clio* (BCMH), 2007.
9. Chandler, D., *Blenheim Preparation, the English Army on the March to the Danube*, 2004, p. 121. See also Dalton, C., *The Blenheim Roll 1704*, 1904, p. 9. Richard King, who was awarded a bounty of £16.10s for his work at Blenheim, eventually served as quartermaster-general in Canada in 1711 with the rank of colonel.
10. Chandler, D. (ed.), *Military Memoirs, Robert Parker and Comte de Merode-Westerloo*, 1968, p. 31.
11. Chandler, *Marlborough as Military Commander*, p. 130.
12. Fortescue, J. (ed.), *The Life and Adventures of Mrs Christian Davies (Mother Ross)*, 1929, p. 106.
13. Millner, p. 83.

14. Chandler, D. (ed.), *A Journal of Marlborough's Campaigns during the War of the Spanish Succession, 1702–1711* (JSAHR), 1984, p. 5.
15. Ibid.
16. Chandler, *Blenheim Preparation*, p. 161. Given this careful calculation of how much and for how long any given district could sustain an army on campaign, it is no surprise that most warlike operations were conducted in fairly well-populated areas, rich in resources, and means of easy communication and well-developed agricultural practices, such as the Southern Netherlands. From this also developed the barbaric practice of eating up a region, stripping it so bare that an opponent could not operate or subsist his own army there – the French were adept at this, particularly in the latter part of the seventeenth century. However, Marlborough's devastation of Bavaria in July 1704 was of a similar nature; if he could not achieve his immediate aim of forcing the elector to come to terms, he could at least prevent the Bavarian and French armies from quartering properly there through the coming winter. The inevitable effect upon the unfortunate civilian population, from either course, hardly needs stating.
17. Fortescue, p. 57.
18. Murray, Volume I. p. 359.
19. Atkinson, C., *Gleanings from the Cathcart Mss* (JSAHR), 1951, p. 66.
20. Anon., *The Origins of Ostomy Surgery*, website, 2007. The material from which the soldiery was drawn was generally pretty rough-hewn; William Hiseland, born in 1620 and a veteran of the English Civil Wars, is perhaps the prime example of this breed, as he fought at Malplaquet in 1709 at the ripe old age of 89 years, got married fourteen years later, and went on to die in the Royal Hospital in Chelsea in 1732, his 112th year. Alexander Kilpatrick, who was at Blenheim, died in 1783, and Ambrose Tennant lived until 1800, before dying in Tetbury in Gloucestershire.
21. McBane, D., *The Expert Swordsman's Companion*, 1729, pp. 108–9.
22. Arni, Gruber von, *Medical Support for Marlborough's Army* (JSAHR), 2008, p. 166.
23. Johnson, S. (ed.), *The Letters of Samuel Noyes, 1703–1704* (JSAHR), 1959, pp. 133–45.
24. McBane, p. 122.
25. Ibid., p. 120.
26. Fortescue, p. 139.
27. Ibid., pp. 152–3.
28. Hennen, J., *Military Surgery*, 1918, p. 2.
29. Spencer, C., *Blenheim*, 2004, p. 186.
30. Scouller, R., *Queen Anne's Army*, 1966, p. 56.
31. Burn, W. (ed.), *A Scots Fusilier and Dragoon under Marlborough* (JSAHR), 1936, p. 58. See also Dalton, C., *English Army Commission lists and Registers*, 1904, p. 62.
32. Murray, Volume I, p. 152.
33. Dugawe, D., *Mrs Christian Davies* (DNB), 2004. See also Falkner, *Marlborough's Wars*, p. 9. Applications for admission to the Royal Hospital in Chelsea in the period 1715–32, which would all have been from Marlborough's veterans, included the following reasons for incapacity:
    (i)   A trooper of Horse who had been shot in the right arm at Blenheim (1704), shot in the back at Ramillies (1706) and then cut over the head at Oudenarde (1708).

(ii)   A soldier of Sabine's Regiment who had been wounded in the left hand at the Schellenberg (1704), in the left heel at Blenheim, and in his right hand at the siege of Ghent (1708).

(iii) A soldier of Howard's Regiment who had been shot in the right knee at Blenheim, and his left leg had then been fractured by a bomb blast and he had been wounded in the left elbow by the thrust of a halberd.

(iv)   A soldier of Sabine's Regiment who had been shot in the right arm at Malplaquet (1709). He had also been shot in the head at Maastricht [1705 possibly], with the ball entering behind his right ear and exiting in his neck.

(v)   A soldier of Sabine's Regiment who had been shot in the left wrist during the siege of Lille (1708), and in his left side, under the ribs, at the siege of Douai (1710).

(vi)   A soldier of the Foot Guards who had been blown up by a barrel of gunpowder at the siege of Tournai (1709), where he had also been wounded in his left shoulder and arm. He was later cut in the thigh at the siege of Bouchain (1711).

(vii) A soldier of Wade's Regiment who was shot in his left thigh at the Schellenberg, and in his right knee at Blenheim.

(viii) A drummer of Wood's Regiment who had lost his right eye during the siege of Lille, and been shot in the right arm and neck at Malplaquet.

(ix)   A sergeant of Anstruther's Regiment who had been shot in the left foot at Steenkirk (1692), and in the head at Nether Hespen (1694), and then wounded in the right arm at Blenheim.

(x)   A soldier of the Foot Guards who had been wounded in the abdomen during the siege of Menin (1706), and in the left leg at the siege of Douai. He had also previously been wounded several times at the siege of Tournai (1709).

See Arni, *Medical Support for Marlborough's Army*, for further useful details on this aspect of campaigning.

34. Crichton, A. (ed.), *The Life and Diary of Lieutenant-Colonel J Blackader*, 1824, p. 364.
35. See Dalton, *The Blenheim Roll*, for specific details.
36. Neuburg, V., *Gone for a Soldier*, 1989, p. 61.
37. Chandler, *Military Memoirs*, p. 149.
38. Crichton, p. 242.
39. Crichton, p. 244.

Chapter 9: Marlborough's Legacy

1. Churchill, W., *Marlborough, His Life and Times*, 1947, Book Two, p. 15.
2. Ibid., Book Two, p. 918.
3. Goslinga, S., *Memoires Relatifs a la Guerre de Succession de Espagne, 1706-1709 et 1711*, 1857, pp. 33–4.
4. The widespread surprise that Marlborough had been caught unawares by the Duc de Vendôme's audacious offensive in northern Flanders in the summer of 1708 indicates very well that this was a most unusual incident. His ability to recover his strategic poise and overwhelm the French at Oudenarde within a couple of weeks speaks very highly for the duke's military talent and resourcefulness.
5. Trevelyan, G., *Ramillies and the Union with Scotland*, 1948, p. 287.

6. It should not be assumed that Great Britain's allies were unaware of the restraining orders which the Duke of Ormonde received in 1712 when appointed to be the commander of Queen Anne's troops in the Low Countries. That the British had been in negotiations with the French to concluded a peace, separate if need be from the rest of the Grand Alliance, would not be kept secret; much was known but much could not be said while the Allied armies, on the face of things, continued to operate in harmony together. Eventually, 'New instructions were sent to the Duke of Ormonde; in consequence of which, he withdrew from the rest of the army, encamped at Aven-le-Sec with all our English troops ... To the end the allies might be rendered incapable to undertake anything considerable against France.' Ormonde also had instructions to withdraw from service those foreign troops paid for by British subsidies, but in this he had mixed success: 'The Prince of Hesse-Cassell, also summoned to follow us, thus addressed himself to the officer who carried the order: "Sir, tell the Duke of Ormond that the Hessian troops desire nothing more ardently than to march, provided it be to engage the French."' See Fortescue, J. (ed.), *The Life and Adventures of Mrs Christian Davies (Mother Ross)*, 1929, pp. 162–3.
7. Black, J., *Britain as a Military Power, 1688–1815*, 1999, p. 59.
8. Churchill, Book Two, p. 99. See also Falkner, J., *Guide to Marlborough's Battlefields*, 2008, p. 96.
9. Holmes, R., *Riding the Retreat*, 1992, p. 33.
10. Keegan, J. (ed.), *General Jack's Diary*, 1964, p. 6.

Bibliography

Alison, A., *The Military Life of John, Duke of Marlborough*, 1848.
Anderson, R., *The Storming of the Schellenberg, 1704* (JSAHR) 1986.
Anon., *The Compleat History of the Treaty of Utrecht*, 1715.
—— *The Diary of John Evelyn* (edited), 1818.
—— *The Origins of Ostomy Surgery* (website), 2007.
Arni, E.G. von, *Medical Support for Marlborough's Army* (JSAHR), 2008.
Atkinson, C., *Marlborough and the Rise of the British Army*, 1921.
—— *Marlborough and the Dutch Deputies* (JSAHR), 1935.
—— *Marlborough's Order of Battle* (JSAHR), 1936.
—— *A Royal Dragoon in the Spanish Succession War* (JSAHR), 1938.
—— *Queen Anne's War in the West Indies* (JSAHR), 1946.
—— *The Journal of William Todd* (JSAHR), 1951.
—— *Gleanings from the Cathcart Mss* (JSAHR), 1951.
—— *Wynendael* (JSAHR), 1956.
—— *Queen Anne's Army* (JSAHR), 1958.
Baignol, R., *La Campagne de 1704 en Allemagne*, 1909.
Bathorp, M., *Marlborough's Army, 1702–1711*, 1980.
—— *British Infantry Uniforms*, 1982.
—— *British Cavalry Uniforms*, 1984.
Belfield, E., *Oudenarde, 1708*, 1972.
Bishop, M., *Life and Adventures of Matthew Bishop*, 1744.
Black, J., *Warfare in the Eighteenth Century*, 1999.
—— *Britain as a Military Power, 1688–1815*, 1999.
Bowen, H., *The Dutch at Malplaquet* (JSAHR), 1962.
Brereton, J., *History of the 4/7th Dragoon Guards*, 1982.
Brown, B., *The Letters and Diplomatic Instructions of Queen Anne*, 1935.
Bruce, A., *The Purchase System in the British Army, 1660–1871*, 1980.
Burn, W. (ed.), *A Scots Fusilier and Dragoon under Marlborough* (JSAHR), 1936.
Burrell, S. (ed.), *Amiable Renegade: The Memoirs of Captain Peter Drake*, 1960.
Cannon, R., *Historical Records of the 2nd (Royal North British) Dragoons*, 1836.
—— *Historical Records of the 1st (Royal) Regiment of Foot*, 1844.
—— *Historical Records of the 14th Regiment of Foot*, 1846.
Carleton, G. (ed. Lawrence, A.), *Military Memoirs of Captain Carleton*, 1929.
Carman, W., *Notes* (JSAHR), 1939.
—— *The Dress of Erle's Regiment in 1704 and 1709* (JSAHR), 1968.
Chandler, D. (ed.), *Military Memoirs, Robert Parker and Comte de Merode-Westerloo*, 1968.
—— *Marlborough as Military Commander*, 1974.
—— *The Art of Warfare in the Age of Marlborough*, 1976.

—— (ed.), *A Journal of Marlborough's Campaigns during the War of the Spanish Succession, 1702–1711* (JSAHR), 1984.

—— *Blenheim Preparation: The English Army on March to the Danube*, 2004 (ed. Falkner, J.).

—— (ed.), *Military Miscellany: The Journal of John Wilson, 1694–1727* (Army Records Society), 2005.

Childs, J., *The British Army of William III*, 1979.

—— *Armies and Warfare in Europe, 1648–1789*, 1982.

—— *The Nine Years' War and the British Army, 1688–1697*, 1991.

Chisolm, J., *A Manual of Military Surgery*, 1864.

Churchill, W., *Marlborough, His Life and Times* (two volumes), 1947.

Cormack, A., *Equine Casualties during the Campaign of 1704* (JSAHR), 2013.

Corvisier, A., *Le Morale des Combattants* (Revue Historique des Armees), 1997.

—— *La Bataille de Malplaquet, 1709*, 1997.

Costello, V., *Huguenot Regiments in the War of the Spanish Succession* (JSAHR), 2008.

Coxe, W., *Memoirs of the Duke of Marlborough* (three volumes), 1847.

Cra'ster H. (ed.), *Letters of First Earl Orkney during Marlborough's Campaigns* (English Historical Review), 1904.

Crichton, A. (ed.), *The Life and Diary of Lieutenant-Colonel J Blackader*, 1824.

Dalton, C., *English Army Commission Lists and Registers, 1660–1714* (four volumes), 1904.

—— *Commissions from the British Ranks* (RUSI Journal), 1900.

—— *The Blenheim Roll, 1704*, 1904.

—— *George the First's Army*, 1910.

Davies, G., *Recruiting in the Reign of Queen Anne* (JSAHR), 1950.

Dickinson, H. (ed.), *The Correspondence of Henry St John and Thomas Erle* (JSAHR), 1970.

Dickson, A., *Red John of the Battles, the 2nd Duke of Argyll*, 1973.

—— *Lieutenant-General William Cadogan's Intelligence Service* (Army Quarterly), 1979.

Dugawe, D., *Mrs Christian Davies* (DNB), 2004.

Falkner, J., *Great and Glorious Days, Marlborough's Battles, 1704–1709*, 2002.

—— *Blenheim, Marlborough's Greatest Victory, 1704*, 2004.

—— *Arnold Joost van Keppel, 1st Earl Albemarle* (DNB), 2004.

—— *Captain Robert Parker* (DNB), 2004.

—— *Colonel John Gardiner* (DNB), 2004.

—— *William, 1st Earl Cadogan* (DNB), 2004.

—— *Marlborough's Wars, Eye-Witness Accounts*, 2005.

—— *Ramillies, Year of Miracles, 1706*, 2006.

—— *Marlborough's Sieges*, 2007.

—— *Guide to Marlborough's Battlefields*, 2008.

—— *Marshal Vauban, and the Defence of Louis XIV's France*, 2011.

Fitzmaurice Stacke, H., *Cavalry in Marlborough's Day* (Cavalry Journal), 1934.

Fletcher, I., *Gentlemen's Sons*, 1996.

—— *Galloping at Everything*, 2001.

Fortescue, J., *History of the British Army*, Vol. I, 1899.

—— (ed.), *The Life and Adventures of Mrs Christian Davies (Mother Ross)*, 1928.

—— *The Royal Army Service Corps*, 1930.

—— *Marlborough*, 1938.

Frances, D., *The First Peninsular War*, 1974.

Fuller, J., *British Light Infantry in the 18th Century*, 1925.

Goslinga, S., *Memoires Relatifs à la Guerre de Succession de Espagne, 1706–1709 et 1711*, 1857.

Grant, C., *Uniforms of the Marlborough Wars* (Military Modelling), 2000.

Grant, J., *British Battles on Land and Sea*, 1880.

Hamilton, F., *The Origins and History of the Grenadier Guards*, 1877.

Hare, F., *A Full Answer to the Conduct of the Allies*, 1712.

Hastings, M. (ed.), *The Oxford Book of Military Anecdotes*, 1985.

Hatton, R., *George I, Elector and King*, 1978.

Haythornthwaite, P., *The Armies of Wellington*, 1996.

Henderson, N., *Prince Eugen of Savoy*, 1964.

Hennen, J., *Military Surgery*, 1818.

Hoff, B. van T', *The Marlborough–Hiensius Correspondence, 1701–1711*, 1891.

Holmes, R., *Redcoat, the British Soldier in the Age of Horse and Musket*, 2004.

—— *Marlborough, England's Fragile Genius*, 2006.

Horsley, W. (tr. and ed.), *Chronicles of an Old Campaigner*, 1904.

Hughes, B., *Open Fire, Artillery Tactics from Marlborough to Wellington*, 1983.

Hussey, J., *Marlborough and the Loss of Arleux, 1711* (JSAHR), 1986.

Johnson, S. (ed.), *The Letters of Samuel Noyes, 1703–1704* (JSAHR), 1959.

Kane, R., *The Campaigns of King William and Queen Anne*, 1747.

Kemp, A., *Weapons and Equipment of the Marlborough Wars*, 1980.

Kenyon, J., *Stuart England*, 1978.

Kipling, A., *Uniforms of Marlborough's Wars*, 1970.

Lang, G., 'Orders of Battle for the Schellenberg, 1704' (unpublished mss), 1997.

Langallerie, M., *Memoires of the Marquis de Langallerie*, 1710.

Lediard, T., *The Life of John, Duke of Marlborough* (three volumes), 1736.

Lee, A., *History of the 10th Foot*, 1910.

Leslie, N., *The Succession of Colonels of the British Army, from 1660 to the Present Day* (JSAHR), 1974.

Levrau, P., *Crippled by a Musket Shot and a Sabre Slash*, 2008 (see also Money D., *Oudenarde and Lille, 1708*).

London Gazette, 1710–1711.

Lyndon, B., *Military Dress and Uniformity, 1660–1720* (JSAHR), 1976.

Lynn, J., *The French Wars, 1677–1714*, 2002.

McBane, D., *The Expert Swordsman's Companion*, 1729.

McKay, D., *Prince Eugene of Savoy*, 1977.

MacMunn, J., *Prince Eugene, Twin Marshal with Marlborough*, 1934.

Martyn, C., *The British Cavalry Sword from 1600*, 2004.

Miller, H., *Colonel Parke of Virginia, the Greatest Hector in the Town*, 1989.

Millner, J., *A Compendious Journal, 1701–1712*, 1733.

Money, D. (ed.), *Ramillies*, 2006.

—— (ed.), *1708, Oudenarde and Lille*, 2008.

Muller, J., *A System of Camp Discipline*, 1757.

Murray, G. (ed.), *The Letters and Despatches of the Duke of Marlborough* (five volumes), 1845.

Neave-Hill, W., *Brevet Rank* (JSAHR), 1970.

Neuburg, V., *Gone for a Soldier*, 1989.

Nosworthy, B., *The Anatomy of Victory*, 1992.

Oates, J., *Dutch Forces in 18th Century Britain* (JSAHR), 2007.

Palmer, R., *The Rambling Soldier*, 1977.

Parker, G., *The Military Revolution*, 1998.

Pelet, J. and de Vault, F., *Memoires Militaire relatif a la Succession d'Espagne sous Louis XIV*, 1850.

Petrie, C., *The Marshal Duke of Berwick*, 1953.

Phelan, I., *Marlborough as Logistician* (JSAHR), 1989–90.

Pigaillem, H., *Blenheim, 1704, Le Prince Eugene et Marlborough contre la France*, 2004.

Porter, W., *History of the Corps of Royal Engineers*, 1889.

Priest, G., *The Brown Bess Musket*, 1986.

Pul, P. van, *In Flanders Flooded Fields*, 2006.

Reeve, J., *The Siege of Bethune, 1710* (JSAHR), 1985.

Rennoldson, N. (ed.), *Renaissance Military Texts, Warfare in the Age of Louis XIV*, 2005.

Robinson, J., *The Princely Chandos, a Memoir of James Brydges*, 1893.

Rogers, H., *The Weapons of the British Soldier*, 1961.

—— *History of the Mounted Troops of the British Army*, 1967.

—— *The British Army in the Eighteenth Century*, 1977.

St John, B. (tr. and ed.), *Memoirs of the Duc de St Simon* (four volumes), 1879.

Sapherson, C., *The Danish Army, 1699–1715*, 2000.

Sautai, M., *La Siege de la Ville at de la Citadelle de Lille en 1708*, 1899.

—— *La Bataille de Malplaquet*, 1904.

Scot, J., *The Scots Brigade in the Netherlands, 1572–1782*, 1901.

Scouller, R., *Queen Anne's Army* (JSAHR), 1958.

—— *The Armies of Queen Anne*, 1966.

—— *Marlborough's Administration in the Field* (Army Quarterly), 1968.

—— *The Clothing of Queen Anne's Army* (JSAHR), 1969.

—— *Purchase of Commissions and Promotions* (JSAHR), 1984.

Scurfield, R., *Smoothbore Firearms* (JSAHR), 1957.

Seignemartin, P., *Les Regiments Suisse au service de la Hollande* (Nec Pluribus Impar website), 2008.

Sichart, R. von, *Geschichte der Koniglich-Hannoverschen Armee*, 1866.

Snyder, J., *The Marlborough–Godolphin Correspondence*, 1975.

Spencer, C., *Blenheim*, 2004.

Stapleton, J., *Forging a Coalition Army: William III, the Grand Alliance, and the Confederate Army in the Spanish Netherlands, 1688–1697*, 2004.

Stewart, P., *The History of the XII Royal Lancers*, 1950.

Sumner, P., *Standing Orders for Dragoons* (JSAHR), 1945.

—— *Military Memoirs of Lieutenant-General Charles Colville* (JSAHR), 1947.

Swift, J., *The Conduct of the Allies*, 1711.

Taylor, F., *The Wars of Marlborough* (two volumes), 1921.

Terraine, J. (ed.), *General Jack's Diary*, 1964.

Tindal, N., *The Continuation of Mr Rapin's History of England*, 1738.

Trevelyan, G., *Select Documents for Queen Anne's Reign*, 1929.

—— *Blenheim*, 1948.

—— *Ramillies, and the Union with Scotland*, 1948.

—— *The Peace and the Protestant Succession*, 1948.

Trim, D., *Logistics in the English and Dutch Armies* (BCMH), 2007.

Turnbull, S., *The Art of Renaissance Warfare*, 2008.

Tylden, G., *Accoutrements of the British Infantryman* (JSAHR), 1969.

—— *The British Infantryman* (JSAHR), 1969.

Vauban, S. (ed. and tr. Rothrock, G.), *A Manual of Siegecraft and Fortification*, 1968.

Verney, P., *Blenheim, 1704*, 1964.

—— 'Papers of Major Peter Verney', Liddell Hart Centre, Kings College London.

Wace, A., *The Marlborough Tapestries at Blenheim Palace*, 1968.

Walton, C., *History of the British Standing Army, 1660–1700*, 1894.

Watson, J., *Marlborough's Shadow, the Life of the 1st Earl Cadogan*, 2003.

Weaver, L., *The Story of the Royal Scots*, 1915.

Weinstock, L., *The Songs and Music of the Redcoats*, 1970.

Whitworth, R., *Field Marshal Lord Ligonier, The British Army, 1702–1770*, 1958.

Willcox, W., *The Historical Records of the Fifth (Royal Irish) Lancers*, 1908.

Williams, N., *Redcoats and Courtesans*, 1994.

Wykes, A., *The Royal Hampshire Regiment*, 1968.

Young, P., *The British Army, 1642–1970*, 1967.

Index